Superhuman
River

dear Bhaskarda & Brindad-di

:) ♡

thanks for your
support!

Bidisha

Superhuman River

Stories of the G A N G A

BIDISHA BANERJEE

ALEPH

ALEPH

ALEPH BOOK COMPANY
An independent publishing firm
promoted by *Rupa Publications India*

First published in India in 2020
by Aleph Book Company
7/16 Ansari Road, Daryaganj
New Delhi 110 002

ISBN: 978-81-943657-6-1

1 3 5 7 9 10 8 6 4 2

For sale in the Indian subcontinent only.

Printed by Parksons Graphics Pvt. Ltd., Mumbai

For my family: blood, chosen, and global

For G. C., without whom this book would never have begun
And for M. B., whose maverick and pioneering spirit taught me that
no dream is impossible
And for S. B., who taught me the power of forgiveness and
the glory of adventure
And for P. T., who held my hand and kept me focused
And for S. P., S. M., and M. T., without whom it would have never
been completed
And for B. M. B-C., my kokoro, who taught me to say
'No, go away!' to all that blocked my way
And for the Ganga River dolphins and those who live alongside them.

To the spirit of warriors/visionaries/healers/teachers such as
Dr B. R. Ambedkar, Dr Bindeshwar Pathak,
Rokeya Sakhawat Hossain,
and Nirbhaya, whose dreams made it possible for us to live in a more
liberated way.

CONTENTS

I bow to Mother Ganga.
Every morning after getting up I repeat your name
—Village woman's song quoted
by Georgina Drew in *River Dialogues: Hindu Faith and the
Political Ecology of Dams on the Sacred Ganga*

Gangájalsparsha: Touching the water of the Ganges, which forms
part of the ceremony [of swearing oaths on the river in a court
of law instead of on a holy book].
—*A Glossary of Judicial and Revenue Terms, and of Useful
Words Occurring in Official Documents Relating to the
Administration of the Government of British India from the
Arabic, Persian, Hindustani, Sanskrit, Hindi, Bengali, Uriya,
Marathi, Guzarathi, Telugu, Karnata, Tamil, Malayalam and
other Languages, Compiled and Published Under the Authority
of the Honourable the Court of Directors of the East-India
Company* by H. H. Wilson, M. A. F. R. S., 1855

Jump into experience while you are alive!
Think...and think...while you are alive.

—Kabir

PROLOGUE
DISPATCH FROM THE BUCKET BATH

My first bathtub was a red bucket. It came with a red mug.

I was small enough to fit inside the bucket filled with cold tap water.

'Ganga, Ganga,' my grandmother and mother taught me to say out loud.

We rarely visited the river, so I didn't know how to picture it; but there it was, at the end of every bath, rolling off my tongue once I'd climbed out of the bucket, punctuating the thrilling moment when the whole bucket was emptied onto my head with a colossal splash. 'Ganga, Ganga!'

I didn't know then that the Ganga was considered especially sacred in Bengal. I was twenty years from learning that in ancient times, Southern Bengal was known as Gangahridaya—the land of the Ganga-hearted. And although I'd been saying it since before I could remember, I did not realize that the Devi Bhagavatam, a sacred text devoted to Shakti, claims that 'he who utters "Gange, Gange" even from a distance of hundreds of miles becomes purified from all sins and attains Vaikuntha, the world of Vishnu'. For my family, uttering the Ganga's name was an unquestioned morning ritual, passed from generation to generation. I certainly had no idea what it meant to live with the understanding that the river had carried away all my ancestors' ashes, not to mention their sins.

My own identity has been that of a bridge. I went from being an unaccompanied minor travelling between Kolkata and Kansas to buying luxury bottles of Gangajal in California to working with young people interested in secular ethics who hailed from dozens of countries. Following the Ganga led me to understand my own personality and motivations, and to discover archetypes that helped impel my growth.

All the same, I won't tell here of my own quest for meaning and purpose in hope of evoking yours.

This is not a book about a few heroic social entrepreneurs whose organizations need support—though myriads exist, and I encourage you to find them if you wish to.

Neither is this a book that analyses multigenerational systemic causes of why things are so stuck—though that is a crucial topic. Nor is it a book about needed sweeping social changes.

My vantage point was a privilege: following the Ganga from source to sea over ten years and deepening my personal relationship to spirituality, meaning and purpose, and lineage.

But neither do I wish to encourage my readers to follow the river like I did. Rather, I encourage my readers to sit with water, any water. Sing to it, pray to it, pen an entry of gratitude in your journal in front of it. And I encourage them to ask their elders and community members about their own relationship with the sacred water. In this way, they too can contribute to the stories of the Ganga.

Bidisha Banerjee

INTRODUCTION

In 2009, I heard that the Ganga was going to dry up by 2035. Although I had been indifferent to the 'dirty, sacred river' for most of my life, this claim hit me like a bucket of cold water. I was studying in the US, and was fortunate enough to be able to return to India and travel along the majestic river. I witnessed a solar eclipse from the river at Varanasi and trekked up to Gaumukh, where its waters begin. By January 2010, it turned out that—even though the effects of global warming are causing the Himalayan glaciers that feed the Ganga to melt—the 2035 figure was an overstatement and the Ganga, at least in our lifetime, will not run out of water.

But that discovery was not the end of my engagement with the river; in fact, it proved to be the beginning. For the next seven years, I kept returning to the Ganga. I made my way from the melting glaciers of the Himalaya to the salty mangroves of the Sundarbans, with their nutrient-rich lagoons and estuaries. I walked on pilgrim paths, sat in crammed train compartments, rode in rickety boats, endured the backache of bhan-garies, and revelled in air-conditioned vehicles. Up and down and down and up, from activists, scholars, and technocrats, I heard the slogan: 'Ganga ko aviral behne do!' (Let the Ganga flow uninterrupted.)

I kept returning because the river kept teaching me how to slow down; I kept returning because I couldn't shake the thought that maybe, and more than once, I'd heard the river whisper in my dreams: *I am Gangaji. I am many rivers. I am your blood. My preferred pronouns are she/they/it. Face the failures haunting me and my banks. I will keep pulling you back until you can feel the karmic traces of your anger, fear, and shame melting into gold.*

I kept returning because she/they/it kept teaching me how to love the river with all my heart; how to breathe deeply and ask for support from the earth and the trees so that I could stay afloat in the dissonance between my grandmother's devotion and my generation's disregard for the river; how to drink in those milliseconds while the glaciers continued to melt and the seas continued to rise. I kept returning because she/they/it kept teaching me how to surf above silence and be splashed by the possibilities glimmering beneath the scum.

I kept returning because climate change and melting glaciers were not the only threats facing the river. At least 1,109 polluting industries discharge toxic waste in the river. Arsenic, cadmium, chromium, copper, lead, mercury, and pesticides plague the river, not to mention microbes more than 3,000 times the prescribed limit. Almost 800 dams dot the river's basin above ground while 15 million tube wells suck water from below. Not to mention, as Nachiket Kelkar has pointed out, the proposed dredging that threatens to turn the river system into a series of canals for transporting coal via barges—a method that would cost about the same as transporting it via rail, while jeopardizing the lives of the elusive Ganga River dolphins.

I kept returning because, in this time of accelerated complexity, I thought the river could teach me simplicity. On the banks of the changeable river where yoga and meditation were born, I kept returning to learn how to transform tension into attention.

I kept returning because I couldn't stomach what a Hindu holy man had told me: that it didn't matter if the physical river dried up someday—devotees would continue to worship the river for its ritual, symbolic purity. I kept returning because I wanted to learn the river's body with my body; to taste its soma-amrita, the nectar of immortality, on my tongue; to make my peace with birth and death; and to sip an elixir with the power to cleanse my sins and free me from the bonds of karma and reincarnation.

I kept returning because I wanted to understand the river's movement through both space and time, in hope that the stories of people and places along the river, where so many bodies had met their ends, could teach me something about how to live and what kind of self to be, in this, our iniquitous age of dissolution.

I kept returning because an ancestor of mine had written a novel about the lives of indigent fishermen who try to found a utopia at the mouth of the Ganga in present-day Bangladesh. I wanted to understand one of the most famous quotes from that book, written in a rich vernacular: 'Padda amago joto daay abar totoi loy' (The river takes just as much from us as it gives). I wanted to visit the island frontier he'd written about, the Sundarbans delta where tigers still roam.

My journeys were not always easy. But the memory of standing with thousands of others in the river at Varanasi during a total solar eclipse in 2009, the likes of which wouldn't occur again for 123 years, kept me going. During that eclipse, I met the legendary priest–hydrologist, Veer Bhadra Mishra, who told me that science and spirituality are like two banks of the same river. He bathed in the river every morning even as he measured increasingly high levels of faecal coliform bacteria in it. What would the Ganga be like in 2132?

The people, stories, and places I encountered during my travels along the course of the Ganga taught me a lot about how much contemplative and rigorous compassion and accountability need to be practised, over a long haul, in order to bring about the social transformation we hope for. And there is hope to be derived—from the clean-up of the Thames, for instance, which took decades for Victorian Britain, as it grew from industrialization to post-industrialization, and then required second-phase efforts in the 1950s and 60s.

I know that this hope, theoretically at least, flies in the face of the division between mind and body that arose in Europe in the late seventeenth century. Many see this dualism as enabling industrialism, which steadily spread from English origins and forever changed our relation to nature. Instead of timing their lives by the seasons, the sun and the river's ebb and flow, people had to obey the ticking of clocks and the pull of capital. And instead of celebrating the interconnectedness of the human body and the environment—the world view that enabled millennia-long reverence for the Ganga—people became disconnected from their own bodies and from the river's body. As traditional society crumbled due to the requirements of industrial production, or rather over-production, the river itself became less 'self' and more 'it'.

Reclaiming the continuity broken in the past between the human body and the cosmic body is critical to the Ganga's continued flourishing—but this is difficult given the legacy of British colonial infrastructure, which was built upon the idea that the human being exists as a result of thoughts, rather than as part of a relational continuum with all other creatures. New practices—of imagination, engineering, and contemplation—are needed.

Writing this book has made it clear to me that our individual and collective sense of self are as malleable as river-mud. I include myself in this collective as someone who has had the luxury of knowing the Ganga from a few different angles of refraction, though millions of others exist. The river is where we've gone to work and rework ourselves, but, as we change, the river has endured. It's the dissolving agent that makes it possible to explore these lofty non-thoughts.

WHO OR WHAT IS THE GANGA?

Kursi pe baithne wale full-pantwallahs (Those who wear trousers and sit on chairs) know the Ganga as a fraught triumph of Indian engineering, declared as India's national river in 2009. The fisherwomen of Bhagalpur in Bihar know their reach of the Ganga as a married goddess and sister river to six other rivers. The hilsa fish, the Anguilla eel, and the Bengali shrimp know the river as a freshwater refuge from the salty sea. The Bihari boatman knows his reach of the Ganga as a sanctuary for smooth-coated otters and the critically endangered blind dolphins, cousins of the Amazonian pink boto and the Yangtze River's baiji, which disappeared from this world by 2006. The Dalit fisherfolk know it as the mother of Toofani Baba, their stormy guardian. The Jains know it as the former home of the forgotten port city of Champa, where their spiritual teacher, Mahavira, liked to wander. The Muslims know the river as the place where tazia is immersed on Muharram to celebrate the martyrdom of the Prophet's grandson and his seventy-two companions. The Sufis know it as the locality where Murshidabadis still celebrate, with crocodile-shaped rafts, the day when the Iranian saint Khwaja Khizr walked across the water on a large fish and saved the Nawab's life. The Sikhs know the river as the backdrop to hallowed gurdwaras, like Gau Ghat and Kangan Ghat in Patna. The Buddhists know the river as the metaphor through which the Buddha illustrated many of his teachings—such as the importance of leaving the raft behind once you reach the farther shore, even though it has carried you safely across the water.

The activist Rakesh Jaiswal knows his stretch of the Ganga in Kanpur as a river plagued with toxic tannery waste, harsh enough to make human skin disintegrate. The National Waterways Act, 2016, knows the river in its current shape as an obstruction to the rapid transport of coal and goods. The Ethiopians might know the river as the site of a ruined tower built by a Mughal-era Ethiopian slave-king on the India–Bangladesh border. Surfers might know the river as a tidal bore site: good surfing! Old-timers know the river as the home of tasty fish like the hilsa, pabda, and mahseer: good eating. And many know the river as the place where the ashes of their ancestors disappeared.

Is your Ganga like Bengali writer Adwaita Mallabarman's Titash River, which curves like a bow, and is bordered in the rainy season by a village which resembles 'the world inside a rainbow'? Or is it like Kannada poet Chandrasekhar Kambar's village pond, Mother Ganga, where 'generations of flies, fleas, bugs of every kind/breed in endless motion, in unbroken exchanges of give and take?' If you live beside it, is it more like your kitchen sink and bathwater?

In March 2017, Haridwar's Mohammad Salim fought illegal mining and stone crushing alongside the Ganga by appealing to the law. In response, a high court in Nainital, Uttarakhand, gave us yet another way of knowing the river. It conferred upon the Ganga and its tributary the Yamuna, the legal status of a human or 'living human entity…with all corresponding rights, duties, and liabilities'. The court appointed three custodians for the river—the chief secretary, the advocate general, and the director of Namami Gange, a five-year plan initiated in 2014 that aspires to enforce protection of the river. A few days later, the court extended the 'living human entity' status to include all their 'tributaries, streams, every natural water flowing with flow continuously or intermittently of these rivers'. However, in July 2017, the Supreme Court suspended the earlier judgment, declaring that the Ganga and Yamuna are not living entities.

The Uttarakhand court was trying to help the river—to bring it into a framework where its needs could be measured and met. But their anthropomorphization raises many questions. For starters: did the living goddess Ganga briefly receive a promotion or a demotion? If she had been found human, would this change the way we make requests of her, or what she requires of us? As environmentalist Ashish Kothari asked, does the decision imply that she is a dependant needing protection and, if so, what does that make us? Perhaps the decision would have meant that we are peers, but considering how humans sometimes treat each other, is Gangaji more or less protected now?

In 2000, Nobel Prize-winning chemist Paul Crutzen proposed that a new geological epoch had commenced. He called it the Anthropocene because humans have reached the level of impact formerly reserved for great planetary events. Human hands have touched the moon, the mythic and astronomical neighbourhood of Akash Ganga, the Milky Way. Human waste now pours steadily into the river—more than a billion litres of waste flows into the Ganga every day. Human feet can now reach downwards to touch the river's bottom, where Patal Ganga was once said to flow. ('Akash-pataler tofat', the difference between heaven and hell, an old Bangla proverb goes.) The Ganga's current state impels us to revisit a question that the river has been begging people to ask over and over, for aeons, well before Manu's ark ponderously came to nestle on Badrinath glacier, where he recreated the human race after the flood and shackled it in superstitions about gender and caste.

A Vedic hymn suggests that a land without the Ganga is like a sky without the sun. But the Vedas were composed during a more expansive time, when India was a loose collection of tribes and kingdoms isolated by frontiers. The Indo-European invaders, to paraphrase historian Steven Darian, were fighting to establish domination over the indigenous people, and inundated the earliest Vedas with their masculine sky gods and their reverence for wheeled chariots.

'The remarkable thing is the speed with which the indigenous values–those of the Indus civilization and the earliest inhabitants of the Ganges Valley–find their way into the Hindu scriptures, starting from the Vedas,' writes Steven G. Darian. Within half a millennium, roughly between 1200 to 700 BCE, as the nomadic Aryans learned how to cultivate rice and barley, and the art of shipbuilding and navigation from the indigenous people, they used these skills to penetrate and farm in the jungles of the Ganga Valley. Sacred texts began to ripple with reverence for the earth, for the mother goddess, and for plants. All three were held in equal reverence, for they were seen as equivalent, allowing humans to grasp the interconnected nature of life.

In the oldest hymns, the paramount river is the Saraswati, now an invisible riverbed spanning western India and parts of Pakistan. As the Saraswati dried, the Vedic people moved eastwards to the fertile and sparsely populated Gangetic plains, where they started growing rice 4,000 years ago; much of the Saraswati's sacred imagery in the Vedas was later transferred on to the Ganga. Currently, the Ganga River basin is one of the most populated in the world. In India, Nepal, and Bangladesh, more than 500 million people live in the Gangetic basin. The river irrigates 47 per cent of India's farmland: rice, lentils, sugarcane, mustard, jute. If the Ganga were to falter (which we are causing the river to do), the food supply of India would falter, and there would be nowhere eastward for more than one billion people to move.

Before the Ganga was a human being, she/they were many other beings, animate and inanimate, young and old, life-giving and sometimes unfathomably menacing: a tree; a pot; a dashing woman holding a pot; a snake; half woman, half snake dancing in Shiva Nataraja's dreadlocks; full woman dancing in Shiva's dreadlocks on the male half of the body of Ardhanarishwar, who is depicted as half female; an adolescent led by the sage Bhagirath; a fertile goddess who birthed Kartikeya, the god of war; one who lounged under a lotus umbrella; a river dolphin gracing the lintel of a palace; a doorpost; a crocodile with a child in its mouth under the wheel of time. She/they were depicted—surely with astonishment, and probably with awe—in the maps of foreigners, albeit initially misplaced. In mythology and legend, we can find a river yielding up gold, and when Columbus landed in Central America thousands of years later, he believed he was only a few days away from the golden Ganga.

In our current age, finding an accurate map of the Ganga River system in India is almost as difficult as in Columbus's time. In 2017, the Survey of India started operating according to a new law. Any maps of India published in India must first be sent there. Often, the maps languish in their office for several months. Nine out of ten times, they send the map back with corrections and changes. Often, they look like the kind of simplistic maps used when we were schoolchildren. Showing Tibet is a no-no, as is showing the borders. Violators risk forty-five days in jail and a fine. Children are growing up with distorted maps of the country. This is an incredible paradox at a time when Google Maps offers such exquisite detail.

Traditionally, Gangaji was the one who did not honour boundaries— she was the place where bodies disappeared, the place where a rigidly bound society slipped off its boundaries. Today we violate her boundaries, half-disappeared and sewage-choked, strapped up with barrages and dams. In the old days, sages would learn how Gangaji changed during the monsoon season. Now, the river's personality is determined more by the opening and shutting of the barrage gates. Time and water are both flowing faster. For millennia, most of the rain in the subcontinent has fallen within one hundred stormy hours during the three-month monsoon season in northern India. With each passing year, more rain falls within a shorter time span. According to the World Economic Forum, out of sixty-seven surveyed countries, India is the most vulnerable to climate change. As peak rainfall becomes more intense, landslides— already an existential threat to thousands of mountain villages—will become more common. The monsoon crops, chief among them rice, will be alternately drowned and starved, and the summer crops will die if more irrigation cannot be drawn from the limited water table. But a lot of solutions exist.

Through this troubled landscape winds the mighty river, now glimmering, now dull, now out of sight. Each day, with our excreta, our disavowal of balance and responsibility and our acceptance of the legacy of industrialization, we are writing a dark chapter in the biography of this ancient goddess, the eternal life force, the Ganga River.

A MAP OF THIS BOOK

The Ganga's physical and symbolic course has shifted as the balance of power in India has changed. Indigenous tribes, invading pastoralists, storied dynasties, Buddhists, prudish Western merchants and engineers and pastors, Bollywood studios, and river-interlinking enthusiasts have all modified her already malleable shape.

One of the first biographies of the Ganga was written in stone for eyes far away from the river. Today, the Gangavatarana, or 'Descent of Ganga', still stands, 56 kilometres from Chennai, in the world heritage site of Mahabalipuram, a port town named after a great wrestler (although Marco Polo called it 'Seven Pagodas' and Thirumangai Alvar called it 'Sea Mountain'). Carved in the seventh century CE, on a pink granite boulder near the seaside, 29 metres long and 13 metres wide, as Darian notes, blurred sculptures of gods, rishis, serpent rajas and ranis, and other celestial beings tense between form and emptiness, permanence and impermanence, eager to greet the Ganga's arrival on earth. Even back then, the Ganga was defined by her flow: water once cascaded into a cleft in the rock from a vessel above. And a book on the Ganga was inextricable from Hinduism, for the sculpture commemorated the triumph of Hinduism over Buddhism.

This book is not meant to be carved in stone. Instead, like the river itself, it is a searching, swirling confluence. While its source is the holy glacier Gangotri, the story flows into questions not just about the river but about what it means to be human and to balance our individual material aspirations, our need for happiness and purpose, and the collective good.

Our journey begins at the Ganga's headwaters, in Uttarakhand, the state that gave the Ganga living human status. In and around Gangotri, the Himalayan gateway to one of the sources of the river, I explore the Ganga's glacial and mythological origins, and learn to call the river Gangaji.

In Rishikesh, where the river leaves its steep, narrow Himalayan bed, and Haridwar, where the Ganga runs broad and flat for the first time, I tag along with the kanwariyas who make an annual pilgrimage in the rainy season to gather the holy waters of the Ganga. They lead me to learn more about the colonial builder of the Ganges canal and Pandit Madan Mohan Malaviya, the freedom fighter who successfully rallied a coalition to oppose the canal. I am struck by how current economics has helped shift the shape of the river. After Haridwar, the river changes course from southeast to southwest and flows through the Gangetic plain. In Kanpur, I visit some of the villages most affected by the toxic waste dumped into the river.

Deeper within the Gangetic plain, I go to Allahabad at the Triveni Sangam, where the Ganga and Yamuna meet and mingle with the invisible Saraswati River. I learn about the surprising history of the Kumbh Mela, and its even more surprising present.

In the holy city of Varanasi, downstream, where the river flows east, I share the story of an engineer cum holy man, from whom the new generation of activists has much to learn. I also visit the government-funded models of the river that have been lying dormant and inaccessible to the public for several years.

In the Vikramshila Dolphin Sanctuary in Bhagalpur, Bihar, where the river—having been replenished by mighty tributaries including the Ghaghara, Kosi, and Gandak—flows south-southeast. I explore the resilience of the natural ecosystem and the unique collaboration between scientists, naturalists, and fishermen under threat from the local mafia. I am greeted with surprising respect because I am related to Manik Bandhopadhyay, author of the classic Bangla novel, *Boatman of the River Padma*.

Next, I cross the border to Bangladesh, where I am confronted by all the ways in which maps and models have failed to do justice to the river. I also examine the relation of maps and geological models to the arsenic crisis.

Back in rural West Bengal, across the border, which didn't exist when my grandparents were born, I attempt to discover what the river's past can teach us about its future. I travel to the graves of the Ganga in Gaur, a medieval city that features a tower built by a forgotten Ethiopian slave-king who ruled Bengal. I also visit the Farakka Barrage which is said to have caused extensive damage to Bangladesh and Bihar. In fact, the then chief minister of Bihar, Nitish Kumar, held a conference in 2017 called 'Incessant Ganga' in which he called for its demolition.

Next, I head to Gangasagar in Sagar Island, a sacred place for Hindus—where the river meets the ocean. There is an ashram dedicated to the Vedic sage Kapil Muni, he of the fireball eyes whose curse caused the Ganga to dry up after Sagar's 60,000 sons ran amuck on the earth committing an early example of ecocide and necessitating Bhagirath's millennium-long penance.

I end up at Satjelia, a forested mangrove island in the Sundarbans, where I describe uncanny visions of the forest goddess Bonbibi, told by a tiger-charmer, recount travels with an anthropologist whose painstaking work reveals the egalitarian and utopian history of the island. Although the area also faces a new potential threat from the National Waterways Act, 2016, this story suggests a more hopeful view of the relationship between the human and more-than-human world.

So far this book may appear to be a travelogue, but it is less about locations than about humans trying to locate themselves in relation to what I have called a superhuman river. The term 'superhuman' in this context resists a succinct definition. Can a river have a nature superior to that of ordinary humans? It certainly shows capacities and powers unimaginable in a single person, but I believe that the Ganga can help us better understand our own superhuman status. For now, in an age of climate change, we have the power to impact the earth and its future in ways unimaginable before.

How might the Ganga help us better understand our own superhuman status? My hope is that each of these stories can give us different yet overlapping perspectives and principles for understanding the relationship between our bounded and boundless selves. In Gangotri, I take a perspective from anthropology: the fraying idea of pehchaan—that our identity as a people, how we recognize ourselves, is inextricable from our relationship with the river. In Haridwar and Rishikesh, I turn to the history of freedom fighting in India. Madan Mohan Malaviya rallied diverse spiritual and political leaders to convince the colonial powers that the river is above and beyond any individual's profit motive. In Kanpur, the perspective is about perspective itself. People from completely different backgrounds can look at the same stretch of the river and reach completely opposite conclusions.

In Allahabad, I explore how the government, private industry, and ordinary people create the world's largest and best-managed spiritual commons during the Kumbh Mela. In Varanasi, I take a fresh approach— the map is not the territory. At the Vikramshila Dolphin Sanctuary in Bihar, my key principle comes from economic history—the tragedy of the commons or the idea that when social norms fail to govern a riverscape, treasures taken for granted start to disappear. Next, crossing the border to Bangladesh, I am struck by a perspective from the humanities—'post-Partition amnesia'—a phrase I learn from a fellow traveller, Professor Ananya Jahanara Kabir.

In rural West Bengal, I take a key principle from ecology—everything is interconnected. So, making major changes in a river's system we don't fully understand that by building dams, drawing on groundwater for irrigation, and interlinking rivers can do more harm than good. In Sagar Island, I take a perspective from economics: small is beautiful. And, finally, in the Sundarbans, I finish with folklore: the uncanny is still alive and well and a potent source of greater connection between the human and the superhuman world.

In this book, then, I have presented these various approaches as having a sacred reciprocity: our identities can span the gamut from our inner lives to our social lives yet there is a life beyond that, the life where we touch and are touched by spirit and landscape.

In an 1855 glossary of key terms in Indian languages compiled and published by H. H. Wilson, librarian to the East India Company, the Ganga is defined as 'the Ganges, the Godavari, any river'. So the Ganga is a river that can grow to encompass any river, but it's also the unique bridge between the sacred and the profane. Terms like 'Ganga–Yamuna'—'a mode of adjusting an account of borrowed money, interest paid to the creditor until the whole debt is discharged, on the other hand, interest allotted to the debtor on all the instalment he may pay'—show how inextricably entwined the Ganga was with the profane world of the bazaar.

But it was also so closely associated with the sacred that the everyday word Gangajal (Ganga water) was synonymous with swearing an oath on the river. Gangajaliya, meaning a person who swore on the river, was sometimes used contemptuously, according to Wilson's *Glossary*.

As a pandit named Kasinath pointed out around 1827, for the so-called 'respectable' or upper-caste Hindus, the Ganga was considered so powerful that innocents would rather pay debts they didn't owe (or even, in at least one case, go to jail over a false debt they couldn't pay) rather than swear to their innocence on Gangajal in court. This was because it was believed that if one misspoke, even by accident, while swearing on the Ganga, one's ancestors would be condemned to the Hindu equivalent of hell for all of Brahma's lifetimes. Of course, perhaps these 'upper-caste' folks didn't need to go to court to prove anything because, according to the law of Manu, a Brahmin's word was infallible whereas being a Sudra was as good as being a criminal. When faced with such caste discrimination, the so-called lower castes took recourse to swearing on the Ganga. 'Upper castes' regarded this with contempt, although from another vantage point it served as a commoner's judiciary.

But let's not get stuck in the swamps of the colonial Ganga; if we swim against the current and travel upstream in time, we'll encounter the Gangaridae, as the Western world knew this region. The historian Dineschandra Sircar suggests that this word means 'people of the Ganga'. To me, this word is best understood as 'Ganga-hearted'. After Alexander's ill-fated excursion to the edges of what is now India in the fourth century BCE, contact between the Greeks and the Indians grew. In Ptolemy's second-century world map, the Ganga is a crude, lush indigo stain on what looks like a bed of silk. Instead of the myriad, sinuous curves Google Earth will show you, the ancient map shows the Ganga splitting into five straight lines. Gangahriday is situated on the banks of the river in Bihar and southern Bengal where the present-day ruined cities of Wari-Bateshwar and Chandraketughar lie. We know about Gangahriday from many Greco-Roman historians including Siculus, Arrian, and Megasthenes. The poet Virgil writes about them too. Sircar remarks that the Vanga people mentioned by Indian historians are likely the same people as the Gangahriday. The Sobhaparvan of the Mahabharata mentions the muslin presented to Yudhishthira by the Vangas. During my journey I was lucky enough to touch the famous muslin saris of Dhaka, which poet Agha Shahid Ali memorializes.

Siculus claims the land of Gangahriday 'was highly renowned for its prosperous and happy condition' and 'had an army of 20,000 horse[s], 200,000 infantry, 2,000 chariots and 4,000 elephants trained and equipped for war'. This massive and seemingly unstoppable elephantpower seems to have deterred Alexander from attempting further conquest.

The Greeks believed that the people from Gangahriday worshipped Bacchus, an ecstatic fertility god also named Dionysus, who had something in common with both Shiva and the ancient god Soma. Soma is the Vedic drink associated with eternal life, perhaps made from a mushroom, or a plant, or from Gangajal itself, and often equated with amrita, the nectar of immortality. William Burroughs, recounting its legend in his confessional introduction to *Naked Lunch*, called it a 'beneficent non-habit-forming [drug]' that was pictured as a 'beautiful blue tide'.

During the reign of Chandragupta Maurya, Gangahriday was an independent kingdom, adjoining Kalinga. It's possible that their domain extended to Orissa and Karnakata, maybe even all the way to Chennai. By Dante's time, a millennium after Alexander, the mouths of the Ganga, where the Gangahriday lived, represented the edges of the world known to the West. (Dante's scanty knowledge of India came from Marco Polo. He wrote about trees in Paradise so tall they shocked even the Indians.)

Not much else is known about the Ganga-hearted people—which makes them a perfect canvas upon which to project my claims. Here are three:

One: whether you are at an ultra-modern yoga studio in Reykjavik, Iceland, or a laughter yoga meeting at a rundown club in Delhi, the Ganga riverscape is where much of what is known to our contemporary world as 'contemplative practice' began. It comes in part from the rich history of exchange between Hinduism, Islam, and Buddhism (and later Christianity) which would not exist unless the river had drawn these traditions together into both collaboration and friction (for example, the Buddha, who criticized the belief that the Ganga had the power to wash away our sins). And the process continues—consider the modern descendants of Kabir and Lalon gliding between and beyond both Hinduism and Islam. The Ganga is known as the healer of trauma, the dissolver of sins and karma, as the flowing borderland between birth and rebirth—something that resonates with people of many different stripes of faith, and people without faith, within India as well as outside.

Two: the domain of the Ganga-hearted has unexpected topographies that are hard to pin on a map. The Ganga's profane, contested, and 'highly engineered hydrological super-surface' (a phrase owed to Anthony Acciavatti) is a collection of waterbodies with highly arguable boundaries. For some, the Ganga does not run in a tidy course from Gangotri to Sagar Island; instead, the Ganga River system's basin extends across China, Tibet, Nepal, and Bangladesh and its sources are myriad. The Ganga's many mouths include thousands of different tube wells, and even the tiny pond outside of Rabindra Sarobar, a performing arts centre in Kolkata. Even the Yamuna floodplains that form the plots for high-rise condos in Delhi after the Commonwealth Games are a part of it. And this vast territory is also a rich ecosystem, increasingly under threat from the fossil fuel and other natural resource needs of a rapidly changing nation. In the Sundarbans Biosphere Reserve, at the mouth of the river, new thermal power plants threaten the integrity of mangrove forests—the home of royal Bengal tigers, and a host of other species. In the Vikramshila Dolphin Sanctuary in Bihar, traditional fishing families struggle with the pressures imposed by a militarized mafia. Meanwhile, the National Waterways Act, 2016, makes a contradictory promise: to render the river into a more convenient transportation corridor. As the river is dredged to make way for coal for new thermal power plants, some of the most ancient, mysterious, and obscure sections of the river are under threat. If you are amongst the 500 million who depend on the Ganges water machine, and despair for its future, know that there are many people of integrity with Ganga hearts who are living, breathing, and learning for the river. You will meet some of them in this book.

Bidisha Banerjee

Three: there is not just one Ganga. The Ganga-hearted don't only live on the banks of the globalized Ganga which flows, unacknowledged, from the yoga class to the meditation hall to the faltering Ganga itself, divided as it is between the centre and the states. The Ganga-hearted have discovered new rivers of imagination: from the pure river to which Rokeya Sakhawat Hossain compares her utopian girls' school, Tarini Bhavan, to Amitav Ghosh's investigation in *Sea of Poppies* into the lives of coolies living close to the poppy fields in the river's floodplain in the nineteenth century.

There is Aravind Adiga's flow of pessimistic darkness into whose 'black mud' his narrator's mother sinks; the river in which Amitava Kumar floated a garland of marigolds to commemorate his mother's pyre; Vikram Seth's river of crocodilian couplets; Hari Kunzru's drone-clogged dry riverbed, 'the worst place in the world, [or] close'. And there are countless Gangas of memory and non-human experience: the Ganga near Vikramshila Bridge in Bihar, where old-timers remember the river emitting a low, resonant echo, one that is rarely heard now; the river that blind dolphins explore with their left fins pointed down. But the dolphins must live in certain reaches of the river. For the Ganga-hearted, in a sense, any drop of water, pool or pond, can be the Ganga. When you start seeing the world this way, you can find your own Ganga wherever you are.

Since at least the mid-nineteenth century, efforts to manage the river have faced what could charitably be called a leadership gap, which unfortunately continues to this day. Since Prime Minister Narendra Modi—who speaks of himself as a son of the Ganga—came to power in 2014, the Ganga's public image changed into a river on the mend: the Modi government has promised an 'aviral Ganga, nirmal Ganga'—a clean and free-flowing waterway. But new leaders, ministries, funding mechanisms, policies, and personnel have overpromised, under-delivered, and failed to live up to our shared environmental values.

There are officials who would disagree and insist that 3,234 villages have been declared free of open defecation. Over 700 industries suspected of dumping waste into the river have been inspected, and 48 were asked to shut down, while 123 new ghats and 65 crematoria have been built. The river flow through Varanasi, Allahabad, Kanpur, and Patna has been cleaned, at least on the surface. But our shit, even in open-defecation-free zones, is far from turning into fertilizer. In many places, sewage still flows freely into the river. Different stakeholder groups blame each other. The task of cleaning the river is more often seen as a technical challenge (one with a clearly defined problem and solution), rather than as an adaptive challenge (one that will require new ways of being and new practices on the civilizational level).

When we strip away gender and caste superstition, when we dare to venture beyond blame-games and the panacea of riverfront beautification, what—if anything—sacred remains to be reclaimed? What does wilderness mean in an ancient and sophisticated civilization facing what Nandan Nilekani and others call a 'demographic dividend'? Unlike in the US, where early forms of environmental protection arose from a desire to preserve what was seen as pristine wilderness, it rose in India only when people started getting displaced due to the building of large dams. How has this strange turn happened, when the river went from sacred to profane? Was it an avulsion, a change of course, a rare flood that flushed rich and strange debris downstream?

We have remade the Ganga in a mechanistic fashion consistent with industrial-age ways of thinking and knowing. The task of the century ahead of us is to remake ourselves as we heal the river. A lot is possible. Restored wetlands, bioswales (human-made pathways for draining and filtering water), rainwater harvesting, compost toilets, reinvented corporations. Valli Bindana, director of the film *Surya Ganga*, told me, 'One look at the impacts of hydro-power on the rivers and mountains disqualifies it as clean and renewable energy. Solar, on the other hand, is the alternative as it does not inundate rich ecosystems, farm and forest land. It does not impact water systems or wildlife. What's more, once installed, solar gives fixed priced energy for twenty-five plus years without any additional intervention in natural systems.' The hope that such shifts are possible arises from the river's history. But it will require massive shifts in who we are, how we heal our collective unconscious, and what we practise.

Occasionally, in this book, I may appear too metaphysical and not scientific enough, even though I have a master's degree from Yale University in environmental science. While pursuing my degree, more than once I was surprised (I would not be now) at hearing many of the world's top environmental leaders claim that we'd understood the science of climate change for decades, but facts and figures hadn't changed the hearts and minds of people. In order to enable civilizational shifts, we need to reach into spirituality and creativity, said Gus Speth, former head of the United Nations Environment Program, and work at the level of conscious and unconscious awareness. I looked for further evidence to ground such claims and found a strong case about how spirituality had enabled many major shifts in the world throughout history—for instance, the abolition of slavery in eighteenth-century England. I looked farther afield and found that similar moral and ethical shifts had helped lead the Chinese civilization away from their foot-binding practices.

Although these examples are compelling, I am the first to admit that looking to spirituality for healing in India is a tricky business. First of all, there are organized religions of all kinds. Many of them see themselves as taking an active role in cleaning the river and take partisan viewpoints. Disillusioned by organized religion, many educated people of my generation aspire to a more personalized spirituality but don't know how to connect it to their politics. There is a general sense that more willpower is needed to ensure a clean, free-flowing, and democratically governed Ganga. But the yogis who meditated beside the Ganga for millennia discovered that the roots of willpower lie in the subconscious—and the collective unconscious—which, so far, mostly demagogues seem to know how to tap. I will argue implicitly and sometimes explicitly in this book that until spirituality, science, and the wisdom of our bodies are combined, more progress—and there has been some—is not possible.

The central questions remain: can these 'dirty, sacred rivers' still have the power to heal us? Equally, do we have, or can we find, the willpower to do what is needed in order to heal them?

It might seem unreasonable to ask a whole society to rethink its master narratives, restructure its economy and politics, face partisan identity politics and, instead, engage with deep individual and collective healing of anger, shame, despair, and fear in the face of a common suffering. Yet, until we do so, the Ganga will not be clean. Nor will it/she/they flow freely.

PART I
HIMALAYA TO PLAINS

CHAPTER I

THE ORIGINS OF TOUCH AND FLOW
(GAUMUKH)

In unbroken exchanges of give and take.
The water has nowhere to go.

—Chandrasekhar Kambar,
'Our Village Pond Named Mother Ganga'
Translated by A. K. Ramanujan in
An Anthology of Writings on the Ganga

RE-ENCHANTMENT AT GAUMUKH

In the summer of 2009, I trekked to the Gangotri glacier, the rapidly melting source of the Bhagirathi—one of the two glacial streams that join to form the Ganga. I longed to touch the glacier terminus, where ice and debris hang in the shape of Gaumukh, the 'Cow's Mouth', before it disappeared. The East India Company sent an expedition to find the source of the Ganga as early as 1808, but the expedition failed to reach Gaumukh and declared that the Ganga 'emerges from a spot beyond human reach'. (Opinions change: in the previous century, British surveyors had emphatically declared that the Ganga was a man-made river originating from ancient canals.)

The region remained unmapped until 1935 and the road to the town of Gangotri was built as recently as 1984. Even today, cell-phone reception cuts out past the town. To reach the 13,500-feet-high glacier, I would have to walk more than 17 kilometres without passing a rest house. For six hours I rode towards the trailhead in the back seat of a shared jeep with a plastic vial of Ganga water dangling from the rearview mirror and a religious chant playing on repeat. My companions were men and women who lived in tiny hamlets along the way to Gangotri. The vial lurched this way and that as we lumbered along the muddy mountainside, waterfalls splattering the roof and windows of the car, a

3

landslide halting us for two hours. No one paid much heed; as long as the water was there, they were safe.

Rattled by the drive, a part of me wanted to share this folk belief as earnestly as I had once chanted 'Ganga, Ganga' while pouring water from the bucket baths over my head when I was a child. Another part of me stood apart. Did venerating Gangajal mean accepting darker superstitions about gender and caste that my mother and I had tried, often painfully, to unravel ourselves from? And why bother with these questions when many people said that the Ganga and its glacial source were receding almost beyond recognition?

Two hours from town, the jeep picked up Mangal Singh, the man who had agreed to guide me through the Gangotri National Park. Mangalji was a small man with a narrow face, broad shoulders, and a Charlie Chaplin moustache. His chocolate eyes glowed as he told me he did his 'B. A. and M. A. at the same time'—when he was fifteen; he'd successfully enrolled in both the introductory and the advanced classes at the Nehru Institute of Mountaineering. He also informed me that he had discovered more than eighty trails in the state of Uttarakhand, trained the Indian army in scaling glaciers during the Kargil War in Kashmir, and walked the entire length of the Ganga with a German scientific expedition researching the river's ecology.

At the end of the road lies the town of Gangotri, a clot of shops and priests where buses bearing pilgrims arrive every afternoon. They go to the temple of the Ganga and walk down to the riverbank to marvel at the statue of King Bhagirath, who is said to have brought the river down from heaven through his centuries-long meditation. For most pilgrims, this is far enough. Long before sundown, they climb back into their tour buses. A handful of people, however, push on to the snout of the Gangotri glacier, one of the holiest spots in Hinduism. In recent years, tourism has massively increased; in the past, when trekking to the glacier was near impossible, people treated their village pond as equally sacred, and occasionally worshipped returning pilgrims as deities.

The first segment of the eleven-mile trek to the glacier is an upward-sloping exposure chamber, vast and isolated. Distant snow-capped Himalayan peaks drift into view now and then, but the barren foothills—craggy, sulphurous heaps of rocks and dust—dominate the landscape. Against this relief of massive lifeless rocks, the Ganga, known here as the Bhagirathi, is a delight: a clear, narrow stream, bounding with energy and potential. Thirsty creatures dot the mountainside—black snakes and ibexes, bulbuls and monals, white birches and junipers. Mangalji greeted, with a namaste, not only the river, but each creek and stream we crossed. Self-consciously, with a when-in-Rome attitude, I too folded my palms before crossing over.

After hiking more than 8 kilometres in five hours, we reached Chirbasa, a nursery of silver pine, spruce, blue fir, and cedar trees; the Nepali guards invited us to stay, but Mangalji wanted to keep going. We were aiming for Bhojbasa, a makeshift camp 6 more kilometres away. We walked through a pine forest, dark and dense after the bald terrain we'd been traversing, and Mangalji told me that there had been more forested paths along the trail until pilgrims cut down the trees for firewood. Below us, a pika scampered away, already on guard.

The altitude made me light-headed and slow and I developed a new-found respect for pilgrims who try to outdo each other in athleticism while travelling to the headwaters of the river, as if feats of endurance are a strategy passed down from Bhagirath himself. I had to rest frequently under rocky overhangs, measuring my distance from one patch of starry wild-flowers to the next, from a stand of pines to a stand of grizzled birches. I breathed heavily, my whole mouth open, and forged ahead only because it would be humilating to collapse. The words of James Baillie Fraser, a Scottish traveller and watercolourist, who, in 1815, trekked to the town of Gangotri with his brother, an officer in the East India Company, spurred me on: 'So painful indeed is this track, that it might be conceived as meant to serve as a penance to the unfortunate pilgrims with bare feet, thus to prepare them and render them more worthy for the special and conclusive act of piety they have in view as the object of their journey to these extreme wilds.' The Gangotri glacier has receded more than one-and-a-half kilometres since Fraser tried—unsuccessfully—to reach it.

I walked on, wondering how long the object of my pilgrimage would endure. I had never climbed so high before. Mangalji found a rough aricha leaf and insisted that I chew it to combat nausea. The aricha tasted like nothing but a leaf, with no distinguishing characteristics or immediate effects, but I kept it in a corner of my mouth, drawing it out, eager to absorb a bit of the unworldly landscape. After eight hours, it finally became clear we couldn't reach Bhojbasa before nightfall, and so we settled in a shack owned by trail workers, where we slept without awkwardness on the same crude planks.

That night I dreamed of a bird I'd seen near a house I once shared in South India—the Asian paradise flycatcher, a small white bird with a long, white, ribboning tail. I'd first seen the bird in a forest in Kerala, then once more on a garbage heap next to my window in Tamil Nadu. I had learned in that instant that wilderness could exist anywhere, not just in the wild. The next morning, I awoke filled with tranquillity and wonder. When I woke up I noticed graffiti on the wall of the shack— crudely formed Hindi letters that read 'Water is Life'.

As we plodded along the icy, burbling river that morning, our path crossed with a swami known as Maharaj. He wore sunglasses and tennis shoes, and was accompanied by four portly women from the neighbouring state of Haryana. The party had turned back after seeing a crack in the ice. 'I would have had to roll these four along like drums,' Maharaj said. I asked him whether he thought the glacier would melt within his lifetime.

'It'll take longer,' he said confidently. 'At least fifty years. But even after she's gone, those of us who truly love her will still be able to see her.'

I asked what he meant.

'Most of you are living in the Kaliyuga,' he said. 'Only a few of us have escaped into Ram Rajya, the age in which we can think completely for ourselves, where our minds are free. We are free of the Kaliyuga.'

But Maharaj had not transcended the physical world entirely: 'We used to take the snow, melt it with some jaggery, and eat it as a snack,' he said. 'Today, we can't do that anymore. The snow is greasy and black from vehicle exhaust.'

A few minutes later we reached a field of boulders, which travellers had piled up like cairns. Ahead, the snout of the glacier gleamed, the river thundering out of its icy encasement. In every photograph I had seen, this spot looked barren, discoloured, and stony. But as I sat there, cross-legged, I marvelled at the spots of colour pulsing all around me: tiny pink, yellow and purple wild flowers, complex leaf patterns, and minute crickets that looked as drab as dead leaves until they unfolded their ruby wings. I poured my Gangajal on a small shrine made of rocks.

I felt good, wholehearted, if not enlightened. The pilgrimage hadn't been so tough—just a series of bus rides and walks and one long haul at the end. I tried to imagine the whole sweep of the river, across time and space—the East India Company sailing down the Ganga into Kolkata, which they made the capital of their empire, with floating logs, opium, and slaves down the river that had received the ashes of my ancestors and millions of others; the industrial effluent from tanneries mingling with corpses, sewage, faecal bacteria, and increasingly salty tides carried in by the rising sea. The Ganga was still alive, in spite of everything. But I couldn't shake the thought that, while the gods had been busy guarding the sun, Rahu, the god of unfettered growth, had swallowed the Ganga, making it a zombie river composed of whatever foetid water had dripped from his throat.

The blind Gangetic dolphin, once abundant in the river, is hard to find these days, as are the Gangetic shark and the crocodile, or gharial. The Asian elephants, tigers, lions, rhinoceroses, Indian antelope, sloth bears, and floricans, common a few centuries ago, have been driven from their habitats and hunted down to a fraction of their former populations. Meanwhile, India's human population has expanded almost fourfold since Independence. Higher temperatures and sea levels may prove to be threats on par with hunting and deforestation. India is almost two degrees warmer than it was a hundred years ago, and the country may be asked to endure an additional two to seven degrees by the end of the century. In 2001, NASA satellites showed that Gangotri had begun melting at an unprecedented rate, its 30-kilometre length retreating more than 850 metres since 1975. Six Himalayan glaciers monitored by the National Centre for Polar and Ocean Research (NCPOR) have been retreating in the range of 13 to 33 millimetres per year. Outburst floods, which can be sixty times worse than conventional ones, are increasingly common downstream. In Uttarakhand, where Gangotri lies, 2.5 per cent of the glacial lakes of the state are considered potentially hazardous.

The Hindu scriptures predict that sometime during the Kaliyuga the Ganga will slip underground into hell. Maybe the river will indeed lurch forward to a dry end, unless Rahu loosens his grip on the coal plants and the stock markets, and the climate stops changing so fast. In the meantime, I wanted to gather some holy water from the embryonic river—Hindus believe that even a drop can purify sins—for my grandmother and her family in Kolkata, so I took out a few small bronze vessels. Just as I was kneeling down, a giant chunk of ice fell from the snout into the Ganga. I looked more closely and noticed chunk after chunk dislodging from the crevasse-ridden glacier. I was horrified. Just then I heard Mangalji whooping, and turned around to see him catching a block of melting ice. I held one of my bronze jars underneath his cupped hands, and he let the water drip into the vessel. I took a sip. Ordinary meltwater tastes recent, infused with yesterday's precipitation. This water tasted original, like dew from the last Ice Age.

PEHCHAAN (IDENTITY)

From the moment that drop of water at Gaumukh touched my tongue, I sensed that it might be possible for me to feel alive in a way I'd never felt before.

Growing up between Kolkata and Kansas, I'd studied Western philosophy. I was struck by the sociologist Max Weber's ideas about disenchantment, in which modern society disavows mysticism in order to distinguish itself from the past. Weber describes traditional society as a place where 'the world remains a great enchanted garden' and individuals are strongly anchored within a collective identity. Priests determine what is sacred, and through sacrifice and ritual they are able to create the sacred from the profane. But it turns out that our longing to be enchanted has endured, even as our societies have rejected the supernatural and turned towards modernity and rationality. This can lead to disconnection and a focus on the individual. In order to find a balance, many have sought re-enchantment from wellsprings ranging from Marxism to psychoanalysis to cinema.

My family always emphasized, both hopefully and critically, how new and different the opportunities I'd enjoyed were from those afforded by our traditional culture and I think that I benefited from the individualistic advantages of my upbringing. So it was new for me that merely tasting Gangajal had the power to make me feel a sense of reciprocity with my family, with other people and with animals and with the earth, water, and sky. For years, I tried to understand what had happened to me during that trek to the glacial origin of the Ganga which, after the trip, I had unwittingly begun to call Gangaji. Did it mean I owed the Ganga something? If so, what?

I knew those who live closer to the river, and are interdependent with it, must wrestle with the dilemma of being touched and touching Gangaji to control her. I wanted to hear their stories. In 2011, I compared notes about my visit to the Gangotri glacier with notes by an anthropologist, Dr Georgina Drew, who has conducted field research amongst Garhwali locals since 2004. We reconnected in 2017, and spoke about her new book *River Dialogues: Hindu Faith and Political Ecology of Dams on the Sacred Ganga*. Drew is very clear that 'when people want dams, it's because they are out of options,' and not because they enjoy seeing their habitat desecrated.

Nonetheless, Drew makes clear that few locals benefit from large dams. Many need to migrate to other regions out of economic desperation. Some local dam operators have suggested that those who are concerned about Ganga's flow could trek up to Gangotri. And they've tried to normalize development by proposing a new name for the Ganga in addition to the 108 sacred names: tunnel vahini, she who travels through tunnels.

For many Garhwalis, the Ganga remains an omnipotent and omniscient goddess, or at least a powerful psychologist. People both with and without a college education told Drew that a mere glimpse of the river relieves anxiety and sharing their aspirations and fears with the river gives them peace of mind.

MYTHOLOGICAL FLOW

In the story of Bhagirath in the Ramayana, every character and plot twist smacks of the superhuman. The protagonist overcomes the excesses of human nature by going to the margins of the known world and performing tapasya—transformative austerities that burn away patterns that no longer serve. Tapasya is most often translated as penance or austerity, but it also means the burning desire for change, and it's related to the idea of cultivating oneself for a greater good anchored in an ethical and spiritual vision.

This story starts with King Sagara, who sent a sacrificial horse to roam the land, since he had the right to claim all the land that the horse wandered through. But the horse disappeared, so Sagara sent his 60,000 sons, who raped, plundered, and pillaged the land, continuing their crimes against humanity and against the earth, leaving no stone unturned in their search for the horse. Finally, they found it—in Kapil

Muni's ashram. Incensed by their audacity, the sage burned the sons to death with his fireball eyes. In the *Vishnu Purana*, the gods beg Kapil Muni to rid the world of Sagara's sons and their 'evil ways'. So he curses their spirits—they can only be redeemed if one of their descendants is able bring the Ganga down from heaven.

Sagara's descendants tried to perform the necessary austerities, but failed to multi-task effectively between penance and the day-to-day running of their kingdom. In Ruth Vanita and Saleem Kidwai's translation of the Bangla Krittivasa Ramayana, the scholar Krittivasa tells of Sagara's descendant, Dilipa, who went seeking the Ganga after failing to conceive a son. When Dilipa died, Shiva appeared to his two widows and said, 'you two make love together and by my blessings you will bear a beautiful son.' The two 'lived together in extreme love' and one conceived and bore a child. But the child was born without a bone in his body. Happily, the Sage Ashtavakra saw him and blessed him into good health, and named him Bhagirath, or he who was born from two vulvas (bhagas).

Bhagirath chose to leave his kingdom and commit, for a thousand years, to the task of bringing the Ganga down from the heavens through willpower alone. He is reputed to have stood on one leg while doing so. Perhaps the mythological Bhagirath represents a collective of people, passing down their burning desire for transformation from lifetime to lifetime, like climate activists working for intergenerational change they will not live to see.

We know that Bhagirath was an ancestor of Rama, but we don't know anything about the family he must have left behind. Nor do we know the practices that allowed him to tolerate the discomfort he must have felt while trying to balance the fierce urgency of the present moment with his vast loyalty to his ancestors, and to his descendants. Did he break down and cry from time to time? Did he feel the urge to cheat and put his other leg down sometimes? Our myths are silent on these points.

Regardless, as legend has it, at the eleventh hour, the gods told Bhagirath to direct his tapasya towards Shiva. (This is where the Bhagirath story starts to echo the simpler one told above.) As patriarchal narrators would have it, Shiva (or, more precisely, Shiva's dreadlocks) alone can contain the intensity of the Ganga's force by imprisoning her. Vibanshu

Dave, who maintains an extensive blog on Hindu lore, tells the story as follows: 'Ganga struggled to set herself free, but Shiva could not be budged. [Bhagirath] worshipped Shiva, who let Ganga free after crushing her vanity. She flowed, and is believed to flow, from Shiva's jata down to earth at a gentler pace.'

But the Chola bronzes of Shiva Nataraja, with Ganga in her half-snake form dancing in his dreadlocks, tell a different story about Shiva's relationship with Ganga's free-flowing nature. The identity struggles experienced by both Shiva and Ganga parallel contemporary challenges faced by both women and men—a more nuanced take than the idea that Shiva needs to imprison Ganga to control the feminine force. In the ancient past, the best-known mythological origin stories are about men trying to grow more powerful by simultaneously trying to control the river while vying for its favours. (In the Jain version of the Sagara story, the eldest of the 60,000 sons destroys the kingdom of the Nagas by flooding it with the waters of the Ganga, and as revenge, the Naga king burns all the sons with his wrath.)

Holy Dham, a site maintained by ISKCON, the International Society for Krishna Consciousness, recounts another origin story that contains anxiety about the human ability to affect ecological balance at its heart:

Jahnu Muni used to chant his Gayatri Mantra as the Bhagirathi River was flowing near his asrama. Once, the muni's [ritual] acamana cup and spoon fell into the powerful river and were carried away by the strong current of the Bhagirathi. Jahnu Muni was furious and drank the entire Ganga. Naturally, King Bhagiratha was disturbed by this and thought, 'Where did the Ganga disappear to?' He became very worried when he came to know that Jahnu Muni had drunk all the water of the Ganga. King Bhagiratha then worshipped Jahnu Muni for some time to please him. Being pleased with the King, Jahnu Muni cut his thigh and let the Ganga flow out from his body. Since then her name has been Jahnavi and she became famous as the daughter of Jahnu Muni.

Somewhere else it has been mentioned that the Ganga flowed from sage Jahnu's ear.

Another myth about the river goddess highlights her ability to take omnipotent actions that would be difficult for a living human entity. This story emphasizes both the beautiful power of the river's flow and the possibility that humans could stop it. In J. A. B. Van Buitenen's translation of the Mahabharata, the Ganga, 'greatest of rivers, came to pay court to the Grandfather [Brahma]. The wind blew up her skirt, which was white like the light of the moon, and the throngs of the Gods immediately lowered their faces.' But King Mahabhisa 'looked at the river fearlessly'. And for this the gods cursed him to be reborn, once again, as the human Pratipa, king of Hastinapura, though he had previously attained godhood.

But according to the Mahabharata, Ganga didn't mind being looked at by King Mahabhisa and she retained a sweet spot for him and his progeny. Enter the eight Vyasas, gods who were cursed by the sage Vashishta to be born in a mortal womb. They earned this punishment because they stole one of Vashishta's cows, offspring of the goddess Surabhi and Kasyapa, the turtle god, thinking that drinking the cow's milk would help one of their friends, a mortal woman, become immortal. But this plan went awry when Vashishta caught on. Plagued by his curse, the Vyasas requested Ganga to be their mother. Pleading that they could only bear to enter a pure womb, they asked her, as the 'goddess who walks in three worlds', to throw them in the water immediately after giving birth so that 'our atonement will not last too long'. Ganga agreed and married a mortal, King Santanu, son of Pratipa. The epic poem is very clear about the superhuman virtues of King Santanu as a ruler: '[I]n all the worlds he was famous for being true to his word. Self-control, generosity, forbearance, resoluteness, perseverance, and a high majesty were the perennial virtues that were lodged with the mettlesome Santanu... His neck was marked like a conch shell, his shoulders were wide, his power was like a rutting elephant's, and Law for him was established over Pleasure and Profit.' In fact, he is so virtuous that 'with that herdsman of the Bharatas all the princes of earth were freed from sorrow, fear, and worry, and woke every morning from happy dreams... and no unlawful death befell any breathing creature.'

Ganga bore Santanu eight sons and, as soon as each of the first seven sons was born, she tossed him into the river, fulfilling her promise to the Vyasas. King Santanu's forbearance must indeed have been considerable, because it wasn't until his eighth son failed to show up that he grew

Bidisha Banerjee

suspicious and 'followed the Ganges downstream and saw that little water stood in the river'. He wondered, 'Why is it that the queen of rivers does not flow as it did before?' He noticed that a young boy had stopped the river's flow with a touch of his arrows. '[T]he king was astounded by the sight of this wondrous, superhuman feat.' The boy tried to hide, but Ganga appeared, and allowed Santanu to take his son, whom he hadn't seen since his birth, back with him. This son, Devavrata, is none other than Bhishma, the mighty warrior celebrated in the Mahabharata for his prowess and his ability to keep a vow of intense self-sacrifice. We don't think of Bhishma as an eco-warrior, but perhaps that is part of who he was. Aware of the power of his touch upon the river, he served as a model of cultivated self-restraint to the many warriors he taught.

Valmiki, Kapil, and Jahnu—these sages attained their power through contemplative practice. At first glance, something so ascetic, self-denying, and enshrined in hierarchies of gender, caste, and superstition seemed irrelevant to me and to our modern, bureaucratic world in which decisions are typically short-term and made by committees. Nonetheless, these stories touched me. In the years after my trek to Gaumukh, as my own interest in contemplative practice grew, so did these bureaucratic attempts to protect the Ganga's flow. How did these bureaucracies, necessarily bound in the profane, material world, engage with the longing for re-enchantment which I, and others, felt after tasting uncontaminated Gangajal?

PROFANE FLOW
In the past, priests mediated between the celestial and human worlds by consecrating profane elements and symbols through ritual so that they became sacred. The sages and kings set ethical standards regarding how to touch Gangaji's flow through the power of contemplative practice and self-restraint. The partial collapse of this system and the possibility of alternatives have been liberating for many. Yet, these alternative possibilities are in their infancy in part because seventy years is a very short time for a nation to build new myths around a river.

Today, a surprisingly large proportion of this task falls to the state. On 4 November 2008, the day the Ganga officially became India's national river, the National Ganga River Basin Authority (NGRBA), a consortium of government officials and NGO experts, was tasked with authority over the river flow. Then, in 2014, Prime Minister Narendra Modi came to power, in part on his promise to clean the river by 2020, and promptly created the National Mission for Clean Ganga. The NGRBA—the river's nominal authority—seldom even held meetings and, in late September 2016, it was dissolved in favour of a new entity, the National Council for River Ganga (Rejuvenation, Protection, and Management).

With the National Council for River Ganga, the state's attempt to control the Ganga reached a new phase. The council members included the prime minister, several union ministers, the chief ministers of all the states that the Ganga flows through (Uttarakhand, Uttar Pradesh, Bihar, Jharkhand, and West Bengal), the head of the National Mission for Clean Ganga, and the head of NITI Aayog (National Institute to Transform India), which succeeded the National Planning Commission in 2015. (NITI Aayog was created to encourage cooperative federalism, in which local, state, and national authorities would work together to solve problems; its creation followed on the heels of a 2014 recommendation from the Independent Evaluation Organization that 'a control commission' should replace the Planning Commission.)

Along with the newly formed National Council for River Ganga, the National Mission for Clean Ganga (NMCG) received the status of an 'authority', which meant that the NMCG finally had the power to fine polluters. Uma Bharti, the Minister of Water Resources, claimed that this would help tackle '22 drains that cause 90 per cent of pollution'. Whether this definition of pollution includes non-drain sources—or, if it does, how those other sources were measured—is not completely clear.

Although no longer current, the Ganga River Basin Management Plan (GRBMP)'s 2013 Interim Report provides a fascinating window into an attempt to craft a definitive account of what constitutes the Ganga or National River Ganga Basin (NRGB). The term 'National River' restricts the river to India, but the Ganga Basin, as the report clearly states, spans India, China, Nepal, and Bangladesh. The report emphasizes that the 'entire river valley (including the active floodplain)' is 'the river space'. It steers clear of mythological stories like the one about sage Jahnu drinking the Ganga, and fails to mention the Jahnvi, a Tibetan river that merges with the Bhagirathi and that sometimes serves as another name for the Ganga.

The report's stiff and punctilious tone oscillates between technocracy and an attempt to remember the unrivalled taste of pure Gangajal on one's tongue. The report writers clearly granted the river a kind of personhood several years before the Uttarakhand High Court did so. They wrote, 'In order to preserve and invigorate the National River Ganga, her essential character needs to be grasped in a holistic manner.' After extensive research and consultations, the 'wholesomeness of the National River Ganga', viewed from a dynamic perspective, was determined to be the sanctity of the river system 'imbibed' in four points:

1. Aviral Dhara (continuous flow)
2. Nirmal Dhara (unpolluted flow)
3. Geologic entity
4. Ecological entity.

'The first two points are based on ancient Indian concepts—a testimony to our ancient wisdom—while the latter two points derive from modern knowledge and understanding.'

What wasn't in the interim report was more provocative than what was. The report made no attempt to value, in economic terms, the cultural, spiritual, aesthetic, and biological services provided by the river and its flora and fauna. Nor did it attempt to peg a monetary amount to the decentralized pre-colonial traditions that protected the river as a commons in which traditional water management practices were adapted to local needs.

The report claimed it would take too long to do such valuation. But, given the thirty years of report writing that has been the primary accomplishment of the Ganga Action Plan, this seems like an evasion of the real question, and significant leaps were made elsewhere without much hand-wringing. For example, the report writers felt comfortable recommending the removal of shanty-town dwellers living in the river's active floodplain, although words like 'power' and 'special interests', and 'reparations' did not make the cut.

But even if the river's countless benefits are hard to enumerate, quantifying specific harms is more manageable. For example, according to a report co-authored by the LIXIL Group Corporation, Water Aid, and Oxford Economics, waterborne illnesses caused by open defecation cost India a staggering 5.2 per cent of the nation's GDP in 2015.

SWAMI V.

The reverence for the Ganga that I first felt during my trek to Gangotri continued to percolate over the years. Studies have shown that spirituality gives people a sense of meaning and purpose that increases their satisfaction with life. Certainly, deepening my relationship with Gangaji changed the course of my life for the better. But I struggled with grief, numbness, overwork, and the need to keep up with what seemed like increasingly rapid changes in the world around me. When I thought of the Ganga, I thought of those who lived along its banks struggling with the same things, even as the river continued to get dirtier and more polluted.

Six years after my trek to Gangotri, in December 2015, a stranger emailed me. His name was Krishnan Unnikrishnan. Like me, he had participated in the Indicorps Fellowship, which had supported people of Indian origin to spend a year or more living in rural India on very little money. Krishnan was inviting me to attend a gathering in honour of Swami Vidyadhishananda, also known as Swami V. The invitation billed him as 'a living saint who hails from lineages of the combined heritage of Vedic rishi sages and nath meditation yogis from the Himalaya', and mentioned that he is 'among the very few scholars in the West to hold the degree of Mahamahopadhyay (Great Ordained Teacher) awarded by the university system in India due to his scholarly and meditative interpretation of Sanskrit literature'.

I was overbooked at the time. I should stick to my priorities, I told myself. I looked at the email. Would it take two minutes or less to answer? I shot off a polite decline, and moved on.

To my surprise, Krishnan immediately sent me a second invite, to a different gathering, at the home of two brothers who lived in San Jose, strongly encouraging me to attend.

No, thank you, I responded. Unfortunately, I'm swamped. I put some sweet potatoes in the oven, and continued racing through my workload.

At some point, I stepped out for a breath of fresh air. When I tried to re-enter my apartment, I realized I had forgotten my keys and the sweet potatoes were still in the oven.

I called two friends who had keys to our apartment. But neither of them could make it. Finally, I called my husband, who left work immediately, fearing that our lives in California were about to go down in flames.

With nothing left to do but wait, I sat outside my front door. Confronted by the increasingly concerning, yet strangely comforting, smell of roasted sweet potatoes, I rolled my eyes at my haplessness, and decided to meditate. During the meditation, I found myself wondering if the Himalayan monk could teach me anything about the Ganga. I realized that I wanted to meet him, even though this seemed like a disruptive incursion into my long yet tidy to-do list.

Fortunately, my husband came home before our oven exploded. As he fanned the smoke out of the window, I found myself calling Krishnan. I didn't know how to vet swamis.

Does the Swami have a caste bias? I asked him.

No.

Does he have a gender bias?

No.

Will he have time to talk with me about the Ganga? Krishnan was unsure.

Now that the prospect of meeting the Swami was starting to seem real, I started having second thoughts again. That's when Krishnan told me that Swami V. had been working on his own book about the Ganga, to be called *Mountain Path by the River of Knowing*, for ten years. And Krishnan also connected me to Maria D'Souza, an Iranian-Indian attorney and disciple of Swami V., who offered me a ride to San Jose. Suddenly, a meeting seemed possible.

In a crowded living room in San Jose, I had my first audience with Swami V. Born in Bengal, he asked my name in clear Bengali. I replied and mentioned that my grandfather had wanted my name to be Annapurna, which means 'complete' or 'full of rice'. He liked that. He led our group through a guided meditation; it hinged upon visualizing a tiny blue heart at the centre of our hearts. (Oddly, the next day, a friend called me and evoked the same image, a tiny blue heart, as he encouraged me to listen to my intuition. At the time, the coincidence didn't seem like one; instead, it seemed an irresistible confirmation that I should keep walking along the Ganga even though returning seemed increasingly difficult.)

When I told him about drinking glacial meltwater at Gangotri, Swami Vidyadhishananda said that I had been drinking 'melted wisdom' from the Himalayan mountains where his order originated. Deeply drawn to maps, he revels in the NASA imagery of the Ganga's glacial origins; he loves to trace them with a yellow pencil, pointing out the tiny rivulets that lead into the six official headstreams. He was inspired to write his book about the Ganga in order to share with the world the insights his monastic order had gleaned over centuries of meditating next to the Ganga.

It felt strange to have permission to converse freely with a Swami instead of kowtowing to him (though I had to do a bit of that too). As I was leaving, I offered to send him the second-century BCE Ptolemaic map of Gangahriday in ancient Bengal, a map that showed only five mouths of the river, and his eyes lit up. He gave me a parting gift—a satellite image of the Ganges delta with all its gorgeous, many mouths, a vision that I've loved since then.

I'd always thought of wisdom as abstract, and after my last trip to Gangotri it seemed safer to separate the material and spiritual worlds, to compartmentalize my grief for the dying river and treat it as separate from my inherited reverence for it. Yet, here was Swami V. telling me that the river's wisdom was something that I could absorb—had absorbed!—with my body. I realized how much I didn't know. What had my ancestors meant when they insisted the river could purify karmic sins and break the cycle of death and rebirth? How were these beliefs changing as the river weathered a world where humans were impacting the earth's climate with geological force? What melted wisdom, if any, could ancient contemplative practices still hold for those of us trying to hold it together in that changing world?

Holding these questions like a heart inside my heart, I found myself heading back to the Ganga.

CHAPTER 2

'THE RIVER, VAINLY, IDOLIZED OF YORE' (RISHIKESH AND HARIDWAR)

[Contemporary man] is blind to the fact that, with all his rationality and efficiency, he is possessed by 'powers' that are beyond his control. His gods and demons have not disappeared at all; they have merely got new names.

—Carl Jung, *Man and His Symbols*

If we look at the body through the Ayurvedic lens then the body is intimately connected with nature and the cosmos and there is nothing in nature without relevance for medicine. This body image, then, stresses an unremitting interchange taking place with the environment, simultaneously accompanied by a ceaseless change within the body. Moreover, in this view, there is no essential difference between body and mind.

—Sudhir Kakar in an interview with Vikram Zutshi

PILGRIMAGE TO NEELKANTH MAHADEV TEMPLE

'Bam! Bam! Bhole!' The words thud out as if involuntary from deep within the chests of the thousands of pilgrims straining up the mountain path that leads towards Neelkanth Mahadev Temple (Temple of Blue-throated Shiva). It's 10 p.m. in the summer of 2009 and I'm sitting on a rock half a mile above the fast-running sliver of the Ganga and the New Age mecca of Rishikesh. Yoga retreats and backpacker hostels now flank the site of the ashram where the Beatles meditated with Maharishi Mahesh Yogi in 1968. Varanasi is roughly 800 kilometres downstream and the glacial headwaters of the Ganga, the farthest point on this seasonal pilgrimage, lie a little over 250 kilometres upstream.

I remember the verses from the Padma Purana: 'What need of expensive sacrifices/ or of difficult penances?/ Worship Ganga, asking for happiness and good fortune/and she will bring you heaven/and salvation.' The pilgrims I encounter move me with their desire and willingness to take on difficult penances and expensive sacrifices. I want to get swept up by the camaraderie on the trail.

Nineteen kilometres beyond Rishikesh loom the lights of Haridwar. The Ganga has been both trained and tamed there, but it still moves forcefully enough that railings have been built on its banks for swimmers to grab if they are being swept away. In Haridwar, you can understand how the word Ganga, often taken to mean 'swift-goer', originated in the Sanskrit root gam—'to go'. The most popular pilgrim spot is the Har Ki Pauri (Footsteps of the Lord) Ghat at Haridwar, where, it is believed, the Ganga leaves the mountains and enters the plains. Within the Har Ki Pauri is an area called Brahma Kund, one of the most sacred spots in the holy town, which is believed to be the place where amrit, or the nectar of immortality, accidentally spilled as it was being carried across the sky by Garuda.

Pilgrims have been coming to Haridwar for thousands of years. Perhaps the earliest recorded description of the place comes from the Chinese pilgrim–scholar Hiuen-Tsang, who travelled to India in the seventh century. In Hiuen-Tsang's account:

> [S]tanding by the Ganges river, is a great Deva temple, where very many miracles of divers sort are wrought. In the midst of it is a tank, of which the borders are made of stone joined skillfully together. Through it the Ganges river is led by an artificial canal. The men of the five Indies call it 'the gate of the Ganga river'. This is where religious merit is found and sin effaced. There are always hundreds and thousands of people gathered together here from distant quarters to bathe and wash in its waters.

Though most tour buses stop at Haridwar or Rishikesh, some pilgrims still walk about 30 kilometres from the latter town to the Neelkanth Mahadev Temple. Many of them are farmers, construction workers, or migrant labourers—most are male. In their zeal, they sometimes overturn vehicles blocking the highways. They take their name, kanwariyas, from the bamboo containers they sling from their shoulders on wooden poles, carrying Ganga water from Haridwar or Rishikesh to the temple of Shiva to thank him for saving the world not once, but twice.

The second time Shiva saved the world, it was, as we've noted, from the river-maiden Ganga herself. In the kanwariyas' version, an ancient king performed a meditation powerful enough to persuade the goddess to come down to the earth in the form of a river, but neglected to consider that the force of the torrent would be so great as to destroy the world. Shiva, in his high Himalayan stomping grounds, interceded. He caught the river's fall from heaven in his unruly locks at Haridwar, allowing the Ganga to flow to earth without shattering it.

Today, instead of bamboo containers, most pilgrims sport plastic canteens. Hundreds of young men carrying torches storm past me on the way to the Shiva Temple, where they'll fill their canteens with the holy water. Their faces are streaked with firelight, and their chant is unrelenting: 'Bam!' Hail, Lord Shiva! 'Bam!' Hail, followers of Shiva! 'Bhole!' Hail, happy-go-lucky lord! 'Bam!' Left foot. 'Bam!' Right foot. 'Bhole!' Left again. 'Chal bam, chal!' Onward!

Their cheer and enthusiasm were infectious as we prepared to hike up to the temple that afternoon. In Rishikesh, packs of pilgrims bought orange—several shades brighter than the signature holy saffron—T-shirts in bulk at the bazaar; T-shirts emblazoned with images of the Ganga straining to escape Shiva's tangled locks. As we trudged up the mountain, only the canteens of holy water kept us from looking like a walking forest of carrots. Some of us wore flip-flops, others wore sneakers, and some hardy souls went barefoot. Two or three especially determined pilgrims had perfected an inchworm-like motion that left their knees dusty and bleeding. When I asked a young woman who was crawling on the ground, a board strapped to her breasts, why she was doing it, she looked back silently at her parents. 'She wants something from God,' they said. 'Chal bam, chal!' The afternoon hike was exhausting enough, but the cheer had given me a second and then a third wind.

After four hours of walking uphill through dust and mud, past troops of black-faced langurs, several hundred slippers abandoned where they had worn out, and stick-thin policemen carrying stretchers bearing the burlap-wrapped corpses of two pilgrims, we turned downhill with the trail, the temple nearing in sight. We were herded into a cramped bazaar filled with a hundred lantern-lit stalls, each selling identical goods. There were innumerable stamped and sealed plastic cups filled with Ganga water, which gave off a hygienic, bluish-white glow, alongside red hibiscus flowers glistening like blood, and packets filled with tiny white balls of sweet prasad.

Suddenly, the crowd stopped moving. The Temple of the Blue-throated Shiva had just closed its doors. We had shown up during the private bathing of Shiva's cosmic privates. Like the hundreds of thousands of Shiva statues in temples throughout the country, this one bore a black stone lingam (phallus), which was bathed several times a day.

I sat down on a sack filled with pilgrims' footwear. This was the first break I'd allowed myself. Ahead of us, the queue had stagnated inside a caged-in metal bridge, and I felt my claustrophobia kick in. A fellow pilgrim suggested breathing exercises; everyone else waited patiently. After an hour the queue stirred. We made it over the bridge and trooped up the white marble steps and into the inner sanctum. Prolonged communion with Shiva was impossible; we had less than five seconds to pour Ganga water onto the lingam before we were pushed away by the unyielding flow of pilgrims. We left the shrine with canteens still half full. A priest in white robes fed us ash from a holy fire that never goes out and ushered us from the temple. The ash lodged in my throat. As I tried to choke it down I was struck by the irony of the ritual: the Himalayan glaciers that had given birth to the Ganga, the swift-goer, were melting, and here we were, showering Shiva with holy water hundreds of times each hour.

As we began to hobble down the mountain again, I noticed that the pilgrims had multiplied in number and sonic power. An implacable parade of flip-flops, tennis shoes, loafers, and bare soles slapped against the rocky trail and the joyous chanting had splintered into menacing non sequiturs. 'Bam! Bam! Bhole!' was undercut by scattered cries of 'Pakistan me gir jaye bam!' (Let bombs fall on Pakistan) 'Chal bam, chal!' (Fire, bombs, fire!) I could almost see Rahu's gleaming eyes amid the procession of flashlights and lanterns, as happy-go-lucky Bholenath transformed into a nuclear warhead.

HAR KI PAURI GHAT

After returning to Haridwar, I wondered: would I have the courage to enter the Ganga, which gets progressively more polluted after Rishikesh, again? One afternoon in late July 2009, on my last day in Haridwar, encouraged by a friend, I walked gingerly down the long, wet stone steps of Har Ki Pauri Ghat. Some devotees call it Hari Ki Pauri, claiming that this place is sacred to Vishnu (Hari); others stand firm that Shiva (Har) claims it but all are in agreement that Gangaji descended to earth here.

I had no suitable bathing costume with me but Anilji, my travelling companion, assured me that there was no such thing as a fashion faux pas in front of Gangaji. He encouraged me to buy a pair of aubergine-coloured cotton pants. Anilji worked for a coal-fired power plant in Chhattisgarh and taught yoga for the Art of Living Foundation in his spare time. I'd met him at the guest house where I was staying and he had accompanied me on my journey to the Neelkanth Mahadev Temple. As a woman travelling alone, I had been prepared to distrust him, but he had put me at ease by sharing stories about his family and by encouraging me to breathe through my claustrophobia when I'd felt trapped on the narrow blue bridge near the temple.

Reassured by Anilji's claim that his wife and kids back in Chhattisgarh would be delighted to hear that I hadn't turned back from Gangaji (and also reassured by the presence of dressing rooms beside the ghat), I wondered if Gangaji would recognize me. Step by step I descended until, finally, my clothes were ballooning underwater like sails and the ice-cold water was tickling my navel.

In 2014, the genes NDM-1 and NDM-4 (NDM stands for New Delhi Metallo-beta-lactamase) were discovered in Haridwar; these were genes that ally with bacteria to form 'superbugs' resistant to most antibiotics. It was the latest aspect of Gangaji that horrified and confounded public health standards. When I took the plunge, the Indian-American doctor Atul Gawande had not yet contracted giardia, a parasitic infection, after swallowing three spoons of river water as a part of the rituals while scattering the cremated remains of his father in Varanasi. (He had taken antibiotics prophylactically, but this didn't help.) Despite the traditional belief that the nectar of immortality lies here, I was braced to be repulsed, to get sick. But I did not.

Instead, my skin broke out in goosebumps, and the hair on my arms and legs stood on end. In the time it took me to wade up to my shoulders and dunk my head underneath, my endorphins kicked in and my sense of time seemed to expand in all four directions. Suddenly, it was wide enough to hold the sunken cities and prehistoric mastodons that had once existed along the river, and deep enough to hold a sense of connection with my rebellious great-great-grandmother, who escaped domestic obligations in Kolkata to trek up to the Himalaya and live a semi-ascetic life along the shores of the Ganga. Buoyancy helped me sense my body in a new way. At my watery core, I could feel the seed of future generations.

My toes gripped the riverbed. I am a mediocre swimmer, and by making this journey by myself, not to mention opening up to my senses underwater, even for the briefest moment, I'd already reached the limits of my self-trust. I was all too aware how easy it would be to let go, to go with the flow, to try to claim the middle of the river with strokes less powerful than those of the bare-chested men in lungis who surrounded me.

I recalled stories from women who had told me about secretly skinny-dipping in the river. One had jumped into the river from a boat, and then taken her kurta off, sneaking it onto the boat and putting it back on when she boarded. Another woman described the bliss she felt while swimming buck-naked on the opposite shore at Rishikesh, where no one goes—or, at least, no one she could see: she didn't have her glasses on, so, for once, she couldn't feel male eyes on her. The cold didn't bother her, and swimming in the Ganga gave her a feeling no other water in the world did, she said, comparing the river both to a nourishing mother and to an exuberant woman rushing to meet her lover, the ocean. And, I remembered my grandmother telling me about her exhilaration while splashing in the river in her blouse and petticoat against my grandfather's wishes, in Haridwar in the 1950s. I had braved the river, but I wasn't so defiant as to splash, much less unclothed.

THE GANGES CANAL

In Haridwar, confined between sloping brick embankments of the Upper Ganges Canal, the Ganga is tamer and more swollen than in the narrow, sinuous, boulder-strewn bodies of water upstream. The flow here is controlled and channelled by gates and sluices. Extending from Mayapur to Roorkee, the Upper Ganges Canal was the longest aqueduct bridge in the world when it was completed in 1854. It diverts much of the river's strength towards irrigating the Uttar Pradesh doab, a 23,000 square-mile area between the Ganga and Yamuna rivers. This long tongue of land created by the deposition of Himalayan sediment was once the site of many significant historical battles. Local water bodies were zealously kept up by community ownership because of water scarcity. The canal allowed millions to survive, thereby changing the face and fortunes of India and the world.

A colonel of the British Army, John Colvin, had first imagined the possibility of the canal in 1836, in the heady days of the railroad, the revolver, the electric lamp and Charles Darwin's voyage abroad on the *HMS Beagle*. That same year, another British officer, Lieutenant-General Proby Cautley, spent six months surveying the river in and around Haridwar, mapping it and measuring its depths to explore the feasibility of Colvin's dream.

Cautley came to India as a second lieutenant in the British Army when he was about seventeen. His career began and ended on the Ganga and was entwined with it as thoroughly as she had been entwined in Shiva's dreadlocks. His entry point was Diamond Harbour, where the Ganga meets the Bay of Bengal. In those days, as Cautley's biographer Joyce Brown notes, cadets needed to hire boats to travel up the Hooghly to Fort William. For travelling up the Ganga, they used the budgerow, 'a decked boat accommodating two passengers and their luggage, with one or two masts for sailing and ten or twelve oars'. Rowing up the Ganga could take between two and six months. According to Brown, when Charles Morrison, registrar of the surveyor general's office, led a small fleet of boats from Calcutta to Mussoorie to open an office, the journey took six months. Squalls along the river often claimed the lives of cadets.

Cautley was the first man to come to Haridwar and witness the Ganga in a way that no one else had known or seen her before—as a collection of soil, rocks and water that could be bent to the whims of the empire. The architect and historian Anthony Acciavatti tells us that Cautley noticed that 'the steep slopes that exist at the immediate debouche from the mountains enable the engineer, by a proper adaption of levels in his artificial channels, to obtain a command of water, which places the whole country under his control'. This new vision, supported by Cautley's command of maps and measurements, helped him defy the long-standing tradition that had placed a taboo against exploiting the river Ganga for profit.

Cautley's feat seems especially striking for an undistinguished student who didn't qualify for the engineering division at Addiscombe, the British school where he prepared for his career in India. Instead, he was assigned to artillery. But rather than letting this detail hold him back from an engineering career, Cautley forged a unique expertise for himself by rearranging earth, water, and history. In his youth, he helped expand the Mughal remnants of a canal along the Yamuna, and, as a middle-aged palaeontological enthusiast, he spent years tramping around the Sivalik Hills with his friends.

These treks led to major discoveries, including sunken underground cities and a superhuman behemoth called the Sivatherium. Brown recounts how this animal was 'almost as large as an elephant with a broad head like an ox's, horns like an antelope's and a trunk'. She says that Cautley and his friends also found 'an enormous tortoise, *Colossochelys Atlas*, estimated to have had a shell twelve feet long and six feet high'. And she recounts how Cautley killed a makar and a gharial—both crocodiles—and then compared their skeletons to those of their fossilized crocodile ancestors. (To me, this detail suggests a brutal demystification, because both these creatures are closely associated with Gangaji's mythical mount, the Makara.)

It was only after the famines of 1837–38 that the British government authorized funds to complete construction on the canal, which was started in 1836. This marked a moment when a newly minted superhuman entity, the British East India Company, co-opted the holy Ganga. Cautley spent six months surveying the river and its khadir floodplains on foot and on horseback, following a route initiated two centuries earlier by the Mughal administrator Ali Mardan Khan. Cautley, however, was armed with a modern instrument of power: the theodolite, a rotating telescope that measures angles. He spent eighteen years building the canal, lost his wife to another man during the process, and employed over 35,000 people in this colossal effort to move the earth and its waters in order to satisfy the British empire's hunger for more revenue.

Anthropologist Georgina Drew notes that Cautley set the precedent of conceiving of a tunnel to channelize water past Haridwar. Here is Cautley on the tremendous effort that canal-building took: 'Every kind of difficulty had to be overcome: orders and counter orders came from the authorities, civil and military, in bewildering succession. At one moment, it was to be an irrigation canal, the next for navigation only.

What was worse, a formidable opposition arose to the idea of the canal at all; notwithstanding the fact that the East Jumna Canal which had originally been built by the Mughals in the eighteenth century had been extremely successful in combating famine in the country which it passed through. It was said that the earthquakes would destroy viaducts, that miasmas would hang over the irrigated land, that malaria would become rife, and that the navigation of the Ganga would be affected.'

Cautley's most superhuman act involved building an aqueduct featuring what he called 'super-passages' that wound the canal amidst the three fast-flowing raos (torrents) that descended upon the Solani River from the Sivalik Hills. 'While the Solani River is either a dry, sandy bed or a small, sluggish stream throughout most of the year, during the southwest monsoon it not only floods, but also hurtles boulders, trees, sediment, and debris at great speed,' notes Acciavatti, pointing out that Cautley needed up to 6,000 labourers per day to create these super-passages. The canal proceeds above the Solani River for approximately 4 kilometres. 'The water bridge is 172 feet wide and 24 feet tall,' according to *Atlas Obscura*, 'and once two lions sat at one end to mark the beginning of the canal's irrigation area. It was, one observer wrote in 1887, "the most stupendous monument of that kind yet constructed".'

More than 50,000 people, including labourers, surrounded by elephants, camels, and tents were present on 8 April 1854 when, after a Christian service, the canal levers on eight newly built gates were successively thrown open and the Ganga began gushing into the Solani aqueduct. Gun salutes were fired, locals shouted 'Ganga Maia ki jai!', and at night, fireworks and strings of lights lit up the fifteen arches of the aqueduct. In many ways, this triumph of engineering marked a turning point in the Ganga's long story.

Some observers present at the festivities intuitively grasped that the opening of the canal marked a symbolic victory against the traditional wisdom that had recognized the river as Gangaji, the goddess. Charles Eliot Norton, a Harvard professor and social critic, who happened to be visiting India during the opening, spoke about the canal as a moral agent of peace, and as a form of 'quiet conquest'. Emphasizing that the canal had cost half as much as the Taj Mahal, Norton wrote: 'The night in which false religion, tyranny and war have enveloped India, is

giving place to the day of Christianity, good government, and peace…
the glow of the morning is in the East, and the first streaks of light
are reflected brightly in the flowing waters of the great Ganges Canal.'

Henry George Keene, a scholar of Arabic and Persian, who was also
present on that day, wrote a poem called 'The Opening of the Ganges
Canal', published in the *Blackwood's Edinburgh Magazine* in 1854. It
encapsulates the profit-driven colonial mentality as opposed to the more
reverential perspective of earlier times:

> I stood among them on the shining morn,
> I saw the ruler of the land
> Let loose the waters with an easy hand,
> The river, vainly, idolized of yore,
> Now first her servants blessed;
> The White-topped mountains never bore
> us benefit before,
> Till taught by those wise strangers of the West.

His legacy thus established, Cautley announced that he was retiring from
service in India. He was sent off with a thirteen-gun salute along the
Ganga and a grand celebration of his intellect and modesty. The London-
based *Civil Engineer and Architect's Journal* noted that the construction
of the canal was the most lucrative British action since the Empire had
begun ruling Bengal. Once back in London, Cautley served as one
of the most senior advisers to the British empire. Years later, William
Wilcox, who worked on irrigation both in India and in Egypt (on the
Suez Canal), named his two horses Proby and Cautley as a tribute.

However, Cautley's reputation was not entirely unchallenged. In
1863, the East India Irrigation Company, considering purchasing the
Ganges Canal from the government, asked Cautley's old school chum,
Arthur Cotton, to estimate how much it would cost to run it more
efficiently. Unlike Cautley, Cotton had actually studied engineering.
Cotton's report was critical: in his view, all had not flowed smoothly in
the early years of the canal. His public *Private Memorandum upon the
Ganges Canal* (1863) suggested that Cautley had misused public funds
and made no less than nineteen design errors. Cotton thought the head
of the canal should have started ninety-five bellows below Haridwar,
via a weir built across the Ganga. Essentially, he claimed that Cautley

had not taken the specific features of the topography into sufficiently careful consideration.

In return, Cautley dismissed Cotton's claims as 'disproved statements' and 'idle calumny'. The Cotton-versus-Cautley debate mounted, with Cautley's *Reply to Statements*, Cotton's *Observations on the Foregoing Reply*, followed by Cautley's *A Disquisition on the Heads of the Ganges and Jumna Canals*. Cotton, refusing to back down, wrote his *Reply...to Colonel Sir Proby Cautley's 'Disquisition on the Ganges Canal'*, to which Cautley responded with *A Valedictory Note...Respecting the Ganges Canal...*to which Cotton wrote a *Reply to Sir Proby Cautley's Valedictory Note*. Eventually, the British government interceded in Cautley's favour, and Cotton's critical voice faded. After all, the British government loved the canal because it increased the capacity of the surrounding farmland and made new areas cultivable.

Ironically, the biggest challenges posed by the canal almost two centuries after its creation could not be foreseen at the time because the new sciences of ecology and demographics were in their infancy. Acciavatti argues that the canal's 'imposed infrastructure provided the perfect alibi in order to incorporate a population into a colonial government and international market... And if engineering could supply freedom from the monsoon, it promised economic liberation, as well. And yet, paradoxically, this "liberation" was supplied from above—from the actions of an unyielding, expanding central authority.'

In other words, the Ganga sustained an intricate web of life bound by an economy that could scarcely be quantified by a colonial overseer. The construction of massive aqueducts along the river jeopardized the world view of the Gangaji as an animate spirit who should not be exploited for profit. This led to a colonization of the bodies and labour of those who lived along the doab; even though the traditional agricultural lifestyle seemed to continue, the revenue generated by the farmers now fed a massive international empire.

Did the spirit of Gangaji cleave from her riverine body when the canal opened? If Gangaji was so beloved, why did she lack defenders at the time? Certainly, the British did not think to consult any local wisdom-keepers during construction and it is clear that the colossal innovation represented by the canal awed the local dignitaries, who may not have thought through the implications of breaching traditional wisdom. As with most industrialization efforts, the effects of constructing the canal did not become clear until decades later.

In the years that followed, the Upper Ganges Canal was further extended into the Middle and Lower Ganges Canals. Acciavatti recounts how, a little more than a century later, the longest canal system in the world, which was prone to seepage, would grow in tandem with millions of tube wells; indeed, in an illustration of what Roger Revelle, the Director of the Harvard Center for Population Studies, along with V. Lakshminarayana, in 1975, called the 'Ganges Water Machine', the water seeping from the canals contributed to recharging the underground sources that fed the tube wells. There is no question that the canal drastically altered not just the river's course, but also the economic identity of those who lived along it. The river-interlinking proposals currently circulating in India are entirely indebted to the precedent set by its colonizers.

PANDIT MADAN MOHAN MALAVIYA

During my brief visit to the Har Ki Pauri Ghat in Haridwar, I witnessed the Ganga aarti, a nightly celebration during which priests standing at the edge of the river perform a synchronized worship of Gangaji with Sanskrit chants accompanied by devotional songs piped on loudspeakers, plus flaming lamps of fire, gongs, flowers, saffron, and ghee. Remarkably, the roots of this ceremony lie in the British re-engineering of the ghat— or, more specifically, in the first organized act of resistance to it.

Like the river itself, Har Ki Pauri Ghat has been reshaped over the centuries. The anthropologist Kelly Alley cites Walter Hamilton, the author of the first *Gazetteer of India*, who wrote in 1828 that 'there is room for only four persons to pass abreast' through the ghat. 'At that time,' Alley adds, 'the Ganga flowed through several channels that lay a mile across an open gorge.' Following a stampede in the 1819 Kumbh Mela in which close to 430 people died due to the authorities' apathy in making proper arrangements, Alley writes that, 'the British Government expanded the access way to one hundred feet and increased the ghat to sixty steps'. By the time I stood there, in 2009, there were thousands of people gathered next to me.

In 1909, the British proposed to alter Har Ki Pauri Ghat further. The real issue at stake then was exactly the same one that is at stake now: the free-flowing nature of the river. Ever since the canal was built in 1854, humans had been interfering with the river's flow, managing it through gates, through levers, through super-passageways, and archways.

Not long after the canal was inaugurated, certain design flaws became hard to ignore. At the Brahma Kund in Har Ki Pauri Ghat, where the nectar of immortality is supposed to reside, periods passed when there was no water for pilgrims to bathe in and farmers to plant autumnal and winter crops. Worse, the riparian crops, which the canal builders had promised to irrigate further, often lacked water. In the 1909 proposal, the British stuck to their modus operandi, consulting no one except a local group of priests, who went along with the suggested changes because they were told that afterwards there would be water for bathing in the dry season. The British administration started to make the changes, but a few years later they modified their plan again and decided to dig a new channel that diverted the river around Laljiwala Island near Har Ki Pauri Ghat.

It was at this point that a young freedom fighter named Madan Mohan Malaviya took a spirited stand for Gangaji's dignity. Born into a Brahmin family in Uttar Pradesh, Malaviya received both a traditional Hindu and a British education. In iconic photographs, he is depicted with a white turban and a flowing white mustache, wearing a white kurta-pyjama. A lawyer and journalist who had spent much of his adult life as a sannyasi, he was reverently dubbed 'Mahamana' by Rabindranath Tagore for his key role in the Indian freedom movement. His response to the British is a powerful and singular example of the human relationship with the Ganga, one that is needed to this day.

Malaviya had spent the prior decade working to establish the Banaras Hindu University in Varanasi, but just as fundraising for the university was in its final stages, the British began construction of the dam that threatened Har Ki Pauri Ghat. Malaviya took action. He roused an alliance of religious and political dignitaries, including a maharaja, the head of a Sikh gurdwara, and a judge of the Calcutta High Court to put up concerted opposition to the attempts to fetter the river flow by the British. Malaviya argued that pilgrims' religious sentiments about bathing in the river should trump the marginal economic gain that would result from the proposed modification. His biographer, Parmanand, quotes one of Malaviya's speeches: 'Even if some extra cost is incurred the feeling of the people should be soothed. It is said that the agriculturists will suffer if the volume of water that passes into the canal is reduced, but no Hindu would place his material prosperity above the dictates of his conscience and his religion.'

In addition to making this crucial distinction between material desires and spiritual and ethical needs, Malaviya also understood and foresaw that public dissatisfaction with impositions upon the 'holiness of the river' would not go away without the disappearance of faith itself, saying that '[e]ven if the cost were one lakh or two lakhs, that should not matter when it was a question of belief with the people. This must be borne in mind. They believe that the Ganges makes people pure and removes sin.'

Remarkably, the British caved in. The proposed expansion was constrained out of deference to the objections that Malaviya and his crew had raised. The British passed a law called the Agreement of 1916 stating that there must always be at least 1,000 cusecs (a volume of water one foot high and one foot wide flowing a distance of one foot in one second) in Har Ki Pauri Ghat during every season. More than a hundred years later, this law is still cited regularly when issues around the river's flow arise. But it's an open question whether the victory of Malaviya and his alliance did enough to constrain modification of the Ganga. For example, in the century that followed, many dams were built upstream of the Ghat despite the concession, irrevocably altering the nature of the river.

Malaviya's network is notable for being the first and most successful alliance of religious and political people on behalf of Gangaji. Nonetheless, some historians claim that the concession was pragmatic and not very costly for the British, especially at a time when their power struggle with Indians was mounting. Kelly Alley tells the story of Malaviya's efforts to rally nationalists and spiritual leaders as the case study of a strategy that once succeeded, but has barely been attempted since. She argues that the majority of religious leaders have not mobilized effectively against environmental pollution because of a peculiarity in Hindu belief (that sounds to me like sophistry): priests have told her that the river could become unclean (aswaccha) but never ritually impure (ashuddha or apavitra).

I wonder what Malaviya would make of this distinction. Throughout his life, he gave diksha to 'untouchables' by anointing them with Gangajal, once narrowly escaping a knife attack at the river's side for the audacity of this practice. Even if his strategy was not successful elsewhere in India, or in the decades to come, he was a pioneer who searched for, and found, his own truth regarding the best way to combine traditional wisdom with contemporary reality. The 1916 law was cited as recently as 2016, in a heated argument about whether more dams should be built on the headstreams of the Ganga. (The Government of India argued that more dams were fine as long as the 1,000 cusec rule was respected.)

Malaviya also founded the Ganga Sabha in Haridwar: an all-male committee of priests that keeps Har Ki Pauri Ghat clean. It's a surprisingly well-functioning body of regulators, a rarity in other key sites along the river. One of the responsibilities of the committee is to perform the Ganga aarti, which Malaviya started in 1916 and I witnessed almost a century later. I doubt he would have put it this way, but I expect that one of his motivations was to re-enchant the engineered river. Just a few years after my visit, the floods of 2012 and 2013 would devastate this region, washing away the statue of Shiva that once majestically straddled the river at Haridwar. So much has changed over the years, including our understanding of the superhuman nature of the river. Yet some preverbal principles clung to my skin like a coat of glistening water following my dip at Haridwar; the deep echoes of reverence, reciprocity, and refuge resonating throughout my body. I did, of course, step into the river again. I just had to allow the water to shock me into being completely present, matching my own rhythm and appetite for risk with the river's rippling, increasingly risky, rhythms.

BIOGRAPHY OF THE TUBE WELL

After the Ganga Aarti, I returned to the National Thermal Power Plant guest house where I was staying, passing innumerable tube wells on the way. These black metal pumps are often surrounded by a cluster of bathers and water-bearers, an unremarkable part of the Indian landscape. In the years when I first began my travels along the river, I was unaware that they were intimately connected to the Ganga.

In his biography of the tube well in India, Acciavatti recounts how, in 1947, another engineer–(dis)enchanter, a British official named T. K. Stampe, left his mark on India by supplementing Proby Cautley's canal with his own 'Himalayan dream' of providing tube wells along the Indo-Gangetic plains. Stampe popularized the tube well technology, which involves drilling a hole into sandy soil and dropping a perforated tube of metal in, using a diesel motor to extract the water lying underground. In a powerful attempt to re-enchant his own project in the Indian context, Stampe referred to the abundant groundwater six metres beneath the surface in the region as a 'silent Saraswati'. But the Ganga groundwater was a very different, much more palpable water source from the intangible, legendary river of yore.

Acciavatti claims that tube wells, originally considered a rural technology, ended up in urban settings as well because the government failed to provide an alternative. This crossover helped Indians obliterate the difference between cities and rural areas and gain independence from both the irregular rhythms of rain and the unreliable water services provided by the state. The fact that a tube well can be dug by almost anyone, anywhere, distinguishes it from the colossal coordination needed to build a canal. Access to this ubiquitous and demystified Saraswati deepened the economic colonization enabled by the Ganges canal. The tube well irrigation helped fuel the Green Revolution, during which, US agricultural interests shaped the cultivation practices of Indian farmers and the need for diesel to power the tube wells drew farmers into a deep dependence upon the global petroleum market.

Today, thanks to the canal, the tube wells and the explosion of the Indian population—all driven by policy and infrastructure designed by officials from the UK and the US to benefit their national interests—the Indo-Gangetic plains support approximately 900 million people—one-eighth of the world's population—whose employment, livelihoods, and income are dependent on one of the most fertile and burdened plains in the world.

PART II

PLAINS

CHAPTER 3

THE DEMON OF KANPUR

Scream! Otherwise people will say Ganga
tolerated being stripped naked quietly.
—*Ram Teri Ganga Maili*, 1985

JOURNEY

Kanpur is one of the country's great industrial centres, a city that came
to prominence in the nineteenth century. Its pollution levels have a
nineteenth-century character, even as the industries of the city grapple
with the needs of a twenty-first-century population in which the upper
class is proud of its vegan, hemp-starch belts, while the others aspire to
buy a belt, in order to gain access into the belted class. The protagonists
in Jules Verne's 1880 novel, *The Demon of Cawnpore*, arrive in the city
on a mechanical elephant towing several European houses complete with
heating and air-conditioning from Kolkata to the Himalaya, following
the Ganga back to its source. Quite in line with this fantasy, our hotel
was one of the fanciest I'd ever stayed in and cost the same as a dingy
room in Varanasi. The hotel insulated us in a bubble of affluence, our
own European house set down amidst the tannery waste.

Lacking a mechanical elephant, however, my mother and I reached
Kanpur via the National Highway 10 on a January night in 2016.
The traffic jams were interminable. Paused at a street corner, I noticed
a strip of garishly coloured belts hanging from a rope tied between a
wall and a street light. The light cast a yellow hue over the curtain of
pink, white, blue, green, black, and brown strips of leather that divided
the street from the sidewalk. They hung like half-curled snakes, casting
diminutive shadows. No vendor was visible and the belts, which were
probably left to dry after being dyed, seemed up for grabs.

The city's past is polluted with blood spilled by the demon in
Verne's story, Bajirao II's adopted heir, Nana Sahib, who instigated the

1857 Siege of Cawnpore, during which Indians held almost a thousand British soldiers at bay for three weeks. The siege began at Fatehgarh, on the banks of the Ganga, and led to a bloody massacre at Satti Chaura Ghat, followed by the deaths of close to 120 British women and children. In retaliation, 'Remember Cawnpur!' became a war cry for the British soldiers as they indulged in merciless violence, burning an entire village of 2,000 people in one case.

AN UNSUNG HERO OF COMPASSION

Rakesh Jaiswal exemplified an engagement with real life outside the bubble. I had been hearing about Rakeshji for years. Born in Mirzapur, he moved to Kanpur to study political science. In 1993, he co-founded Eco Friends, an organization devoted to cleaning the Ganga. He was awarded an Ashoka Fellowship and lauded as an Unsung Hero of Compassion by a San Francisco-based charity. An understated man, he was soft-spoken and dispassionate, as if dedicating his life to cleaning the Ganga had scoured him of inessentials.

Rakeshji began: 'In 1995, the Ganga Action Plan report came out. The government made claims the river had been cleaned by 70 per cent... We started verifying their claims. In Kanpur, we found all the claims were false. Almost twenty drains were going into the river. The water intake point [from where water is taken] was receiving two drains, including contaminants from a T. B. hospital. We highlighted the failures of the Ganga Action Plan. And since then I've been working on the issue of the Ganga. In and around Kanpur the ground water is contaminated with chromium. For five years, we worked on arsenic contamination in a nearby district. In more than twenty years there is no change on the ground.'

Our first stop was Bhagwat Das Ghat. The Ganga here looks orderly and straight. We encountered the priest of a small Hanuman temple at the ghat. He was a formidable, pot-bellied man with a moustache and a blue-and-white knit cap, sitting on a purple plastic lawn chair, reading a newspaper, enjoying the riverside air. Next to him shone a number of metal pots filled with water drawn from the river. 'I drink the river water every day,' he claimed, adding that he never got sick and took a regular dip in the river as well. 'It has cured my diabetes. Ganga apne aap saaf ho jayegi,' he said, reiterating an old belief that 'the Ganga will clean itself'.

He gestured to a silver-haired man who had been sitting in a contemplative posture nearby and who, without saying a word, brought over a shiny pot full of Gangajal. What did tuberculosis-infected water that had washed over corpses taste like, I wondered? The priest offered it to us; his demeanour held such authority that I found myself extending my cupped palm out to receive it, eyeing Rakeshji sidelong. To my surprise, Rakeshji too accepted the Gangajal and sipped it from his palm with an appreciative slurp, wiping his mouth with his scarf. So, I slurped it too. Immediately, my abdomen tightened and my breath became shallow.

'You drank it!' I said accusingly, back in the car.

'I never drink it,' Rakeshji said.

'It looked like you drank it.'

'I wiped my mouth with my scarf,' he said, his fingers brushing the understated grey fabric protecting his neck.

I gulped, this time tasting the way in which the priest's bulky insistence had broken through my defence. No one had forced me to drink the water. I hadn't wanted to drink it—but I had.

GANGAJI'S PAIN POINTS

En route to Kanpur, I'd read *Ganga: A Water Marvel* co-written by Dr A. C. Shukla—Rakeshji's co-conspirator and a specialist on algae—whom I was looking forward to meeting. Along with the Sangam (the confluence of the Ganga and Yamuna at Allahabad) and Gaya, Varanasi is one of the three most important Hindu tirthas—a Sanskrit word meaning 'to ford or cross a river'. Shukla quotes the Rig Veda on Prayag, the ancient name for Allahabad, and close to the current name, Prayagraj:

Sitasite-Sarite-Yatra-Sangate
Tatralupta so Divmutpatanti
Ye Vai Visrajanti Dhira
Stejanasomritatvam Bhajante

This selection was the first time I'd encountered the word 'somrita' (within 'Stejanasomritatvam'). Soma, of course, is the nectar of immortality, and so is amrita. Both can refer to Gangajal, or, loosely, any drink that heightens the inner perceptions. Back in the safe cocoon of my hotel, I swished cool water in my mouth, and spat it out. I wondered how some people continue to drink Gangajal as nectar and survive, despite the high levels of pollution in the water.

My question would remain unanswered for over a year until my interview with Dr Dhruv Kazi, a public health specialist and cardiologist, who participated in a cutting-edge study of the river sponsored by Harvard University during the 2013 Kumbh Mela in Allahabad. Dr Kazi emphasized that, except for the TB contained in the guts of some cows, most tuberculosis is airborne. Contracting TB from the few sips of Gangajal I'd swallowed was unlikely. Even if I'd ingested heavy metals like chromium or arsenic or some foul bacteria, I was most likely safe. I'd only swallowed a tiny amount and, simply by virtue of having spent the first decade of my life in India, I was probably immune to Hepatitis A (which results from ingesting tiny amounts of faecal matter, often borne by water).

However, this hardly means that polluted Gangajal is safe to drink. Dr Kazi explained that over time, these same contaminants build up or overwhelm the body and lead to illnesses like acute diarrhoea and other gastro-intestinal diseases as well as a greater likelihood of kidney and bladder cancer. The incontrovertible evidence is there; the link has been widely documented in other water bodies, though it's harder to carry out a long-term study in the Ganga's basin. 'The story has not been communicated very well,' Kazi emphasized—a simple phrase, but one which stayed with me.

'How do you think about the pollution of rivers? What do you consider as the main threats?' he asked. 'There is chemical contamination from tanneries, there is micro-biological contamination from human and animal waste, and then there is biochemical contamination which is more relevant for lakes than it is for rivers where if you use too much fertilizer on the riverbanks it causes algal blooms and overwhelms the underwater life. All of these contaminants are a function of how much is deposited and how much the flow rate is. For all of them, as the flow rate goes up, the contamination goes down... Are you thinking about contamination as a yes or no question or as a continuous scale? E-coli for example, for the bacterial contamination, we often think of it as a threshold. This is safe, this is not safe. It's hard to imagine a river not having any contaminants at all, particularly when it flows through such a densely populated region.'

When Rakeshji started monitoring the river in 1995, the presence of a hundred corpses in a 10-kilometre stretch of the river was an everyday occurrence, albeit 'offensive and repulsive'. I had already been to Varanasi, so it didn't surprise me that the river had once hosted a constant stream of bodies. Rakeshji gained a local reputation for good deeds by mobilizing a team of volunteers to remove more than 180 corpses. The idea was to sensitize people and also galvanize government agencies into action. Initially, though, there was no response from the government, he claims. So, Rakeshji and Eco Friends filed a two-paragraph writ petition to Justice Giridhar Malaviya at the Allahabad High Court. Eventually, in 1997, the court heard the case, whose scope was widened to include the entirety of the Ganga throughout Uttar Pradesh, which included Uttaranchal at that time. 'For two years it was a very high-profile case. Several orders were passed by the court: 250-odd polluting factories were closed, including 127 tanneries in Kanpur,' Rakeshji told me. The court banned the immersion of dead bodies and restricted the dumping of industrial effluent. It also mandated septic tanks in Uttaranchal and demanded the safe and scientific disposal of sludge.

'It must have been a huge victory. How did you feel?' I asked.

'On the ground, I am concerned with the cleaning of the river. I want to see a clean and healthy river. Even today that is not there. Earlier it was cleaner. What kind of victory is this?'

'What makes you say it's more polluted?' I asked. Somewhere below my ribs, the Gangajal I'd swallowed still swirled uneasily.

'There is less water, less flow; more sewage, more industrial effluent is entering into the river. It's frustrating. I have lost hope. I do not see a clean Ganga happening.'

'How did you feel when Prime Minister Modi spoke about Swachh Ganga Abhiyan?'

'Always hope is ignited. When Dr Manmohan Singh declared the Ganga the national river, then again there was new hope. When Modi came to power and talked about cleaning the Ganga, again hope was raised. But already eighteen months are gone, again there has been no change, no activity on the ground. Nothing has happened. Every day I read in the newspapers, see on the TV, that meetings are taking place. There are reports—this will happen, that will happen. Money—20,000 crores have been allocated. Nothing is visible on the ground. Some bold decisions need to be taken by the government. The flow and quantity of water needs to be augmented in the river. We do not need any money. Only a bold decision needs to be taken at the central level.'

Rakeshji paints a bleak picture of one of the bleakest stretches of the river. He and a small group of dedicated volunteers have spent their lives putting forth a superhuman effort: getting writs against many different industries, and changing the infrastructure through which the waste is disposed. Yet, out of some combination of humility and his ability to face the dire on-ground realities of the rising pollution in the river, he denies that he has been able to achieve any victories.

Rakeshji's stance on hope reminded me of the words of Tibetan Buddhist teacher Chogyam Trungpa: 'Give up hope completely, accept what is totally.' After wrestling with this for years, I discovered the rich fruits of accepting terrible confusion and grave disappointment. For me, these fruits involved understanding my personality, and my gifts, motivations, limitations, and fixations better so that I could better understand how I could best contribute to the unfolding story of the Ganga. In this way, Rakeshiji's wisdom was ultimately galvanizing.

I was struck by the way in which Rakeshji's catalogue included both point and non-point sources of pollution. Environmental experts use these terms to distinguish industrial and sewage wastes (which originate in specific, predictable locations) from more diffuse sources with no fixed origin, like run-off from pesticide-sprayed fields or bacterial contamination or construction debris or corpse disposal. Although he distinguishes between point versus non-point sources of pollution, when he speaks, he also tends to lump together different types of pollution: tannery waste, sewage, corpses. It made me wonder whether a more nuanced presentation—one which sorted the monolithic problem of pollution into addressable (or at least less overwhelming) individual issues, and which acknowledged that some areas had seen real improvement— would make it easier for new volunteers (ideally, millions of people, from every sphere of life) to join the cause.

Anthropologist Kelly Alley describes meeting Rakesh Jaiswal on Ganga Dussehra in 1995, when Rakeshji attended religious celebrations and tried to persuade religious leaders to care about material pollution. But mainstream religious leaders had a different perspective on the Ganga, and were able to hold thoughts like: 'It is only because that power must be accessed in radiant place and time. Ganga occupies a fixed sacrality beyond space and time (acyut). Therefore, she is imperishable in both space and time.'

Alley writes that the VHP leaders gathered with swamis, Sankaracharyas, and members of Parliament on Har Ki Pauri Ghat and performed pujas. Afterwards, as the yatra moved from the banks of the river, the conversation around it barely mentioned the call to save Ganga. This was even though the objectives of the yatra explicitly included the aim 'to build up assertive public awareness to ensure maintenance of sanctity and purity of the Ganga; and also awareness against environmental pollution'.

She continues, 'The interest in demonizing Muslims and using calls to reappropriate Hindu sacred spaces controlled by them was not linked to the environmental concern about the river because an easy transference could not be made. A Muslim enemy could not be created to mobilize audiences behind the call to save the Ganga. While Hindu nationalists cast Muslims as the demonic other in struggles for sacred space, they have no basis for treating Muslims as enemies of the river. Although one could argue that Muslim industrialists pollute the river, Hindu industrialists do the same, and the two groups are often little different in their behaviour.'

Together, Rakeshji and I travelled to Jajmau, an industrial suburb of Kanpur where hundreds of tanneries discharge waste into the Ganga. Unfinished leather heaped on the sidewalks, the hides of hundreds of cows are to be found here, a pitiless place where the sacred becomes the profane.

We passed numerous tanneries with evocative names like M/S Skin Finishers and M/S Baba Hide. They all said the same thing: NOTICE OF HAZARDOUS CHEMICAL WASTES. But the chemicals and other features listed underneath were strangely vague and mysterious to the uninitiated: hazardous chemicals, acid (Sulphuric, formic, etc.), basic chrome sulfate, dyes, capacity CA Pest as registered CETP, E. T. P. Particulars, P. H., S. S., C. O. D., Biochemical Oxygen Demand (B.O.D.) etc. There was room on the board to list the specific quantities of these substances on site, but the amounts were almost invariably blacked out.

Our first stop was at a treatment plant for sewage and tannery waste.

As we drove away I saw a man amidst a rising cloud of dust beating at the ground with a branch still thick with leaves. This seemingly ineffectual gesture in such a desolate place—with broken doors, empty rooms, a rusted-out water tank—Rakesh Jaiswal said there is a landfill some 80 kilometres away, but the municipality doesn't want to pay transport costs due to corruption.

There are four tannery canals which flow directly into the river. With a weary air, Rakeshji only showed me one. 'There's a small tributary called Pandu River; a lot of waste goes into Ganga via Pandu. It has been converted into a drain. It's a carrier of raw sewage and industrial water. It doesn't carry any fresh water. When the river enters Kanpur, it receives a huge amount of raw sewage and industrial effluent.'

He continued, 'Tanneries use hundreds of chemicals: dyes, large amounts of lime, chemicals with heavy metals like basic chrome sulfate, and also chemicals which have cadmium, lead, mercury. This waste water is highly toxic. It's a cocktail of deadly chemicals. There are 400-odd tanneries in Kanpur right on the bank of the river. They generate roughly 50 million litres per day of waste water. Most of the tanneries use groundwater. But the waste water goes to the river.'

He explained that, under the first phase of the Ganga Action Plan, a plant was set up in Kanpur which would have been adequate if the tanneries had accepted their shared responsibility to undertake primary treatment of their waste water (including chromium removal) before sending it to the plant. But the tanneries simply sent all the waste water to the treatment plant directly, resulting in chromium levels rising up to a hundred times higher than the permissible limits. After Rakeshji's 1998 court case, 127 tanneries were directed to shut their business down until they installed a Primary Effluent Treatment Plant (PETP). But, as of 2018, most ETPs are lying unused or are underutilized and the primary treatment is unsatisfactory.

Again, I tried to commend Rakeshji for the victory he and Eco Friends had won. But he would not admit any significant success. Over the years, the amount of waste water discharge has steadily outpaced the treatment capacity. 'Almost all the tanneries have chrome recovery plants. And for small tanneries there is a common chrome recovery plant. So there is a treatment system. But there is a gap. We have treatment capacity for 9 MLD of tannery waste water, but the discharge is 50

MLD. So 40 MLD of waste water is going into the river without any treatment.'

The first tannery drain we saw was filled with a metallic grey-blue effluent. 'This flows into the Ganga,' Rakeshji said. Pigs rooted in the garbage nearby, several of them asleep on a dirt island in the middle of the blue-grey pool. From time to time, one would nuzzle the other. I wondered if they were superhumanly robust, the survivors of ancestral pigs who thrived on effluent. I regarded them regarding me.

We did not go inside a tannery, but I was able to walk into a toxic waste site. Rakeshji did not enter, preferring to wait outside. The area was vast and dusty. A few massive concrete pipes lay on the ground covered with mounds of dried waste. The more recent pile was a sickly grey-blue; the older pile was the colour of dirt. A young boy was defecating amidst the leavings. Nearby, two other boys grazed a herd of goats. Dust blew into my nose. I couldn't believe how easy it had been for me to walk into this place, and how casually these boys were using it. I had seen dumps in India before, but surely toxic waste deserved more precaution?

Rakeshji pointed to a long canal filled with sacred, foaming water. 'This irrigation channel carries so-called treated tannery waste water and sewage. You can see the quality of the treated water. This finely treated waste water is used for irrigating 2,500 hectares of farmland… We can talk about the impact of this on irrigation, the environment, and the health of the people. You can see many unorganized factories using the waste water for making glue, chicken-feed, etc.'

We stopped at a village called Sheikhpur. Rakeshji estimated that 1,500 to 3,000 people live on both sides of the canal in front of us. He pointed out that the waste water in front of us affects soil, and thereby crops. He also asserted that chromium had been found in local cattle milk and in other produce. The locals are suffering from skin diseases and cancer. They have no choice but to drink groundwater, which is contaminated as well.

'People have become immune,' Rakeshji said. I laughed nervously. He laughed too, as if out of politeness. I don't know what was beneath our laughter. Despair? My own inability, in that moment, to hold so much complexity, so much toxicity? And yet, toxicity only runs generationally deep; success stories about public health are typically quite long. I thought again about the Victorian efforts to clean up the Thames—how very long it took, even for the world's superpower at that time.

Lala Nishadh and two other middle-aged locals perch atop a cement wall near the waste water, using a seemingly gratuitous pipe that bisected the wall as a footrest. Lala Nishadh knows the ins and outs of the tanneries—he's worked in the industry and understands the elaborate process of finishing the leather.

'Yeh pani bohuth ganda hai (This water is very dirty),' he told me. 'If you stay with anyone here and wear gold or silver, in the morning your jewellery will turn black. We don't drink the water here; we go and buy it from elsewhere. But we use it for crops. The water is yellow. We often get sick. The livestock get sick.

'The gram pradhan doesn't do anything. Koi fayda nahin hain (There's just no point). If you put a blade in the water, it will melt—I've tried it myself and seen.'

I was struck by his emphasis on pollution that was visible to the eye. Because, of course, many of the numerous toxic chemicals in the water are completely invisible.

The most disturbing thing Lala Nishadh said was: 'We sell the crops—wheat, rice, and vegetables. People don't know it's coming from here; we don't know where it goes. Maybe to Delhi. We don't eat the crops we grow.' I started to realize how transmissible the pollution was in Kanpur. I couldn't walk away from Sheikhpur and rinse the taste of contaminated water out of my mouth. My gold and silver were in no danger of turning black, but the contaminants could be in a plate of food I ate in Delhi.

We walked a few hundred metres into Sheikhpur, where we stood outside the home of Ajay Kumar and his family, Munni and Gita. Ajay described how the dirty water had caused spots to appear on his mother's skin which the doctors had been unable to treat.

The spots had affected Ajay's four-year-old son too. He had skin sores and rotting teeth. 'When he touches the water, the spots immediately appear. The gram pradhan and other people don't do anything. The water from the handpump is yellow. The water has chromium in it. It's not drinkable but people drink it. What else can they do?

'The waste water from the tanneries flows into the river water. Even when they are forbidden, people don't obey the law. If everyone is awakened, the Ganga can be cleaned. It's not that it can't be cleaned,'

Ajay said. I was unable to ask whom Ajay meant when he said 'everyone'.

'This is shocking,' Rakeshji said. 'In the village, did you see anyone healthy? Everyone seemed to be unhealthy or sick. People don't care; they do not die instantly if they consume that water. It accumulates. Symptoms become visible only after some time. People are being affected, but what can they do? The industries are powerful. The government has been struggling for the last thirty years to deal with tanneries. Things are immovable. The situation is the same. Everyone is responsible. There are so many actors. State level, central level, local level, the UP Jal Nigam. As far as implementation of environmental laws, rules, and regulations are concerned, the state pollution control board is also corrupt; it turns a blind eye to the corruption.'

Although I only visited that one village in Jajmau, the Centre for Science and Environment team's report entitled 'Can We Save Ganga?' compiled similar interviews with people living in nearby villages. 'The water and soil here are extremely poisonous. Everyone here, man, woman or child, is extremely sickly,' their report notes, quoting Anil Kumar, resident of Jana village, Jajmau. Most people living there have deformed fingers and toes, he says, claiming that doctors have told them that this leprosy-like disease is due to the toxic tannery chemicals and that they should not drink the local water or eat locally grown crops. Another resident, Rajan Kashyap, told the CSE team about a man from a non-profit who collected money and documents from residents to file a court case against the tanneries and then disappeared. Kashyap alleges that the tanneries paid off this man.

Walking around Jajmau, I remembered some odd local history: the visit of Madam Blavatsky, the founder of Theosopy—a Victorian hodge-podge of Indian and Western spirituality—to the caves of Jajmau. The editor of the *Bombay Gazette* in 1881 quotes a letter referring to her as 'the imperious Russo–Hindoo lady,' who claims to have unearthed 'mysterious subterranean passages' in the caves. This reminded me of the term Tripathaga—occasionally used to describe the Ganga as the confluence of three worlds: one of the sun and the stars, one of human affairs, and one of chaotic, baleful spirits. And here, uniquely, the tube wells lead to a malevolent underworld.

Rakeshji took me to the house of Dr A. C. Shukla, with whom he co-founded Eco Friends. Mr Shukla is an algae expert and the co-author of the aforementioned *Ganga: A Water Marvel.*

'The most important thing is that the Ganga is an extremely enchanted river,' said Dr Shukla, who holds fast to a more old-fashioned, more hopeful view of the river than Rakeshji's. 'Much has been written. Much is in the public domain. Much is hearsay. Much is in religious texts. It has vast religious significance. There is no ritual in this country, from birth to death, where its water is not used.

'From time immemorial to today, it has been believed that Ganga water does not degrade, it remains pure. The scientific community has been interested in this—why is this river's water so pure, so clean. The investigations were piecemeal, so there was no consolidated picture. Why don't bacteria develop in this water, even after prolonged storage for a number of years?

'The Ganga is one of the most important, widely written about, mysterious, enchanted, religiously and culturally important, and economically useful rivers of the world. Like the Volga, Thames or Mississippi are for their respective peoples, even greater is its religious significance for India. Its biological, chemical, and physical attributes are even greater. And there is still a lot to be known.' Shukla emphasized that there are more than 500 species of algae in the river in Kanpur appearing in different seasons, depending on where you look. There are many possibilities for commercial exploitation that, mercifully, are yet to be tapped.

Shukla's love for the Ganga had a way of kindling curiosity. I asked him about the old belief that the pujari had shared: Ganga apne aap saaf ho jayegi.

'There's a bacteriophage available in the Ganga which kills bacterial growth,' he said. 'The study of phages started in India. The concept of bacteriophages is old. In the National Botanical Gardens, Lucknow, they had kept Ganga water stored for fifteen years. It did not deteriorate. Phages are highly specific. Each is specific to a particular bacterium. It's hard to detect.' He referred to the work of Julian Crandall Hollick, a journalist who has written about how these phages, which he calls a 'Mysterious X Factor', customize themselves specifically for the purpose of destroying certain bacteria, like cholera.

'The Ganga receives water through 250-odd glaciers. I don't think that any of those glaciers have been studied. Whatever happens upstream beyond Narora…does not reach downstream. There is a barrage there, the Lower Ganga Canal. First at Haridwar—Bhimgoda, and then the Middle Ganga Canal.'

Rakeshji interrupted, 'All of the water is being put into canals. It's debatable if even a few drops of Himalayan water are entering Kanpur. We need to increase the flow in the river, and, of course, to stop the pollution. Stop industrial effluent from entering the rivers. These non-point sources, 5 per cent, are contributed by them—dead bodies, polluting social practices.'

'The water is less polluted but water use is little less during monsoon because few people go to take a dip. It's a problem only during the dry six months. During monsoon you won't see any pollution in the river because there is so much water in the river. The pollution going into the river is insignificant because during the monsoon there is 100 times more water,' Rakeshji added.

Any layperson would imagine that toxic chemicals like chromium would be hazardous to health no matter the volume of water they were submerged in. But later public health specialist Dr Dhruv Kazi confirmed that if the river flow is ample, hazardous contaminants get diluted. So the Ganga really does wash away the sins of humanity—but only during the monsoon.

In light of this, the recommendation of the Centre for Science and Environment that the river's ecological flow be increased so that its self-cleansing properties could be utilized makes even more sense. I had learned in Allahabad that during the 2013 Kumbh Mela, when tanneries were shut down for three weeks, the incidence of diarrhoea amongst pilgrims was considerably lower than predicted by a team of public health specialists.

But Rakeshji observed that in Kanpur, during less significant festivals, when the tanneries remain open, the incidence of disease is low. 'Even during the Magh Mela, most of the tanneries remain open. During the Ardh Kumbh, I have been to the CETP. During the main bathing days, 7–8 MLD of waste water reaches the CETP. This means that most of the tanneries are working. Even during these bathing festivals, there hasn't been a major epidemic. It's difficult to correlate the pollution and the health impact,' he says.

THE LEGACY OF *M. C. MEHTA VERSUS UNION OF INDIA*

As I tried to wrap my head around the scale of changes needed, I remembered *Ram Teri Ganga Maili*, the 1985 Hindi movie in which the indignities suffered by the character Ganga that add up to a metaphorical trial are intended to parallel the indignities suffered by the river. Unbelievably, the river itself literally suffered this fate—it caught fire—the year after the movie was released.

Georgetown-based economics professor Shareen Joshi recounts how in 1985, a smoker strolling by the riverbank in Haridwar casually flung a match into the river. Immediately, the Ganga caught fire and burned for more than thirty hours because of being coated in toxic chemicals.

Consequently, in the late 1980s, a decade before Rakeshji began his mission to clean the Ganga, the environmental lawyer and activist M. C. Mehta filed a writ petition in the Supreme Court of India, which became known as *M. C. Mehta vs Union of India*. Mehta initially included the entire 2,500-kilometre span of the river in his writ. In response to the court's professed inability to legislate at this scale, Mehta—although he had no personal connection to Kanpur—decided to focus on this city as an epicentre of pollution and therefore a useful index for the condition of other cities in the Ganga basin.

The court split Mehta's petition into two cases; one focused on Kanpur's tanneries and the other on the municipal corporation. In 1987, the court ordered the tanneries in Kanpur to stop polluting in six months, or close shop. A year later, the court demanded that Kanpur municipal corporation take bold steps ranging from relocating 80,000 cattle to treating sewage more effectively; it also banned the dumping of dead bodies and mandated weekly environmental education classes in schools.

Kelly Alley describes the subsequent expansion of this writ: 'From 1992 to 1995, Mehta expanded his original petition to cover over 5,000 industries in more than 300 towns along the Ganga basin. The court set aside every Friday to review his petition… In its biggest sweep, the apex court fined 191 industries in a single day. Over several years, it closed more than 500 plants along the Ganga basin for failing to set up effluent treatment plants.'

Policy changes of this magnitude, well-documented and taking place gradually, have created a remarkable data set for analysis. While comparing the areas upstream and downstream of Kanpur, Joshi found that the environmental legislation led to 'evidence of a significant drop in both river pollution and health risk' during 1986–2004. She and her fellow researchers used BOD as a measure of river pollution because it's relatively easy to monitor and because it changes in response to pollutants injurious to humans. In addition, they focused on infant mortality as a measure of health because infants are the group most vulnerable to pollution and that data were readily available.

Joshi writes: 'The ruling increases the likelihood of the river water in the area around the tanneries being in the "fit-for-bathing" category by 40 per cent. In terms of health risk, our results indicate that mortality among one-month-old infants dropped by 3.2 percentage points (50%) in areas around the tanneries.' This is very different from Rakeshji's perspective. Joshi claims with empirical support that environmental laws have decreased pollution and improved human health in Kanpur.

Could other variables, like increased awareness of pollution among people living along the river, have contributed to the decrease in pollution and infant mortality? Such questions are difficult to answer, but Joshi's team concluded that the environmental legislation itself had a significantly beneficial impact. Of course, they did not study long-term implications for adult health as a result of pollution in the river. We don't know whether bladder and kidney cancer rates in the area have been impacted by the rising pollution in the Ganga. But I wondered if future scholars would find similarly beneficial effects resulting from Rakeshji's path-breaking work, despite his hopelessness about the situation.

Unlike M. C. Mehta, who lives in Delhi and has a foundation named after him, Rakeshji said he doesn't mentor any youth because hardly any Indians come to him. I am disappointed and at a loss. I want to tell him that there are dolphins downstream, regardless. That there are myriad Gangas: the Himalayan one, the canalized one, the one that's renewed by so many tributaries and distributaries.

I want to tell Rakeshji that there is a brighter way of telling Gangaji's story. Visible corpses in the river have decreased considerably. Industrial pollution is less significant in the monsoon season, although we all need to do a better job of understanding its impact. The state government in Uttar Pradesh has the political will three weeks of the year, every twelve years, during the Kumbh Mela, to keep the river clean, as I discuss below. This suggests that something meaningful and positive can be done, at least under some conditions.

As I prepared to say goodbye to Rakeshji, he mentioned the work of Dr Vinod Tare at IIT Kanpur. 'A consortium of IITs, whose convener is Dr Tare, received 20 crores for preparing a Ganga Environmental Management plan. They took five years in preparing the plan. I don't know if anyone has gone through this report or if any recommendation has been accepted by the government. Some of the reports are available online.' Rakeshji said that what's new about the plan is that zero liquid discharge is recommended for the tanneries.

According to the zero liquid discharge ideal outlined by IIT Kanpur, tanneries would share the cost with the government of installing facilities that would treat contaminated water such that it could be recycled by the tanneries; contaminated sludge would be processed separately. In 2015, the Central Pollution Control Board greenlighted a Zero Liquid Discharge plant to be built in Jajmau as part of a public-private partnership. It would send recycled and treated water back to tanneries for use and dispose of sludge separately. Although tannery owners opposed this innovation, claiming that it had failed elsewhere, the CPCB said that tanneries would be held accountable for paying 25 per cent of the cost of installation.

In May 2017, almost a year and a half after my visit to Kanpur, then Union Minister Uma Bharti expressed confidence that the delayed plans to clean the Ganga would progress under new UP Chief Minister Yogi Adityanath. During the same meeting, Adityanath said the state had decided to phase leather industries out of Kanpur and Kannauj.

What can we learn from history about the proposal to relocate Kanpur's tanneries, which have remained operational despite many threats issued from the courts? According to the 'Can We Save Ganga?' report, 'the tanneries in Tangra, Kolkata, were shifted to Bantala Leather Complex, close to East Kolkata Wetlands [in 2005]'. The Industrial Development Organization of the UN suggested that a certain number of chemical waste treatment units should be built to accommodate this move, but fewer units than the recommended number were built, and ones that were soon stopped functioning. 'The Bantala plan proved to be a failure and the tanners returned to Tangra.'

Despite this discouraging example, I wondered about the social, human, and financial consequences of shutting down the tanneries and converting them to a type of industry that has clean waste. Another option would be for some of the funds allocated to cleaning the Ganga that are not being used (or that are being misused) could be relegated to needs like redesigning industrial processes to generate less waste, retraining workers to adopt the new processes, building more effective treatment capacity, and incentivizing people to rent or lease products rather than purchasing them.

The focus on zero liquid discharge could even be the gateway into a new section of the Indian economy. In an article in the *Indian Journal of Science and Technology*, Nisha Rani Yaduvanshi, Rupesh Myana, and Saravan Krishnamurthy explore the urgent need for India to transition to a circular economy in which industrial processes are redesigned in order to prioritize recycling, zero waste, and the extension of product life cycles. Green consumerism and existing waste management practices derived from India and from developed countries (like enforcing landfill taxes on the polluters) will not be enough to meet the needs of India's growing middle class, they argue. 'The contention that "the poor cannot afford eco-friendly products" needs to be replaced with "the poor can be enabled with circular economy policies and sustainability practices". The transition from a linear to a circular economy in developing countries like India may prove to be challenging in the beginning, but is a necessary challenge to overcome.'

To put this bold vision in perspective, one has to consider that there are close to 700 polluting industries in Uttar Pradesh that currently discharge waste water into the river, according to the Central Pollution Control Board. While there are about 442 tanneries, their toxic waste only contributes 8 per cent of waste water to the river, primarily in Kanpur; a *Down to Earth* report mentions that the clustering of these tanneries near Kanpur is what makes the pollution concentration so high there. Sugar, pulp, paper, and chemical industries also contribute to polluting the river. And the government has published the names and locations of all these offenders.

THE DEMON OF KANPUR
As I left Kanpur, I had much to reflect upon. Since Rakeshji admitted he doesn't believe in the sacredness of the river, how, then, had he mustered the strength to keep going? How can his knowledge of the

history of pollution in Kanpur, grounded in specific neighbourhoods and drains, be codified for future generations to learn from? Was our flawed system of governance to blame for the pollution, or did it predate our independent government? Was the blame to be shared by colonialism, industrialism, the failure-to-thrive of Malaviya's 1916 moment, and the Green Revolution that led to India's sudden spike in population? We live in an era in which capitalism is the dominant paradigm, the engine that powers the contemporary demon of Kanpur. Yet Dr Shukla still sees the Ganga as an enchanted river, embodying the sacramental attitude to nature. For days, I tasted the Gangajal that had been thrust upon me; my insides felt coated in the dust from the toxic waste dump.

CHAPTER 4

THE CONFLUENCE OF WORLDS
(ALLAHABAD)

If like some insubstantial elephant of the sky
you would tumble from heaven
and taste the crystal stream,
so would your darkened shadow swell her
as the Jumna does at Prayag,
lending substance to a dream.

—Kalidasa, *The Cloud Messenger*

Gang-shikast: Encroachment of the Ganges, or any other river
—Wilson's *Glossary*

THE TRUTH ABOUT THE KUMBH MELA

I wondered if anything I'd believed about the Maha Kumbh Mela—
the largest gathering of human beings in the world, located within a
temporary 20-square-kilometre radius that Harvard researchers call a
'pop-up mega-city' spanning the confluence on the Allahabad and the
Jhunsi sides of the river—was actually true.

The only thing everyone can agree on is that the phrase Kumbh
Mela unequivocally means 'festival of water-pots'. (Astrologers equate
Kumbh with Aquarius, the water carrier.) It's a poignant name because
it suggests that our ancestors have been trying to contain the river in
some form for a long time. Beyond that, almost all key facts about
the festival—when and where it began, why it is celebrated, when it is
celebrated, how long it is celebrated for and even whether there is really
an authentic scriptural justification for it—are up for grabs.

The beginnings of the festival supposedly lie in the story of sagar
manthan—the battle in which gods and demons churned the oceans for
soma, amrita, the nectar of immortality—the same battle commemorated

by the Neelkanth Mahadev Temple I'd visited near Rishikesh, dedicated to the moment when Lord Shiva drank the halahala poison, which turned his throat blue. The celestial medic, Dhanvantari, put the nectar in a pot (kumbh) and carried it to paradise; on the way, as the story goes, he stopped in Prayag, Haridwar, Ujjain, and Nasik, spilling a few drops in each place. Today, the festival rotates among all four sites; the Maha Kumbh Mela in Prayag, which occurs every twelve years in order to mark an astrological milestone, is the largest.

One of the most oft-repeated superhuman claims is that the Maha Kumbh Mela has been celebrated since time immemorial, an unchanging and enduring tribute to Gangaji. For example, as historian Kama Maclean notes, in January 2001 *India Today* described the festival as follows:

> In Prayag, Allahabad for modern India, it's the biggest show on earth, conceived by Hinduism's antique memory, conscripted by mythology, history and tradition, and enacted by keepers of wisdom and seekers of moksha. It's the costume drama of nirvana and the passion-play of the East and the naked dance of asceticism and the hara-hara delirium of the hippie and the raw picturesque of pure faith rolled into one oversized panorama of India in its divine diversity—even in the digital age.

All this just modernizes the sentiments of Jawaharlal Nehru, who grew up in Allahabad, and wanted a portion of his ashes scattered at Triveni Sangam. Although Nehru was a staunch modernist, he justified his pride in the 'eternal' tradition of worshipping the Ganga:

> I have had an attachment for the Ganga and Yamuna ever since my childhood, and as I get older this connection strengthens.[...] The Ganga is a symbol of India's age-long culture and civilization, changeless, always flowing, but always the Ganga.... Of course, I have abandoned the old-fashioned traditions, and I want to break the chains which constrain India and oppress innumerable people and which prevent the development of their minds and bodies. But even though I want all of these things, I cannot completely separate myself from these old traditions. It is a great source of pride to me that this magnificent succession of heritage is ours, and will always be uniquely ours, and I know very well that I,

like all of us, am a part of this chain, which will never, ever be broken, because this chain has gone on since the beginning of India's eternal history. I could never break this chain, because I see such unbounded worth in it, and it gives me inspiration, courage and spirit.

Maclean asserts that it was the Magh Mela, not the Kumbh Mela, which has taken place for millennia. She suggests that in *The Discovery of India*, Nehru conflates the Magh and the Kumbh, since he says:

> In my own city of Allahabad, or Hardwar, I would go to the great bathing festivals, the Kumbh Mela, and see hundreds of thousands of people come, as their forebears had come for thousands of years from all over India, to bathe in the Ganges. I would remember descriptions of these festivals written thirteen hundred years ago by Chinese pilgrims and others, and even then these festivals were ancient and lost in an unknown antiquity. What was the tremendous faith, I wondered, that had drawn our people for untold generations to this famous river of India?

Wade backwards and even deeper through the murky details, and you will find that, due to the astrological disagreement and lack of authoritative claim, in some years, like 1941 and 1942, or 1965 and 1966, the Kumbh Mela was held twelve months, not twelve years, apart in Allahabad. What's more, there's no Puranic mention of amrita falling in the four different cities. Some historians, like T. K. Bhattacharya, speculate that priests in the four cities, who were competing with each other for pilgrims, each grafted the Kumbh legend onto their own little stretch of the Ganga.

According to Maclean, 'The British took a condescending view of religious flexibility of this kind.' She quotes Edward Connolly from 1837, who damningly characterized the Hindu practice of naming local spots after more famous sacred places elsewhere: 'By this simple process, the Hindu thinks to concentrate a quantity of holiness into a small space, and needy, feeble, or business-bound piety indulges in the plausible consolation of worshipping at home and at ease, the objects of a difficult and expensive pilgrimage.'

This condescending attitude downplays the extent of competition for choice riverside real estate amongst militant sadhus. The bottom line regarding the Kumbh Mela at the confluence of the three rivers is that the Triveni Sangam has long been a contested site where sadhus and the government have uneasily shared power. But, to put it in perspective, according to Lord Elphinstone, who served as the Magistrate of Allahabad, during just one of many turf battles between jousting Naga sadhus representing the opposing camps of Shiva and Vishnu at the Haridwar Kumbh, the body count was supposedly 18,000—in 1760! While that number may be an overstatement, Elphinstone summoned it in order to justify why the British government needed to oversee the religious festival.

Indeed, this tension between the colonial government and local religious leaders may have actually spawned the modern Kumbh. Maclean suggests that the Prayagwals invented the Kumbh around 1860, after the Mutiny, in order to drum up business more effectively. The Prayagwals are Brahmin priests who steer pilgrims through rituals at Prayag. They 'establish their exclusive rights to serve pilgrims at the Triveni' with reference to a firman by Emperor Akbar, dated 1593. After the British claimed Allahabad in 1801, the East India Company soon established a one-rupee-per-person pilgrim tax (plus parking fees). At the time, a person could have lived comfortably for a month on that amount. But it's not just that; prior to the British, no one would have dreamed of associating fees with access to the river for spiritual purposes.

According to Maclean, the British and the Prayagwals didn't trust each other. In the British view, the Prayagwals did everything they could to '[squeeze] those who come for salvation', as a British writer in the 1830s noted. Meanwhile the Prayagwals did their best to convince pilgrims that the British were trying to convert everyone to Christianity. Because pilgrims came to the Sangam from all across India, this rumour spread throughout the country. Tension mounted over the decades and in June 1857, the Prayagwals joined the Mutiny of the 6th Native Infantry.

Colonel Neal's 'pacification' of Allahabad involved attacking Daragunj, where 'a nest of pryagwalas [sic] has been very troublesome in stopping communication over the Ganges by taking control over the bridge of boats.' Many Prayagwals were persecuted and their land was confiscated. (It's possible that the modern-day festival takes place on part of their ancestral land.) Nearly 1,500 families 'were thereafter forced to live as beggars in obscure towns and in jungles to evade capture. The Prayagwals took aim against their rivals, the missionaries who often vied for pilgrims' attention; they smashed the mission press and churches in Allahabad.'

Eventually, an uneasy and pragmatic truce was reached. This led to the increased importance of the Kumbh Mela as the place where religious authority figures could exercise their power, which was otherwise co-opted by colonial officials. This impulse to redefine the priests' power seems to have been a life-preserving act on part of the British. Maclean cites a report in Allen's *Indian Mail*, after the 1860 Magh Mela:

> The spot opposite the confluence is covered with rude flagstaves; and it is strange that upon the flags themselves there are many allusions to occurrences which one would little expect to see commemorated close to the fort, and just under the muzzles of its guns. One flag represents a set of black soldiers, whom it is easy to identify as pandies (rebels), portrayed in the act of triumph over fallen enemies, and the faces of the slain are *white*. On another flag are seen a group of artillery men, engaged with a fort, which it is plain to see was intended to represent an English one. In every place are to be seen symbols of the bloody and cruel nature of heathenism, and it is not difficult to divine, from the scowls and mutterings of men as Europeans pass by, what they would do if they dared.

Even today, pilgrims rely on the flags to identify their own family's Prayagwal and some flags have sepoys painted on them.

Despite so much contestation, it's clear that the sandy floodplain across from the imposing fort, lined with the colourful flags and tin-shed enclosures, continues to play an integral role in the evolution of Indian-ness.

As modern Hinduism developed in reaction to colonialism, perhaps the bathing festival, which feeds an age-old impulse to connect with others, and to co-create rituals celebrating the sacredness of water, needed to be re-dreamed and re-branded as limitlessly ancient. But the core message was the same one I'd grasped in my red bucket bath, the one I'd seen scrawled inside the cabin near Gaumukh: Water is Life. Ganga, Ganga.

'PUL MELA'

The 1993 short story 'Pul Mela' by Vikram Seth takes place shortly after the Indian independence, in a fictional town called Brahmpur, during a fictional spring bathing festival upon the 'beautiful and placid' Ganga. The festival seems to be modelled upon the Magh Mela, and many of the elements Seth describes are still very much in play today: the 'ocean of tents', a 'semi-permanent pontoon bridge' that crosses the Ganga, temporary roads made of metal plates, akharas of militant sadhus vying for proximity to the holy river, and a plethora of babas, including an Engine-Driver Baba.

The protagonist, twenty-year-old Dipankar Chatterjee, has come to the mela to sit at the feet of Sanaki Baba. A family friend introduces him as follows: 'His father is a judge of the Calcutta High Court. And he is searching for the truth.' The story focuses on a stampede at the festival; special trains continue to admit incoming pilgrims even though the crowd has no space to move; a thousand people perish within fifteen minutes, and the river turns to 'bloodied slush'.

Chatterjee asks Sanaki Baba, 'Today, Baba, how do you explain all this?... Is it all the sport of the universe, the games of God? Are they fortunate because they died in this auspicious spot on this auspicious festival?'

The Baba offers an 'interim' response: 'I think there was a flaw in the administrative arrangements,' he says.

There is a real-life precedent to the stampede Seth fictionalizes. In 1954, at the first Kumbh Mela after Independence, a stampede started by an elephant killed up to 800 people. Since then, ensuring a safe and calm festival has become a matter of the utmost political importance. In 2013, according to the state of U.P., 100 million pilgrims attended the Kumbh Mela. However, independent observers suggest that there were only a scant 40 to 60 million.

Prayag, which means foremost place of sacrifice, is a tirtha, or spiritual crossing place; it's believed that rites here, especially when performed at the right time, lead to superior spiritual results. Since the confluence is the sum of many rivers, religious studies scholars Diana Eck and Kalpesh Bhatt suggest that it's believed that other tirthas come to Prayag to be cleansed and that 'all the Hindu Gods [are] congregated in the landscape and river setting'. During the Kumbh, the waters are supposed to be

Bidisha Banerjee

alive with the nectar of immortality. Eck and Bhatt describe snan, a rite in which most people simply dip into the river and then take the water into their cupped hands to pour back into the river as an offering to their ancestors and gods.

Pilgrims from all over the country vie for bathing spots with the akharas—collectives of ascetics who disdain the trappings of the material world. Some akharas are interfaith; the Juna Akhara celebrates Buddhist and Muslim members, like His Holiness the XIV Dalai Lama and Multani Baba, a Sufi saint. Some akharas are comprised primarily of Sikhs. These ascetics build their encampments around dhuni—sacred fire pits. According to Eck and Bhatt, these represent—but in a different way than I would find elsewhere along my travels—all five essential elements of the universe: earth, water, fire, air, and space. The ancient idea that the microcosm mirrors the macrocosm suggests that the fire pit symbolizes both the psychological body and the physical body. Like all the pilgrims, the members of the akharas come from 'diverse traditions that have partially sacrificed...their...differences to seek understanding and even harmony'.

It seems safe to assume that since humans create stress on the river, which then increases the stress on humans, the world's largest accumulation of people on the river's banks would have an extremely significant impact on the ecosystem. Yet, this contested battleground is also the site for the world's largest example of effective human cooperation. It wasn't until I met Dr Dhruv Kazi that I realized that the Sangam is not just a collection of historical and mythological tales, but a fertile intersection for re-imagining the possibilities ahead of Gangaji.

POP-UP MEGA-CITY
'The river is the deity. The temple is just an anchor point for the deity,' Dr Dhruv Kazi emphasized, pointing to a photo he had taken near Gangotri. Kazi is the cardiologist, economist, and public health expert I had consulted earlier when I was trying to understand the pollution in the river at Kanpur. He was born in Mumbai to devout parents. Splashing around in the river during pilgrimages to the Gangotri and Yamunotri was an integral part of his childhood.

Asked about his personal relationship with the river, his confident, expert voice softened. 'For me, it's almost magical to see the river going from this roaring young person up in the mountains to this gentle, serene, older person as it meanders through the plains. Because it's honestly a living metaphor for our lives.'

Kazi offers a metaphor inspired by his cardiological training. 'I don't think the scale of it came home until I did this Kumbh project and saw what the river means to such a large swathe of humanity. Rivers, by virtue of their role in commerce, have been the arteries of the continents. To think that we could in some ways reduce them to canals is unfathomable. Future generations will look back and say, what were we thinking?'

Dr Kazi was part of an interdisciplinary Harvard team of scholars of religion, public health, business, governance, technology, and urban planning who descended upon the 2013 Kumbh Mela in order to learn from it. The team collected its findings about the 2013 festival, which they called the 'Big Data Kumbh' in *Kumbh Mela: Mapping the Ephemeral Megacity*. Here are some of the marvellous facts that they report:

In the Ganga's floodplain, near the confluence with the Yamuna at Allahabad, a city is virtually built once every twelve years. 'The sense of elastic accommodation within the temporary settlement is outstanding and unique,' write design scholars Rahul Mehrotra and Felipe Vera. They are enthralled by the temporary sturdiness of the Kumbh Mela as a 'pop-up mega-city' with its seventeen floating pontoon bridges, the roads built from steel plates locals carry without heavy machinery, the degradable thatch and bamboo, the reuse of tents at other festivals throughout the country, and the 'unspecific and adjustable technology of simple metal clamps used for connecting pieces of infrastructure' that can be easily taken apart. Reversibility—of both materials and governance structures—and openness—to improvise and leave plans incomplete—are the key lessons that the Kumbh Mela holds for them.

Since the area is flooded during the monsoon from June to October, organizers only have two months to build the mega-city and two months to disassemble it; moreover, since the river shifts every day during the festival, sandbags and safety barricades have to be shifted along with it. More than 250,000 people were treated free of charge by the health facilities, and electricity flowed abundantly throughout the settlement, completely free. There were no epidemics or massive accidents, other than a horrific stampede at the Allahabad railway station that left thirty-six people dead.

Because, by tradition, the riverbank has been free for ages (until the British imposed the one-rupee tax in the nineteenth century), no one pays an admission fee, and, thanks to wealthy patrons, many pilgrims received free meals. The entire festival cost about 1.55 billion rupees, or 300 million USD (the current budget is almost 4,200 crore rupees). Infrastructure included building 45,000 toilets, and 9,000 sweepers who patrolled the area at night, picking up faeces left in the open, spraying it with DDT, and burning it. The pollution was minimal; polythene bags were banned. Swami Chidananda patrolled the temporary city; he and his followers attempted to enhance the role of spiritual leaders at the festival to include raising awareness about ecological toilets and breathing new life into a tired acronym (G. A. P.). This entailed shifting blame from the failed Ganga Action Plan to the Ganga Action Parivar, or family, in which everyone bore equal responsibility for the Ganga.

The 1954 stampede at the first Kumbh Mela post-Independence was embarrassing for Prime Minister Nehru and other newly appointed government officials who had seen the festival as an opportunity to connect with the populace of the new country. (The families of the victims were never compensated and MacLean claims that the illiterate pilgrims were blamed by the government for listening to god-men.) Following the stampede, a judicial review committee suggested better management in order to avoid a future tragedy and ordered that dams upstream release more water into the river during the Kumbh. Lo and behold, the Ganga started to look more like her old self. Many safeguards were put in place to ensure swimmers wouldn't drown in the swift-goer and the tanneries were shut down for the duration of the Kumbh, dramatically reducing the amount of heavy metal pollution in the river.

Delivering a safe, healthy religious festival has become a matter of pride for the Uttar Pradesh government, which at all other times seems beleaguered and stagnant in terms of its ability to clean the river, even when, if not especially, the funds are available. In their contribution to *Kumbh Mela: Mapping the Ephemeral Megacity*, business experts Tarun Khanna and John Macomber questioned how the Kumbh Mela managed to successfully serve millions more people, for a longer period of time, with less central government support than the notoriously ill-fated

Commonwealth Games in Delhi or the 2014 FIFA World Cup in Brazil.

ACCOUNTABLE RE-ENCHANTMENT

In sum, these experts suggest that having a singular shared purpose—facilitating a good experience for pilgrims—allowed the Uttar Pradesh government to match its ambition with its capabilities. Its minimalist approach was to ensure that the pilgrims were safe and had access to electricity; it then stepped back and allowed civil society and the private sector to do the rest. In keeping with their training, the Harvard experts predicted that, as even more people try to access the Kumbh in the coming decades, charging visitor fees during future Maha Kumbhs will ensure a high-quality festival; nonetheless, the experts acknowledge that this will create even greater class stratification in terms of access to the Ganga. Other members of the Harvard team—design scholars Benjamin Scheerbarth, Alykhan Mohamed, and Vineet Diwadkar—concluded, 'Dignity and cultural tolerance are pursued over individual ego and identity. This...allows a form of collaboration with non-governmental actors that is agile, flexible, and responsive.'

Notably, Kazi and his team of public-health experts found that faecal coliform levels were much lower in the river than they had expected both upstream and downstream of the Mela. 'We were surprised that diarrhoeal diseases were not very high. In hindsight, it makes sense because [the U.P. Jal Nigam] made a lot of effort to provide potable drinking water,' Kazi told me. A research team led by Annu Baranwal from the Tata Institute of Social Sciences notes that the U.P. Jal Nigam provided 45 litres of water per person per day through forty-two high-pressure pumps connected via a 550-kilometre network of pipelines. The Tata Group of Companies added to this resource.

I remembered what Dr A. K. Shukla, the co-founder of Eco Friends in Kanpur, had told me about bacteriophages—the viruses abundant in the Ganga that target and devour extremely specific strains of bacteria, apparently controlling diseases like cholera. Did bacteriophages bridge the gap between modern science and mythical claims about the Ganga's self-cleansing properties? Cautioning that he was not an expert on the subject, Kazi expressed scepticism that this was the reason why he and the public health team saw less diarrhoea than expected. His doubts stem from the fact that in many places, the river is so polluted that phages, which are sensitive to their breeding conditions, cannot survive there.

He did, however, confirm what Rakeshji had suggested back in Kanpur. Pollution is most intense during the dry season. During the monsoon, the flow in the river is so great that the contaminants are flushed out to the ocean—a reminder that in some sense, the Ganga can still wash away sins. Of course, we are not used to talking about faecal matter, let alone heavy metals, toxic waste, or the factories that produce them, as sins. Nor are the sins really gone: I pointed out that once the waste reaches the ocean, it may be eaten by fish that people might eventually consume. Dr Kazi admitted that this was a problem. Nowadays, TV and newspapers carry so many reports about micro plastic, mercury, and other chemicals in seafood as well as country-sized masses of debris floating across oceans.

I told Dr Kazi about people I met during my travels, like Veer Bhadra Mishra in Kanpur who claimed to drink Gangajal every day and thrive. 'I would caution against using the anecdotes of people who have used this water and seem to be doing well. That's called a survivorship bias,' he said, noting that the association between heavy metals and kidney diseases and malignancies is well documented.

Dr Kazi also warned me against conflating 'the absence of the evidence with the evidence of absence', and insisted that the public-health argument would be strong enough to carry the day if the political arguments weren't even stronger. 'Beijing comes to mind as a directly equivalent example where there is a clear desire to clean up the air. There are so many entrenched stakeholders when there is a price to be paid for cleaning up the air. And the same is true for the river.'

I shared with Dr Kazi my frustration with the NMCG Interim Report, which refrained from estimating the cost of the damage to public health posed by the river's current levels of contamination and flow. It could also be argued that the NMCG has shied away from the work required. When I visited their headquarters at the Central Government Office Complex in New Delhi in 2015, I saw the following words on a multicoloured sign:

> Work is a never-ending process. It can never be completed. Life is
> not only about work, office, and client. You need time to socialize,
> entertain, relax, and exercise. Don't let life be meaningless. A person
> who stays late at the office is a fool who does not know how to

manage work.... H/she is inefficient and incompetent... You did not study hard and struggle in life to become a machine.

In all fairness though, as I told him, it's hard to assess the actual cost of cleaning the river because the balance sheets are falsified and the public has been told that a true accounting of the hazards to health and culture posed by the contamination in the river cannot be done.

Dr Kazi's response was at once challenging and hopeful. 'What's important,' he said, is to understand 'the order of magnitude rather than an exact number... You don't have to get an exact dollar value. You can say X million versus X billion versus X trillion.' That has been done, he told me, with other evaluations involving the environment and public health. 'It's not trivial,' he admitted, 'but it's not impossible.'

I asked him why the Uttar Pradesh government couldn't perform as effectively all the time with regard to the river. After all, it comes through every twelve years during the Maha Kumbh. Dr Kazi took me from background forward, surprising me with his emphasis on publicity—but I came to see his point.

After the 1954 stampede, he explained, it was necessary to have a 'successful' Kumbh Mela (the scare quotes are his). That became 'a litmus test for the government's capacity to deliver', and it gives a government like that of Uttar Pradesh—notorious for its executive inability—the sudden opportunity to show that they can take accountability seriously. It becomes 'almost a singular marker' of the capacity to get something done, 'all the way up the chain of command. It's a matter of pride for the chief minister.'

But there's a subtle problem. There's no 'breaking news' for the media barring a stampede or a major disaster. Unfortunately, 'the taking down of the Kumbh is far more haphazard and a lot more chaotic, with far less concern for the impact on the environment. The clean-up leaves a lot to be desired.' That's not considered big news and hence, does not get the requisite coverage in news media: 'If we had a major outbreak of infection along the river then we would clean it up. But when there are steady-state infections, diseases, destruction of the environment, no one is accountable.'

Kazi continued, 'Particularly in northern India, if we made small investments in cleaning up the river, or cleaning up our environment and our health, we would make such tremendous gains that in hindsight it would be a no-brainer. But we're trapped. We've built a system where the population can't envision a better way. In order to fix something, you have to be able to imagine a better world. And we're so entrenched in the status quo, we've so accepted that this is how things ought to be that we can't even imagine a better world. And that's the trap I would like to see us get out of. Because there are real public health consequences to what the river is dealing with and there are real economic consequences. You can, if you do it thoughtfully, put a dollar value on the consequences of these infections and malignancies that are associated with the contamination of the water. And when you do that, the case for fixing it is self-evident,' Kazi said.

'Don't you think some sense of re-enchantment with the river is needed?' I asked. I felt uncomfortable bringing up my closeted worship of Gangaji, except in the most general terms.

He agreed with me, but was quick to add, 'Re-enchantment *plus* accountability.' For Dr Kazi, it's no longer enough to trust in the river's omniscience or omnipotence. 'Humans need to take responsibility for what they are doing to the river.'

'Some say the top level mean well but the middle managers get in the way,' I suggested.

'When people really care, in India, the accountability is there,' Dr Kazi responded, refusing to give the central government a pass. 'The Kumbh is emblematic of that. People do care, but do they care enough to take on the deeply entrenched stakeholders?'

I asked him what might be possible for the river a hundred years from now. He spoke about imagination as the capacity that's most needed in order to escape from the unnecessary trap of living with the status quo. The social and legal steps necessary to negotiate an accountable re-enchantment with the Ganga are important to understand: 'We constrain our young minds to say this is how things are; these are things that are taken as a given. Imagination is a skill that we sometimes don't teach well. And it can be taught.'

The vision of a clean and sustainable mega-city being built and disappearing in a period of months left a deep impression on me. It helped me synthesize my visit to Haridwar and my exploration of the history behind the building of the Ganges Canal and Malaviya's opposition to it. In particular, it helped me understand the dynamics behind the population explosion in the Ganga River basin and the consequent change in how people relate to the river. Certainly British and American economic interests, aided by local elites who also benefited from those interests, had a lot to do with the change in behaviours and attitudes towards the river. When the canal was constructed, little was known about the wisdom of letting lands lie fallow, or about the consequences of exponential population growth. But given the current state of arguably the most important river of the country, the efforts taken by the government during the Kumbh Mela need to be carried out at a much larger scale and at much more frequent intervals than a few months every twelve years.

CHAPTER 5

MODEL BEHAVIOUR
IN THE AGE OF DISSOLUTION (VARANASI)

> After washing the Lord's feet, Kevat drinks some of the Ganga jal
> and distributes the rest to the members of his family who gain
> great merit as a result.
>
> —Verses translated from original in Kevat Anurag [booklet in
> Hindi and Bhojpuri], *An Anthology of Writings on the Ganga*

TOTAL SOLAR ECLIPSE

At the beginning of time, the great gods churned the ocean and found the nectar of immortality, only to have it stolen and gulped down by Rahu, the astronomical body that causes eclipses and oversees meteors. The sun and moon gods tattled to Vishnu, who beheaded the demon; his body perished, but his head, having absorbed the nectar, had become immortal. Since then, whenever he can manage it, Rahu, also the lord of petroleum mining, fertilizers, chemicals, stock markets, and destructive growth—the lord of contemporary India—swallows the sun and the moon. But they always sail back out of his gaping throat and rearrange themselves in the sky. (It's worth mentioning here that Rahu isn't simply, or always, a villain. Some members of the Dalit Dusadh caste trace their lineage back to him and honour him.)

At 6.24 a.m. on 22 July 2009, I stood with 70,000 people hip-deep in the grey, gluey mud of the Ganga, swirling with ashes, flowers, sloughed-off sin, and faecal bacteria. Although the sun had stumbled into a stratus sky only an hour ago, the clouds gave way and starlight began to play on the opalescent river. We battled a compulsion to stare straight into the cosmic misalignment; we mutely implored the sun to pass through Rahu's mouth, throat, and neck once again. The monkeys of Varanasi had turned their backs to the sun as soon as the strangeness started and the city's birds began to fly in erratic patterns. The total solar eclipse was a cosmological epic—the longest such eclipse in this century. The darkness revealed itself most fully to North Iwo Jima, an uninhabited island off the coast of Japan, where the eclipse lasted for six minutes and thirty-eight seconds. Varanasi, where darkness lingered for three minutes and ten seconds, had cloudless skies and the best view in India. The next eclipse to outlast this one will not occur until the year 2132.

At Tulsi Ghat, one of the city's hundred stone-stepped entranceways into the river, more than a thousand of us pressed close, clapping and cheering with the rapidly darkening sun. Our quotidian star glows at 10,800 degrees Fahrenheit, but a total eclipse reveals the sun's own atmosphere, the corona, white-hot at 3.6 million degrees and poised to slice vision out of an upturned eye. Some viewers wore cardboard 3D glasses. One family peered through an X-ray of a child's femur—deeply opaque, as long as the light didn't pass through the white bone. I looked through my pitch black rectangular sheet of welder's glass. The after-images return to me to this day—dim yolks and certain radiant surfaces (glinting buttons, a refrigerator's bright white reflection, the liquid rays of sweat running down a cold plastic bottle) have the power to bring them back.

Bit by bit, the moon's shadow slid over the sun, hooding its glow until only the thin corona encircled the erasure. Some call this sight 'God's eye'. In the few seconds before the moon extinguished the sun, a flash ate through a lunar valley. We gasped. God's eye had morphed into a diamond ring. The national networks would later obsessively replay this moment, like a cosmic DeBeers commercial.

That darkness reigned long enough for a boatman's wordless song to propel his oars to the middle of the inky, glittering river. It was long enough for me to screw my eyes shut, clamp my nose against the faecal bacteria, and dip my head along with everyone else under the warm water. I expected to be revolted, but I wasn't. During my childhood in Kolkata, my great-grandmother and grandparents had regarded both faeces and the gods with a singular affection—two parts awe, one part comedy. My great-grandmother used to croon about a legendary queen's impressive bowel movements: '*Nyar, nyar nyareshwari, tumi go ma parameshwari*' 'Turd, turd, supreme darling turd, you, my mother, are the empress of all beings.' Head held under the dark water, I imagined unclamping my nose. With my right nostril I would breathe in the river's might and muck, with my left breathe out the mantra vibrating up and down the currents: 'Sita Ram, Sita Ram.'

When I came back up, the scene was playing backward—the boatman departing, the shadow sliding off the sun, the diamond ring iridescing. The horrific, seductive misalignment of the world, compressed into three minutes, could be—was being—reversed. Everyone was cheering and taking a ritual second dip. A few exulting men swam out towards the vast centre of the river, their bare chests tiny and distant, as if bobbing out at sea. 'Sita Ram, Sita Ram,' I mouthed along with everyone else, hoping that the once-human deities would annihilate the rumblings of my belly, ritually empty except for a sneaked cup of predawn tea. The light was so powerful that it seemed to penetrate my retinas and reach into my gums. I had a scorched flavour in my mouth well into the evening.

That afternoon, I walked until I found the virtually dry river Varuna, which, along with the river Assi, gives Varanasi its name. Flowing until about 1998, Varuna is just a drain now, choked with plastic diapers, rotting vegetables, construction waste, and sewage sludge, attended by a small army of pigs and goats snuffling about in the mounds of garbage. As I walked past the sewage, I was joined by Chhotu, a Dalit man who works as a day-labourer and lives in a riverfront slum named Gangotri Bihar. I told him that some climate scientists feared that the Ganga would severely recede in a couple of generations. We also discussed the eclipse. When I asked him what the Ganga might look like in 2132, he laughed and remarked that wise people were saying that the whole world would be under water long before that.

While I was in India, rumours—now discredited—were flying that the mighty river might be gone within a generation. A 2007 report by the Intergovernmental Panel on Climate Change had suggested that all Himalayan glaciers could disappear by 2035. As it turned out, the original source, a paper from 1991, had estimated that all non-polar glaciers might disappear by *2350*. This typographical confusion was not cleared up until January 2010, six months after my trip.

Relying on the error, I baited my host in Varanasi, Veer Bhadra Mishra, a hydrological engineer and spiritual leader, by telling him that the river might dry up in thirty-five years if nothing was done to stanch the melting of glaciers. Mishra, who died in 2013, two years after I met him, was appropriately sceptical, even though his concern for the Ganga was beyond question: he had spent much of the past three decades working to clean the river, starting a foundation that is hoping to use algae to eat the five hundred thousand gallons of raw municipal sewage dumped into the river each day. 'You're talking like a politician,' he told me, insisting that climate change was America's problem. 'And even if the glaciers melt, Gangaji is mostly rain-fed.'

'Faith and rationality are like two banks of the same river,' Mishra told me, while quizzing me about the possibility of getting carbon credits for his algae scheme. 'Paying equal attention to both ensures a happily flowing life, and a happily flowing Gangaji.' Mishra's views on the conjunction between faith and rationality are subjective and his views on the impact of glacier-melt on the river are problematic. Moreover, as far as I know, his algae-powered waste water treatment system was never implemented. But his contribution to the cause of the Ganga—and its conservation—is legendary and continues to inspire environmentalists.

In the weeks after I stood in the Ganga at Varanasi while Rahu swallowed the sun, the swallowing seemed seasonable and lasted much less than a day; the monsoon, far from appearing unexpectedly, was late, stunting crops throughout the region. While the auguries of the climate modellers seemed less hazy than those of the mythological sages, from the comfort of one's home, there were probably just as difficult to imagine unless one actually travelled along the course of the entire river. As a social ecologist born at the mouth of the Ganga and trained in the United States, I felt an odd responsibility to imagine the river's future as clearly as I could. I began to wonder whether those like me, galvanized by the prospect of the river drying up, were starved for a kind of clarity that our information age, with all its uncertainties, failed to provide.

At one point in my conversation with Mishra, I asked him about the Gayatri mantra, which Jahnu Muni had chanted by the river in a yuga far before Kali. I settled onto Mishra's divan, eagerly waiting to accompany Mishra to his evening lesson with one of the foremost teachers of Hindustani vocal music. The songs he sang—from obscure ragas to super-hits—are now inextricable for me from the rhythm of the Ganga at Varanasi.

COSMOLOGICAL CONNECTIONS AND DISCONNECTIONS

History palpably lingers in Varanasi, tempting, and sometimes masking, the dangers of nostalgia—especially, looking to the past and to organized efficient structures that made cosmological connections between the human body and the cosmos while privileging some groups at the expense of others. Varanasi has been settled since prehistoric times, and the cosmological connection exemplified in the city's pilgrim routes is a lesson in not moving too quickly into elegant models that easily include abuse and exclusion.

Scholars describe how pilgrims come to Varanasi on yatras, or pilgrimages, to find tirthas, or crossing points, between the mundane and the sacred:

> At dawn on the ghats of Ganga as pilgrims dip into the Ganga, they move back in time, symbolically die to the world and then are reborn into the light of the rising sun which is itself reborn every morning.... The Panchakroshi Yatra covers a distance of 5x5 krosha (i.e. 55.2 miles/88.6 km), requiring five nights and six days of walking and 108 shrines.... The circuit has two centres, the ancient centre of Kashi at Madhyameshvara and the ritual centre of Kashi at the Jnanavapi well where the initiation and concluding rites for most of the yatras take place.

There are five sacred pilgrimage routes in Varanasi that affirm the similarities of macrocosm (the five elements) and microcosm (the human body): Chaurashikroshi (sky and head), Panchakroshi (earth and legs), Nagar Pradakshina (air and face), Avimukta (water and blood), and Antargriha (fire and heart). This is only the beginning of a multidimensional cosmic trigonometry that is fascinating. At the same time, it's also a way in which the religious elite of Varanasi have perpetuated mystification and caste-based inequity. Perhaps the most telling example is the second route. The geographer Rana P. B. Singh describes its meanings:

> A total of 108 sacred sites and shrines are found along this route [Panchakroshi]. The number 108 has a cosmogonic scope related to the constellations (lunar mansions) and the rhythm of human cognition. It defines cardinality, centrality and circulation. Further,

it refers to a product of 12 (the yearly cycle of months in a year) x 9 (the cosmic space denoting nine planets in Hindu mythology). Other cosmogonic parallels are: a product of 27 constellations, and four parts of the day, of four directions; a product of 36 crores (360 million) divine beings, and three mythical realms; and also the product of the powers of the three basic integers, i.e. 1^1 x 2^2 x 3^3.

The fifth and final route, Antargriha, with meanings as complex in the second, culminates in a ritual bath in the Ganga at the Manikarnika Ghat after which, in the inner sanctum of the Vishveshwara Temple, supplicants 'receive the highest religious merit, resulting in peace and relief from transmigration'. This final route has a spiral shape and is related to the seven chakras. Travelling this path empowers pilgrims to feel as if they are 'a vital part of the energy vortex behind all life' and that they have the power to reshape their world.

This is a landscape rich in memories, as many generations of Hindus have followed the same pathway, visited the same shrines, watched the same sun rising through the mists, and performed darshan to the same gods and goddesses.

In the Puranas, the Ganga exists in three realms: the celestial Milky Way, or Akash Ganga; the earthly river we revere and befoul today; and Patal Ganga, which flows through the netherworld. Those who want to taste this third Ganga go to the Gyanvapi well at the centre of Varanasi, which marks the start and end point of the Panchakroshi pilgrimage. The Gyanvapi well (the name means well of spiritual knowledge) was once considered more sacred than the river itself. It is located between the Vishwanath Temple and the Gyanvapi Mosque, which replaced a temple, and therefore is a source of simmering conflict.

I have always wondered why communal violence and war seem to be easier than facing our own repressed emotions and attending to our communities' health. To bring the Ganga back from the brink, we will have to stop averting our eyes from our waste products, bodily and industrial. This is what I thought of when I read civil engineer U. K. Chaudhary's book, *The Living Similarity Between Ganga and the Human Body* (2003), to which I will return later.

We seem to be willing, for as long as possible, to ignore the toxic sludge that pours into the Ganga, the shadow of the steady accretion of pulp, paper, sugar, oil, and leather—not to mention industrial and pharmaceutical pollution—in our lives. It's untouchable. After all, capitalism idealizes cleanliness and orderliness, as Dipesh Chakrabarty, an anthropologist and expert on the lives of Varanasi boatmen, has remarked.

The prime minister has asked every person in the diaspora to build one toilet back in India (or at least to pay for someone to build it). Yet we already know that numerous counterproductive attempts have been made to improve sanitation in India. However, according to Assa Doron, these attempts have been counter-productive because they focus on throwing money and technology at the issue and seek to impose middle- and upper-class sensibilities upon people without cultural and infrastructural privilege. Former Environment Minister Jairam Ramesh conceived the 'Bride for Toilet' scheme, which encourages families to gift a toilet as dowry. However, the scheme ignored the water shortage and people's natural inclination to troupe down to the fields in order to socialize while going about their business.

One reality is that newly constructed toilets funded by this scheme and numerous others have been used as storerooms and garbage dumps. Another reality, although relatively rare, is the eco-san (ecological and sanitary) toilet. It separates urine and faeces, uses little or no water, and lasts a family of five for one year. The gap between pulling down one's pants and flushing away the deed into our rivers involves a habit, only about a century old (and a legacy of the British Raj), which deeply disconnects us from the fouler parts of the circle of life.

MODEL BEHAVIOUR

Today, the evolution of virtual modelling technology allows us to inhabit many rigorously quantified imaginaries: how many million litres of water could break the Tehri dam? How much sewage could the sandy bank on the shore across from Varanasi withstand? The more dynamic the model, the more ways it can be used to simulate the future and perhaps even control the pace of change.

In this heyday of virtual modelling, it was refreshing to read Binay Singh's article about an 80,000-square-foot physical scale model of the Ganga. Built on the campus of Banaras Hindu University (BHU) in

1985, the year before Rajiv Gandhi announced the first Ganga Action Plan, the model is known as the Ganga Research Centre, or Ganga Laboratory. Retired civil engineering professor U. K. Chaudhary, who built the model, called it 'the first and only one of its kind in India'. I decided I had to visit the Ganga Lab and see the model for myself.

There was only one problem: in 2014, when journalist Binay Singh tried to visit the '42,000 cubic feet of Ganga soil and nearly 280-ft straight rigid boundary channel with 7,000 cubic feet capacity sump tank' during working hours, he found the gate locked. Professor P. K. Singh Dixit, who was nominally in charge of the laboratory, told Singh that there was a PhD student who still used the lab, but Singh's article alleged that it had actually been neglected since U. K. Chaudhary retired from BHU in 2011. Singh questioned why the laboratory should be in disrepair at a time when Prime Minister Narendra Modi had just announced the formation of a new Ganga Knowledge Centre (GKC), which the National Mission for Clean Ganga envisioned as uniquely generating 'state of the art scientific and technical knowledge' accommodating 'traditional and local knowledge' yet 'focused on relevant issues' and 'connected to the stakeholders'.

For months, the image of a massive, earthen model of the river situated near the banks of the actual river, about as old as the first Ganga Action Plan, built with public funds but barricaded from the public, haunted me. In my imagination, the model fell just short of capturing the beauty and fluidity of the entire meandering river in its wholeness of headstreams, tributaries, and distributaries. I visualized tiny papier mâché Himalaya and a fang-toothed crèche where the Bhimgora barrage diverted the river into the Upper Ganges Canal. How did the model represent upper Tibet, where the sinuous Yarlung-Tsangpo, the upper arm of the Brahmaputra, sometimes called 'the Everest of Rivers', originates? Did the model hint at the canyon the Tsangpo has carved out over centuries, now considered the world's largest? Would the model do justice to the Tsangpo as it became the Siang in Arunachal Pradesh, and then the Brahmaputra in Assam, and then the Jamuna in Bangladesh, where it joined the Ganga, now called the Padma, and flowed into the Meghna before following its many mouths into the Bay of Bengal? Were magars, gharials, eight kinds of freshwater turtles, sarus cranes, and tiny river dolphins unexpectedly swimming in via the Chambal River (which flows into the Ganga via the Yamuna) too much to hope for?

At the very least, I imagined that the model would help me better understand what had happened in the thirty years since it was built—three decades during which 2,000 crore had been poured into the increasingly degraded river. And those were just my personal hopes. As a society, we had collectively looked away from the Ganga. Maybe the model, if it were open to the public again, could help undo that?

I tried emailing and calling the BHU Civil Engineering Department, but no one ever responded. I tried tracking down U. K. Chaudhary through a friend who had been involved in efforts to clean the Ganga at Varanasi for decades; she said she couldn't help—her contacts were aware of U. K. (as he was known at the University), but had only a string of imprecations reserved for him. I got a hint of his wilfulness, which I would come to admire, in an online excerpt from a 2011 letter U. K. had written to the then President Pratibha Patil protesting the fact that he had not been paid since 2010: 'The twenty-five-year-old centre is without funds. Due to severe mental torture, damage and delay in research on Ganga, I have no option but to sit on a symbolic dharna with my family members and students.'

Eventually, I was able to contact U. K. through the website of the Mahamana Malaviya Institute of Technology for Ganga Management (unwieldily known as MMMIT-GM). He invited me to visit him at the institute, which turned out to be in his home in Varanasi, near the Assi sewage canal, the fallen form of the eponymous river Assi.

One dusty January afternoon, I made my way to U. K.'s front gate. It was decorated with gaudy blue tridents in honour of Shiva, who, in some stories, is Ganga's husband. I puzzled over the giant sign advertising 'The School of GANGA-GEETA ATOMIC THEORY' that offered special training in 'Ganga Model and Ganga Field', along with humbler subjects like Science and Maths, to those in classes 6-8, as I waited outside. 'No Fee, Only Donations in the Name of Ganga', the sign continued.

Eventually, I let myself in, and walked up the stairs, past a dusty, broken sump pump. A plaque near the entrance noted that various prominent politicians had graced the inauguration of this home-based institute. I had to knock a few times before U. K. opened the door and led me into his office.

U. K. is in his early seventies. A Bihari by birth, he received his PhD in river engineering from IIT Bombay in 1974. He started lecturing at BHU's civil engineering department the following year; by the late 1990s he was running the department. He sported a white moustache and a thick saffron dot on his forehead below a woollen cap drawn at a rakish angle. On the bookshelf next to him sat a black-and-white photograph of himself as a handsome young man. He looked pleased when I commented on it.

'Why do you love the Ganga?' he asked me right away. I tried to explain that the Ganga was in my blood, that Bengal had once been known as the country of the Gangahriday. I thought this explanation would suffice for U. K. of all people, since his heart clearly beat in tune to the rhythms of the Ganga. But he wasn't buying it.

'Why do you, personally, love the Ganga?' he wanted to know.

As I fumbled for words, he broke in.

'Every time I was coming to Varanasi, I was taking hundreds of dips in the Ganga at Mughalsarai while travelling from IIT Bombay to Bihar. My heart was never satisfied by how much eternal joy I was taking from these dips in the Ganga system. I might have love for the Ganga since several births. Therefore, I started doing my research only on the Ganga.'

U. K. listed all the questions that had haunted him: Why do all the rivers join the Ganga, yet the Ganga does not join any river? Why are there pollutants in the Ganga? What are the eternal characteristics of its water? Why are there no microbes in the Ganga water? Why do confluences occur only at certain locations? Why does the Ganga spread sand on one side, soil on the other side? Why do different types of unique aquatic life grow in the Ganga? In what distinctive ways does it meander and erode? During his career, U. K. had supervised about forty master's theses and one PhD thesis focused on these questions. Many of his students used the Ganga Knowledge Centre to ground their research.

He explained: 'It is Ganga System. System, you know, means it has different organs. Different organs have different energy levels, which indicate different important functionings, which have different problems associated with them, which have different methodologies for management.'

This mystical line of reasoning sounded familiar; it is echoed in

U. K.'s 2008 book, *Five Theories of River Management*, which I'd puzzled over online. This book, in turn, quoted heavily from his 2003 book, *The Living Similarity*. The way U. K. spoke was powerful but sometimes hard to follow. He sounded like an orator, or a politician, because of his sonorous Hindi, and his abundant use of figurative speech. His writing was even more exaggerated: it read like a mix of stream-of-consciousness civil engineering interspersed with extremely extended metaphors and unanswerable, efflorescent questions that had something in common with Zen koans. The text was peppered with equations that mapped the river flow and hand-drawn diagrams of sand and sediment beds. Infrastructure and cement were floated on extravagant rhetoric.

U. K. always connected the Ganga back to the human body; some echo of ancient wisdom. But it seemed that he had failed to convert his enthusiasm for this philosophy into an ability to positively influence river management by building a coalition.

'I am a simple servant of the Ganges,' U. K. said. 'Just like a son watching his mother. He may not be capable of doing anything. A small child, he sees his mother restless in different conditions, he might not be capable, but is certainly very upset from the inside.' U. K. pointed to an article in that day's Hindi newspaper that mentioned the 2,000 crores spent so far on the Ganga, to no avail. (This number has since risen to ₹7,000 crores according to the National Green Tribunal.) After his thirty-four years of work, he said, more than thirty drains in Varanasi continued to discharge sewage in the river. 'And nothing constructive has been done.'

He continued, 'If a doctor is treating a patient, and he does not know anatomy or morphology, can he be a doctor? No minister, no IAS officer, no lawyer, knows the ABCD of the river. They don't know anything about the Ganga River system. But they are monitoring the river. Most of them are pathologists—they know how to test the water quality, quantity. Simply water testing does not make them a doctor. Ninety-nine per cent of the Ganga's doctors don't know the anatomy or morphology of the river, nor the cross-section of the river. The basic problem is that the river doesn't have her own hospital with doctors knowing her anatomy, morphology. Under these conditions, what would be the fate of the patient? The Ganga is on the verge of death. Your parents may invite doctors from America, London...but if five out of six litres of blood has been taken out, can anybody save you?' U. K. was referring to the fact that 80 per cent of the Ganga's waters are redirected, in most dry months, by the barrage at Bhimgora, near Haridwar, to the Upper Ganges Canal. The river is recharged with groundwater, and again most of the river's water is removed by the Narora Barrage in dry months, and diverted to the Lower Ganga canals.

I mentioned that the Ganga downstream of Narora, despite the degradation, still looked impressive. U. K. replied, 'Suppose an elephant takes 40 kg of grain per day. If you only give it 10 kg, 20 kg, it is not fulfilling the elephant's requirement. The Ganga is a mighty river. It is discharging lakhs of cubic metres per second. And if you reduce this flow to 6k, 7k, 8k cubic metres, that means the Ganga is hungry, is it not?' I was still trying to wrap my mind around the image of the Ganga as a hungry elephant but U. K. kept going, stressing the 'unscientific withdrawal of water, in quantity, methodology, and location' without 'knowing from which location we should take out water in what amount, with what methodology rate. The outflow you are taking from the body is entirely wrong.'

U. K. pointed to the photograph on his bookshelf of Pandit Madan Mohan Malaviya, who almost a hundred years prior had opposed the British dam. 'He saw that once you take water out in one location, the time will come when people will take out waters at other locations. The greatest personality in the entire world at that time. Can you imagine his greatness and boldness? Can you imagine a person with a roaring practice in Allahabad High Court start begging for the Ganga? For Banaras University?'

'But Malaviya was only partially successful, right?' I said.

'Partially, yes,' he replied. '[Malaviya] convinced the Angrez that some water should be allowed to flow past the barrage. A small gate was provided; 600 cubic feet per second was the minimum quantity of water which should have been allowed to flow—but today I don't feel that this much water is passing out.' But this also seems to avoid the question whether the antiquated 1916 agreement reached by Malaviya with the British government is still adequate for the rapidly growing population in the Ganga River basin.

U. K. went on to enumerate two challenges faced by the Ganga basin today. These include massive salination of the soil because of the amount of water that's been taken out of the river for irrigation, and changes in the intensity and frequency of rainfall.

He concluded, 'There is no college to study the Ganga. Therefore, the first solution is an institute.' He described in loving detail the Ganga Model Centre he had set up in 1985 on the BHU campus. 'It's been locked since 2011, when I retired,' he said. I asked him if he had any photos of it, which led to quite some time during which he pored over old photo albums while I sat across from him in suspense, hoping to catch a glimpse of a model now grown to mythical proportions in my imagination. But nothing resembling it appeared. As U. K. became more and more engrossed in the past, it got to the point that I had to nudge him. 'So, do you have any photos of the model?'

Without looking up from his albums, he repeated 'Model?' in a gentle, querulous way, as if he had forgotten that that was why I'd contacted him in the first place.

It was my cue to leave. I walked out past two whole shelves of master's theses filled with insights gleaned from the Ganga Laboratory. They reminded me of the image that concluded the NMCG Interim Report: twenty volumes containing all the research that has gone into the Ganga so far. The Ganga Laboratory theses were covered with pastel chart paper, and their spines were unmarked. They rested next to a few severely moth-eaten copies of *The Living Similarity*. U. K. seemed moved when I recognized them.

'GANGA APNE AAP SAAF HO JAYEGI' (SHE WILL CLEAN HERSELF)

Confusingly, the Mahamana Malaviya Institute of Technology for Ganga Management has a fraternal twin: the Mahamana Malaviya Research Centre for Ganga, River Development, and Water Resource Management. I wondered why Malaviya's role in the biography of the Ganga is not better known, so I asked Dr Vishwanath Pandey of BHU, an eminent authority on Pandit Madan Mohan Malaviya. He spoke about the 'fake science' being done on all sides. It seemed that the actual Ganga was too dirty, too fraught with division, for him to focus on. Disturbed, I tried to find other authorities who could help me understand Gangaji's story.

One of the Malaviya Research Centre's affiliates, Professor

B. D. Tripathi, is also an expert member of the NGRBA and at least two other central agencies, plus a state-level committee devoted to the Ganga. If there is a doyen of all the bureaucracy surrounding the Ganga, it is Professor Tripathi. But this is not to question his experience or his sincerity. Like U. K., and many of the other scientists I interviewed, Tripathi has spent his life studying the Ganga. In fact, in 1972, he pioneered the first research on pollution in the Ganga.

I visited Professor Tripathi the morning after my inconclusive encounter with U. K. The front entrance to his well-appointed home in Varanasi boasts a laminated photo of the Ganga, in which it appears pure azure, like some Photoshop genius's fantasy about the ocean. Unusual houses with quaint wooden roofs grace the riverside. Looking at it reminded me of the floods on the Mandakini a few years earlier, which had washed away those very homes.

I had been connected to Professor Tripathi through Kanak Dwivedi, a classical Sanskrit scholar and former BHU professor who oversees Swami V.'s ashram in Varanasi. Tripathi agreed to see me at short notice because he is a relative of hers. One of the ashram administrators, Avinash Ojha, accompanied me to the interview and genuflected before Tripathi. I'd heard him characterized as a 'whistle-blower'—the first person to draw attention to pollution in the Ganga. Today, he is a canonical personage. The Government of India is publishing his biography in six languages. And, as with any canon, what is left unsaid in Tripathi's narrative is as interesting as what is said. We spoke for nearly two hours; it was hard to get a word in edgewise. Occasionally, he would direct an aside, in Hindi, to Avinash.

'Ganga ko maine padha nahin, Ganga ko main jiya hu' (I haven't studied the Ganga, I've lived the Ganga), said Tripathi, immediately launching into an abbreviated biography.

He was born in a small village a few kilometres away from Varanasi. As a young man, he took his mother to bathe at Dashashwamedh Ghat, where the floating body of a cow repulsed him. 'In those days, the word pollution was not in fashion,' Tripathi said, noting that the word has come into common parlance only since the early 1970s when both Earth Day and World Environment Day were inaugurated.

Observing his disgust, Tripathi's mother, whose religious beliefs did not allow her to see the river as polluted, told him, 'Your education has compelled you to lose faith in the Ganga.'

Goaded by these words, Tripathi completed the first PhD on Environmental Pollution at BHU. He examined the impacts of cremation at Manikarnika and Harishchandra ghats. As part of his research, he forecast the number of bodies that would likely be burned during 2010–15 and tried to anticipate how much wood would be needed.

By 1977, the media had picked up on Tripathi's core message: the Ganga was polluted. 'This was highly opposed by religious people,' Tripathi said. 'I was told I am not a Hindu. I almost lost my job, and I was to be hanged by the university. How could I say the Ganga was polluted?'

I asked Tripathi where he found the courage to speak up under these circumstances. He said that he got the courage to speak up from Gangaji herself. 'I liked the thought that swarg mein ek chair rahega mere liye' (A chair in heaven will be reserved for me).

Tripathi has had early front-row seats for the slow-motion disaster of government spending on the Ganga, and by his account has made several powerful interventions with powerful people. In 1980, he met Indira Gandhi. 'On 21 July 1981,' he said, 'Parliament accepted the truth: pollution is dangerous and it must be cured.'

A meeting with Rajiv Gandhi followed in 1985 and the year after that, the Ganga Action Plan was launched. In 2008, Tripathi met Prime Minister Manmohan Singh, and claims he requested Singh to declare the Ganga a national river. In 2009, Singh followed through with this request, establishing the NGRBA with the PM as the chairman and Tripathi as an expert adviser. However, Tripathi soon realized that the 'national river' status didn't amount to much.

'The PM wanted to know why there had been no action. I said: lack of coordination between central and local and state agencies, and no accountability... The Ganga is being managed by five states with different rules.' In other words, the Ganga is a national river in name only (and this doesn't even address the fact that the Ganga basin extends into Tibet, China, Nepal, and Bangladesh).

Tripathi is a fan of the Adarsh Gram Yojana, the scheme through which each Member of Parliament (MP) is encouraged to take ownership over the section of Ganga in their respective constituency. And he noted that there is now yet another bureaucratic body, the Ganga River

Conservation Authority, which was established in the five basin states that Ganga flows through—Uttarakhand, Uttar Pradesh, Bihar, Jharkhand, and West Bengal—will also incorporate local bodies and have power to take any or all steps 'it deems necessary for abatement of pollution and conservation of the river Ganga'.

Throughout the 1980s and 90s, Tripathi continued to study pollution in the Ganga. During this time, he observed the river's flow diminishing. In his view, pollution is now a 'secondary problem'; if flow, the 'first problem', is improved, he believes that 60 to 70 per cent of the pollution issue will be addressed. Tripathi claims this based on a study he conducted in Allahabad, at the Sangam, during the Kumbh Mela, when millions bathe in the river. Tripathi was interested in how much of the river's Biochemical Oxygen Demand (BOD) would rise during this time. The BOD is 'the amount of dissolved oxygen needed by aerobic biological organisms to break down organic material present in a given water sample at certain temperature over a specific time period'. It's often used as an index of pollution in the river. Notably, it only covers organic matter, not heavy metals or toxic waste.

The model of the study conducted by Tripathi predicted that the BOD at Sangam would rise to 25 million litres per day. But he found that in reality the BOD rose to 7.4 mg per litre on 14 January from 4.4 mg per litre the previous day, subsequently falling to 4.8 mg per litre. He attributes this to enhanced flow in the river thanks to the massive amount of water released by the government during the bathing festival.

Tripathi was clear-eyed about challenges facing the river at present. 'The Ganga is struggling for her existence—will there be a Ganga or not?' He told me in January 2016, when we met, that the river's flow was the lowest ever recorded (reports from April 2016 recorded the river at its lowest in five years).

I pressed him about the issues concerning BOD as an effective pollution index since it didn't address the other kinds of pollutants in the river. Tripathi did not shy away from speaking about these other challenges. 'There are 300 million litres of sewage per day and 500 million litres industrial waste per day,' he said. He explained that only 102 million litres can be treated (at present) by Varanasi's three treatment plants; none of the three can treat heavy metals, which accumulate in flowers, fruits, and grains. 'Instead of minimizing pollution, the plants are spreading pollution,' says Tripathi, because the surrounding land is now irrigated by toxic water after it leaves the treatment plants.

Once, at Bhagirathsila, near Gaumukh, a swami had told him the story of how Bhagirath brought the Ganga down to earth in order to liberate his ancestors, the 60,000 sons of Sagar who were scorched to death by Kapil Muni. Tripathi understood the story to mean that at some point, the population of the whole Ganga basin was around 60,000 people, and they were nonetheless dying for lack of water. Today, the lives of approximately 500 million people will be threatened if the river dries up.

Initially, Tripathi said, he had hope in the current government's vision. 'Modiji made a ministry, arranged money. Money is flowing like water, but water is not flowing. If the system isn't working, how to blame him? Ownership is a problem. Where is people's participation? Why not establish community treatment plants? This is a rotten system. It seems difficult to achieve the goal. Implementers are not experts of the system. People shift around; there is no accountability, no skin in the game. There is khichdi (chaos) from top to bottom. Until there is strong political will, no big work can be conducted. How can we import a design from America or Japan? Our environment is altogether different from a temperate country. Why compare the Ganga with the Rhine?'

I asked Tripathi about the algal waste water-based sewage treatment plant (which would not have required electricity to operate) which was Veer Bhadra Mishra's lifelong dream. Mishra's plans, grounded in state-of-the-art waste water engineering research conducted at the University of California, Berkeley, met with Tripathi's scorn.

Turning to Avinash, who had been listening respectfully, Tripathi said, 'Ganga ko chhod dijiye. Apne aap saaf ho jayegi' (Please leave the Ganga alone; she will clean herself).

◆

By now, I had heard this belief in the self-cleaning properties of the Ganga a few times. I took Tripathi to mean this in a secular way, but it was still a view that I disagreed with. Even Veer Bhadra Mishra, who was a priest, was very clear that human intervention was necessary in order to clean the river.

I was curious about how Tripathi balanced faith and science. He was extremely meticulous and precise about units of measurement and very clear about environmental distinctions. He explained the difference between contamination (undesirable changes in chemical and biological composition—for example, the changes caused by idol immersion) and pollution (that which is harmful to life). He did not betray any reverence for the Ganga; he did not speak of the river as a goddess except to touch on its miraculous antibacterial properties. For Tripathi, the river's antibacterial property is what makes it Mother Ganga. Thus, the fact that this antibacterial quality is diminishing concerns him. 'Due to continuous decrease in flow, the dilution or self-purifying capacity of the Ganga is rapidly decreasing. The flow has been converted to stagnant water.' He also mentioned the instability of the Tehri dam. 'Water is seeping,' he said, implying that the ground it was built on might not hold forever.

Near the end of our time together, Tripathi made two prophecies. He said that the government would change its laws in twenty-five years, but, by then, 'the Ganga will be dry'.

Yet he also said, 'One day, the Ganga will make everything saaf [clean]. Apna ilaka bhi khali karengi' (She will clear her own territory).

I was painfully aware of the double consciousness in Tripathi's claims. In Hindi he came across as devout and orthodox—he suggested that the Ganga still had a vast amount of power to determine its own future. But in English, he spoke of the river as doomed by the 'system', and its self-purifying properties as contingent upon the government's decisions about the amount of flow in the river.

To be clear: I am uncomfortably familiar with ideological inconsistency of this kind—it's hard to navigate between tradition and modernity without it. Indeed, his eloquent inconsistency is probably part of what has allowed Tripathi to be so successful within the 'rotten system' that has twisted the river out of shape and short-changed future possibilities. We can't talk our way out of this mess; words are not enough.

And yet, I wanted to argue with Tripathi, to plead with him. Surely he'd read Anthony Acciavatti's *Ganges Water Machine*? Acciavatti spent ten years mapping the upper Ganga in U.P. and Uttaranchal and suggested a plan for dismantling the infrastructure that is draining life out of the river. He believes it is imperative to regulate the millions of tube wells stuck in the earth like straws and he advocates paying farmers to turn their unproductive fields into bio-swales—human-made pathways for draining and filtering water—and to recycle the sewage entering the river.

I wanted to convince Tripathi to embrace solutions like the ones Acciavatti spells out, to admit that there are pathways forward for the Ganga. At the very least, I wanted to understand his dire predictions better. But, after two hours of sharing his perspective, he kindly but firmly showed me the door.

Even in the end times, though, I still wanted to see the scale model of the river. As I was leaving, I asked Tripathi if he could help me access the Ganga Laboratory. In response, Tripathi dismissed U. K. As for the model itself, Tripathi called it, 'Simply a few truckloads of soil. It was [U. K.'s] personal shop... U. K. is an expert in the meandering of the river. He doesn't know the ABCD of pollution. He speaks in parts per million when milligrams per litre is key.'

Adrift in all these allegations, I almost gave up my pursuit of the Ganga Laboratory. I'd been calling the BHU Civil Engineering Department, but, despite the plethora of numbers on their site, no one ever picked up the phone. Eventually, I took the only option I had left—I jumped into a cycle rickshaw to the BHU campus.

'PURE BHARAT MEIN AISA MODEL NAHIN HAI' (THERE IS NO MODEL LIKE THIS IN ALL OF INDIA)

The civil engineering department of BHU lies inside a vast, spacious tree-lined campus—Madan Mohan Malaviya's most famous legacy.

I walked, uninvited, into the department office and asked to speak with P. K. Singh Dixit, the ostensible head of the Ganga Laboratory. I was told that he was away and that he was the only one who could grant me access. A master's student informed me that there were no students working in the Ganga Laboratory anymore. She was kind enough to give me Singh's mobile number. I tried calling, but there was no response. So far, no surprises.

I was about to head back to my hotel when a custodian, whose name I am withholding, asked me what I was looking for. 'I want to see the Ganga Laboratory,' I said.

'Let me call my friend. He has the keys.'

In a few moments, a second custodian, who will also remain unnamed, appeared. 'You want to see the Ganga Model? There's nothing to see there now. It looks like a field,' he said.

'I'd really like to see it anyway,' I said.

'I see. Please wait,' he said, and disappeared into a department building. Soon, he reappeared, carrying a massive key ring filled with keys. 'Please, sit on my scooter,' he said.

I looked tentatively at my new friend, the first custodian. 'Should I go with him?' I asked. My other new friend nodded. I looked the second custodian in the eye and trusted what I saw enough to climb on to his scooter and hold on as he drove a half-kilometre up the road. I had exactly enough time to wonder—was I endangering him—or myself by being there?

Soon, we pulled up to a locked gate next to a dusty soccer field. The gate reminded me of U. K.'s entrance; it, too, was emblazoned with metal tridents, a few of which were bent backwards. A faded sign in Hindi demarcated these grounds as the Ganga Research Centre. The bas-relief of a Shiva lingam guarded the entrance.

My new friend sifted through his key ring, found the right key and, after a few agonizing seconds, we were inside the fabled Ganga model.

I say inside because, as soon as we entered the spacious, tree-lined grounds, we found ourselves standing on a cement path next to a long, straight, white concrete ditch. It was about two feet deep and filled with cracked soil and dry leaves.

So this is what 'a nearly 280-ft straight rigid boundary channel' looked like. This hardly met my expectations for the first and only model of the Ganga in the whole country.

But my new friend, the public servant, looked proud. And, to his credit, I must say that the channel could have been dirtier—indeed, apart from its blankness and rigidity, its cleanliness was its most distinguishing characteristic. Clean, blank, and rigid. Not the first three words that come to mind when the name 'Ganga' is uttered.

The channel led to an abandoned-looking pump-house; next to it was a broken sump pump and a perpendicular side-channel filled with stagnant water connected to the boundary channel. Most of the grounds, however, were occupied by tiny, burr-filled hillocks—the final resting place of the 1,600 truckloads of Gangetic soil that I'd heard so much about. When the model was functional, water was pumped through the channels and into the hillocks in order to understand the river's meandering.

Together, we walked up to the pump house. My friend unlocked the door. There was a rusted, broken motor for the pump, amidst abandoned desks and chairs.

We approached an inner chamber. 'The Chemical Room', my friend said. Inside, there were tiny tables covered with dusty, pigeon-shit-streaked brown bottles and plastic casings for obscure electronics (I didn't dare to touch them). Across from these glories was a large hand-painted wooden sign so battered and faded that I almost missed what was written on it in red, white, and blue letters:

In Honour of Prof. K. G. Ranga Raju,

50% discount on the book 'THE LIVING SIMILARITY BETWEEN THE GANGA AND THE HUMAN BODY.'

The next line bore the book's title in Hindi.

Ganga Research Centre, BHU Varanasi.

I didn't know what to make of this desolate sign. It was at most thirteen years old, since the book dated from 2003. So I stood looking at the nearly obscured words, 'The Ganga and the Human Body.' So finally, after getting to see the all-but-hidden model, I ended up at this advertisement for remaindered books. I don't know what was most anticlimactic: the 50 per cent discount announcement, the fact that the title was illegible or the actual model itself.

Still, there it was: the one and only Ganga Model. Proby Cautley, the builder of the first Ganges canal in 1854, would have been happy with its containedness, its rectilinearity. That was not a comforting thought. If macrocosm and microcosm are truly meant to rhyme, as I'd learned at Varanasi's pilgrimage routes, then surely the Ganga Model should be a moment of arrhythmia, a metric miscarriage.

We turned around and walked out of the laboratory. I took one last look at the landscape. Forget the human body—I tried to find a 'living similarity' between the model and the river I knew. There was none. If the Ganga Model had a saving grace, it is that it was cleaner than the canals that channel waste water upstream, in Kanpur. That was it.

At least, I thought that was it. But it turns out that once you gain access to one model of the Ganga, other, unsuspected models are only a few footsteps away.

Back at the Civil Engineering Department, the public servant offered to show me something. He unlocked a giant room with green stained-glass French windows. A curving concrete ramp bordered by a Shiva lingam-esque pump dominated the room. Tiny grids of varying sizes were chalked upon the ramp, which was dusted with fine sand.

'This is the river from Ramnagar to Rajghat', the public servant told me, describing the northern and southern bounds of Varanasi. He glowed with pride as he said, 'Pure Bharat me aisa model nahin hai' (In all of India there is no other model like this). After the pump is turned on, after three hours, they see where deposition and erosion occurs.'

There were eight chairs set up in front of the model, possibly for committee meetings. A bamboo ladder leaned against broken, askew bookshelves. 'This indoor lab is used sometimes,' my friend said.

I offered him a token amount of money—for friendship, for tea. But he, and his friend, the first custodian I'd encountered, adamantly refused.

'We only care about the growth and development of young researchers such as yourself,' they said. They invited me to come back the following day, when P. K. Singh Dixit, who headed the Ganga Lab, would be present. 'He can explain everything,' they said.

The following morning, I was finally able to get in touch with Dixit, but only briefly. He said he was too busy to speak to me, but suggested that I contact his friend, who was working on remote sensing models of the river in Delhi.

Our conversation left me in a reflective mood. 'We can't forget that the river is a basin, not a pipeline,' a Delhi-based activist named Gopal Krishna, who had worked with the Ganga Bachao Samiti (Committee to Save Ganga) for about fifteen years, had told me. Perhaps remote sensing and other computer models made it easier to see the Ganga as a basin, as opposed to U. K.'s model.

Indeed, U. K.'s obsession with the similarities between the human body and the river's body seemed a bit preposterous after visiting his model. Maybe it deserved to be rendered to the anonymity of history. Maybe civil engineers had moved on to purportedly superior computer models that allowed one to simulate the river's movements more precisely. Still, the decrepitude and inaccessibility of the Ganga Laboratory spoke

Bidisha Banerjee

volumes about our willingness to look away from the past thirty years of history.

For me, the outdoor Ganga Model, locked away from sight, represented the slow gutting of possibility. From the busted pumphouse, the river's future looks fatalistic, predetermined, stagnant, like a drain. The indoor Ganga Model, however, was very different: small, unpretentious, curved, hidden, and apparently reflective of the actual river's sinuous reality. The jerry-rigged nature of the model suggests jugaad—the Indian ethic of innovation by cobbling things together. It's this model that suggests the possibility of a different future for Ganga, one that's more grounded in the river's natural dynamics.

The best thing about models is that you can make and remake them. U. K. and the custodians are right to celebrate the unique nature of the Ganga Laboratory. Both Ganga models should be open to the public that helped fund it. We live in a disembodied time; the internet allows us to be everywhere and nowhere. Each time we visit Varanasi, we should go to see U. K.'s channel and think about how different it is from the river. We need to taste the outrageously stagnant water. We need to walk, two feet above the ground, atop the choices that condition the limited, sluggish responses that are conceivable in the present. We need to feel how much more fluid, organic, and responsive the future we create can be compared to the obsolete legacy of our colonizers and the heirs to their two-century-old vision of canal building.

VARANASI IMPRESSIONS: MY GREAT-GREAT-GRANDMOTHER

In the little time I had remaining in Varanasi, I paced the ghats with my mother. We visited the Shiva temple my great-great-grandmother had built in her home in Bangalipara, a neighbourhood in Varanasi where Bengalis still live. For four decades, she lived alone on the shores of the river in Varanasi, a city as old as Babylon, exultantly awaiting death. She was confident that dying there, 400 miles upstream from her family, would let her climb off the eternal merry-go-round of life and death. The Ganga was her portal out of the Kali Yuga. Before death finally came for her in 1971, she had travelled alone, on four pilgrimages, to the glacial sources of the Ganga in the Himalayas—apparently oblivious to the fact that to any onlooker, she must have seemed unusual at best, this woman by herself and for herself.

We watched priests wearing blouses of white silk worship the river each evening. In sets of three, they brandished silvery puffs and fire carried in containers shaped like snakes. One evening, we took a boat ride. From the middle of the river, we could see the priests dancing and hear the devotional music of the Ganga aarti (a fire ceremony to the goddess Ganga that I first witnessed in Haridwar) at Dashashwamedh and Rajendra Prasad Ghats, which sit side-by-side. Like the Ganga experts I'd spoken to in Varanasi, the priests were out of sync with each other.

Moon, our boatman, was short, wore a smart checked shirt, and looked very professional. He spoke Korean, Japanese, English, Hindi, and a little Bengali. *Joy Baba Felunath*'s Machhli Baba scene was filmed at Dashashwamedh Ghat, he informed us, a factoid to gladden any proper Satyajit Ray-loving Bengali's Ganga-heart.

'Harishchandra Ghat is Delhi, and Manikarnika Ghat is Mumbai. Chitrakoot, on the opposite shore, is Goa,' claimed Moon, who had never travelled far from Varanasi. His father and grandfather weren't boatmen—they worked on the land; Moon, whose parents named him Monu, is a boatman because he loves it. He sleeps on his boat, not in his rented room, because he likes the boat better.

'Five types of people are not cremated,' he told us. 'The holy man who does not like his beard to burn. The Brahmin who does not like his pigtail to burn. Lepers because they have already suffered fire; they want coolness. Pregnant women and children under five because God does not want them to burn—they don't understand anything.' We looked at the water nervously, but no dead bodies, only water bottles, floated there. There are fewer partially decomposed corpses floating past Varanasi these days, perhaps due to the widespread horror and outrage they were causing.

At Manikarnika Ghat, Moon showed us the pyres of fourteen souls busily going 'directly to nirvana'. A traditional pyre takes three hours to burn. Do people burned via electric fire also go to nirvana, I asked him. Yes, they also go to nirvana, he said.

A man had built a tiny, cave-like home in the boat where the logs for burning were kept. We saw him popping out of the window hole, washing his pots. Moon pointed out Kashi Karbad, a temple that was believed by the locals to have become crooked after a mother cursed her son for insulting her.

Varanasi's boatmen are part of a complex history and economy. Moon revealed that he identifies with the Kevat, or the boatman caste. They have their own ghat, Nishadh, and an arrangement whereby certain Kevats enjoy hereditary rights to the waters of each ghat.

'Yes! Previously we used to be turtles—well, not I personally,' he said, dimpling, his smile brilliant in the dark waters.

'Kachhwa, our turtle ancestor, wanted several types of fluid to cross the seven seas. Salty, watery, poison, blood.' Using these, 'Dhire, dhire, dhire Kachhwa paar ho gaye (slowly, slowly, slowly, the Turtle crossed over). Sheshnag, the serpent-king, struck him. Kachhwa died. The gods said, this is not right. Kachhwa will be born as Kevat (boatman).'

Suddenly, at that moment, still spluttering from the taste of ashes in my mouth from the cremation ground, being rowed around by a brilliant tour guide descended from a very slow, very heroic turtle, I felt calm and joyous. All the same, I wondered if, when my time comes, there would be room for me at a waiting house for the dead beside the river. What will accountable re-enchantment look like then?

DEEPA GUPTA AND THE 2014 ELECTION

I spoke to many eminent experts on the Ganga during my travels in Varanasi, but I was curious about what a young generation of activists had learned from the previous generation's work. In October 2017, I had a chance to interview Deepa Gupta, the co-founder of the Indian Youth Climate Network and, later, the founder of Jhatkaa.org, which empowers citizens to utilize digital platforms to hold political leaders accountable. (Full disclosure: I have travelled across parts of India with the IYCN and have donated to Jhatkaa.) When I spoke with her, Deepa was in Delhi, having just returned from a trek to Tapovan, which she described as a 'stereotypical heaven' above Gaumukh, the glacial origin of the Ganga. The landscape she described had changed since my visit there in 2009. A new sewage treatment plant was just about to open in Gangotri, courtesy of campaign promises. But landslides had closed off the trail I'd taken past Bhojbhasa. Instead, she, her guide, and the others in their group had had to scramble over rocks for several kilometres. Within the past month, the shape of Gaumukh had changed—it no longer looked like a cow's mouth, as it had for generations.

An Australian citizen with deep roots in India, Deepa spent her twenties as a grass roots organizer in India. I asked her about her reflections on the 2014 election, during which Jhatkaa, which had launched only six months prior, helped mobilize 8,000 residents of Varanasi over a period of six weeks to demand that leaders of all political parties commit to cleaning the Ganga. I found this extremely impressive, but Deepa contextualized the accomplishment by pointing out that there were over one lakh campaign volunteers from all over India in Varanasi at that time. She emphasized that other organizations, particularly the Sankat Mochan Foundation, which Veer Bhadra Mishra (my host in 2009) had founded three decades ago, had done the core work, and Jhatkaa had focused on magnifying their message. Political leaders were a lot more open to talking with the Sankat Mochan Foundation because of Mishraji's spiritual significance in Varanasi.

Since 2011, when Deepa started collaborating with the Sankat Mochan Foundation, she was shocked to realize that cleaning the Ganga hadn't been a campaign issue since Rajiv Gandhi. When both Modi and Arvind Kejriwal decided to run their campaign out of Varanasi, she thought: 'Let's use this spotlight on Varanasi, the birthplace of the Clean Ganga movement thirty years ago, where the testing of the river [for faecal coliform levels] first took place, to bring attention to cleaning the river... We had two purposes: to get the issue to national light again and to get whoever would come to power to commit to cleaning the river,' Deepa says.

The campaign excelled at gaining media attention. 'Us showing up and creating missedcall campaigns made it a sexy thing to get behind.' Deepa recalls that it was relatively easy to get the different political parties on board, although she felt that the BJP party workers weren't interested in talking to young women. (They had separately met with Veer Bhadra Mishra's son.)

'We were saying that the plan should adhere to three principles. First, make sure you're capturing all the open sewage; second, make sure you have sufficient capacity for the growing population's needs, and third, make sure you actually get the job done. And then we shared some research on what the Sankat Mochan Foundation had done,' Deepa said, alluding to the algal waste water ponds that treat sewage where it lies which Mishra had told me about in 2009 (since his death in 2013 his son, Bedu, has taken over the foundation).

I asked Deepa what she had learned from the 2014 campaign. She mentioned her surprise that there was less corruption amongst government officials than she had originally thought. When insiders did have vested interests, it was a real challenge, but lack of capacity was usually a bigger issue. She also mentioned the apathy that many people feel towards the current state of the Ganga; the sense that they have more important or at least more controllable things to think about. Meanwhile, there is no watchdog organization with its eye on the whole river. Deepa regrets that Jhatkaa did not have the capacity to employ someone to remain focused on the Ganga after the 2014 elections—which would have been her dream. Other commitments have kept her from working on these issues after 2014, but when she stepped down as the executive director of Jhatkaa, she left it in good hands.

A FIVE-POINT PROGRAMME FOR RE-ENCHANTMENT

More than a decade ago, a Sanskrit scholar, Lina Gupta, outlined a five-point programme. I interpret her manifesto as a starting point for re-enchanting our relationship with the Ganga.

'In all her myths and symbols, the Ganga reflects the need for self-transformation,' she wrote. Knowledge is the first pillar of her programme. Not just technical knowledge of pollution, but first-hand witnessing of it. 'One knows how and to what extent individuals as well as the society failed to fulfill their obligations toward the rest of the earthly community.'

But, 'knowledge alone…is not sufficient to bring about lasting change'. Thus, the second pillar is understanding. 'One has to understand and internalize the very essence of her being, her status as a river, her role as woman and mother. The more one becomes absorbed in her true status, journeys through her flow, and is mindful of the true meanings of prayer and rituals toward her, the closer one becomes to her. The more one sees her as an individual in her own right, the fewer chances there are to destroy or dominate her.'

Devotion comes next. 'Until one is thoroughly satiated by being in love with at least one particular part of Nature, one would not be able to comprehend what it is to love all of this physical world,' Gupta says.

Then there is attitude. 'Grounded in knowledge, renewed with the deeper understanding of the Ganga, and thoroughly motivated with a personal feeling and concern, one is ready for a radical change in one's attitude—an attitude that will require developing a set of virtues which will be pertinent to a removal of the Ganga's pollution. [These include] reaffirmation of the traditional virtues prescribed in the Hindu scriptures, such as nonviolence; remembrance of the virtues such as gratitude, reverence, and humility; and reinvention and reinterpretation of the virtues that are not being used in recent times, such as asceticism and endurance.... Once the Ganga is seen in terms of a manifestation of the divine energy...one realizes the equality of all created beings, one recognizes the intrinsic value of all. The result is a profound sense of gratitude, reverence, and humility.'

But all of this is for naught without action, Gupta's fifth and last pillar. 'Learning to live with less, avoiding the overusage and misusage of Nature, enduring certain discomforts for the sake of our earthly community—in this case for the Ganga—will create a brighter future for all concerned. The possibility of reclaiming the ecological balance of the Ganga depends to a great extent on Hindus being able to put aside their emotional commitment to the bare structure of ritual, and comprehending the true meaning of liberation explained in the Vedas, the Upanishads, and the Puranas as loving oneself and others equally. That requires changing cultural practices with the explicit goal of reducing inequality and extraction. As the Agni Purana explains, "whoever does not see another as different from his own self becomes Brahman itself. One who rejoices in his own self is said to be free from impurity"'.

In the battle between fast and slow, it seemed slow had lost. Then I looked in the river. The place of ultimate groundlessness. Time seemed to have slowed down. I thought of the ancient Indian water clock, one of the oldest ways of telling time, which measured not by the minute, but by a unit called naadi, a word that sounds like the word that means 'river' in many subcontinental languages. This kind of clock was of course eventually replaced by the pendulum clock, a mechanism that seems to force time on swing by swing. Luckily, all we have to do if we want time to flow more slowly is look at the river, or remember it, or invoke it.

CHAPTER 6

THE SOUND OF RESILIENCE: (VIKRAMSHILA GANGETIC DOLPHIN SANCTUARY, BIHAR)

Some observers are not optimistic. They think another ten years could wipe out a species that has lasted for one hundred million years. The susu [the Ganga river dolphin] was already in these rivers before the Himalaya were born.

—Cheryl Colopy,
Dirty, Sacred Rivers

Gangá-Rám, Thug: Ráma and Gangá, two divinities; but, as used by Thugs—a hint that danger is nigh.

—Wilson's *Glossary*

SHUSHUK, SONS, HIHO, SUSU

After ten years of longing, I saw the shushuk for the first time. It was on a bright winter afternoon in 2015, that I glimpsed the river dolphin's grey dorsal fin arcing through the air like a question mark. I was on a boat near Barari, in Bhagalpur, Bihar with Dr Sunil Chaudhary, a river ecologist who teaches at Bhagalpur University. The Ganga's rolling grey depths run seven to 33 metres here. Our boatman, Pradeep Mandal, was one of the few people on earth whose lineage involved a generational relationship with the creature.

I strained to hear the creature make the exhaling sound from which it takes its name—in Bhojpuri, sons. In Bangla, shushuk. In Assamese, hiho. In Nepali, susu. In most languages of the subcontinent, the sound of its name falls somewhere between an awed sigh and a shush. Its clicks are inaudible to human ears, a low, mute call to attention, alertness, presence—interrupted, intensified, as the dolphin flashes through the air, its toothy mouth gleaming like a curved sword.

The chance to finally witness the creature I'd dreamed about for so long was bittersweet. I wondered: how optimistic should we let ourselves feel about the Ganga River dolphin's future?

Dr Chaudhary, a botanist by training, had started teaching at Bhagalpur University in 1981, just before the start of the Ganga Mukti Andolan, or Free Ganga Insurrection, an uprising in which the local fishing community had challenged a centuries-old feudal regime. He had a slow start in cetology, having not even realized that the shushuk was a dolphin until a meeting with a British scientist in the mid-1990s, but his research now encompasses many facets of the river.

I'd met Dr Chaudhary through his colleague Dr Sandeep Behera, a dolphin expert at the National Mission for Clean Ganga in New Delhi, and a pioneer in researching the Ganga River dolphin. Behera did his PhD on the Ganga River dolphin in the early 1980s and walked large stretches of the river, from Kanpur to Rishikesh. In 1998, he found some Indus River dolphins living in Punjab's Beas River. They had not been seen since the partition of India and Pakistan.

Because of the Ganga River dolphin's sensitivity, he explained, they cannot be bred in captivity. Their physiology depends on thermoregulation, so they need free-flowing water and deep pools to go to in summer, seeking slower, shallower, warmer water in winter. 'They also need a big boundary for their movement,' Behera told me. 'Because they are blind, their echolocation is very strong. They avoid hard areas. No stony areas. Only sandy and muddy. That's why they are not found in Haridwar.' Their blindness also makes them try to avoid humans. 'Just imagine, if I am blind,' he said, closing his eyes, 'I will be very sensitive to touch, to sound, to anything.'

Sitting across from him, watching his closed eyes flutter, I longed to see the exquisitely sensitive dolphins he was describing. I asked Behera what it was like for him to touch them. 'It was like holding my baby. The first time, I was a little afraid I would hurt it, because the body is so soft. You have to treat them as your kid. Pet them.'

Behera is one of the authors of the Ministry of Environment and Forests' Dolphin Action Plan, 2020. This document outlines best practices for river dolphin conservation. It claims that the river dolphin is the apex predator in the Ganga, like the tiger in the jungle. Its presence is an indication of the river's health. Conserving it will also help other endangered river species like the soft-shell turtle, the gharial, and the Indian smooth-coated otter. In 1981, there were 5,000–6,000 shushuk—or *Platanista*, as they are known to scientists—in the river. Today, there are less than 2,000 alive. If the Yangtze River dolphin is extinct, as it appears to be, then *Platanista* is one of two remaining freshwater dolphin species in the world. In 1996, the International Union for the Conservation of Nature declared it an endangered species.

EVOLUTIONARY AND CULTURAL HISTORY OF THE DOLPHIN

Most of what we know about the multi-million-year-old history of the Ganga River dolphin has emerged in the past thirty-five years. *Platanista*'s evolutionary 'choice' to give up the sea for the river is all the more stunning when you remember that the ancestors of modern whales were originally land dwellers that wanted to wander in the salty marshes and shallow seas. 'There was no straight-line march of terrestrial mammals leading up to fully aquatic whales, but an evolutionary riot of amphibious cetaceans that walked and swam along rivers, estuaries, and coasts of prehistoric Asia,' claims science writer Riley Black. He suggests that over the past three decades, new discoveries have turned 'the origin of whales into one of the best-documented examples of large-scale evolutionary change in the fossil record'.

Indeed, the whale, ancestor of the dolphin, most likely originated in and around the area now known as the Indian subcontinent. Today, most scientists believe that the Indohyus, or Indian pig, a creature the size of a domestic cat, is an ancestor of the modern whale. The fossils of Indohyus were discovered in Kashmir by Indian geologist Ranga Rao around thirty years ago. His widow gave them to Hans Thewissen and his group, who in turn analysed the scraps and published their report in 2007 on the reconstructed forty-eight-million-year-old fossil. The analysis was further confirmed in 2009. Indohyus may have ventured into the sea in increments, at first building its tolerance for hiding from large predators underwater for up to four minutes, and eventually going the whole hog!

The ancestor of *Platanista gangetica gangetica* (the Ganga River dolphin), along with other toothed whales, lived long ago: before Chinese and South American river dolphins, marine dolphins, and porpoises. At this time—around thirty million years ago—the Himalaya were unformed, and the Ganga, Indus, and the lower reach of the Brahmaputra may have been one river, known as the Indobrahm, which flowed west; or, there may have been many rivers there, flowing into the long-lost Tethys Sea, where the dolphin originated. (Or, as some scholars now believe, the Himalaya may have formed over 400 million years earlier.)

This ancestral river dolphin could navigate both freshwater and seawater. Sea levels were much higher 16 to 11 million years ago, in the period that geologists call the Middle Miocene, and the ocean spilled into the Indo-Gangetic plain. Later, as sea levels fell and the ancestor of humans and chimpanzees evolved many miles away, the plain became a freshwater ecosystem. The Shushuk's ancestor continued to thrive in the subcontinent's rivers, even as it went extinct in the ocean, where other whale species flourished.

To live in the Ganga, which was clouded with Himalayan sediment, *Platanista* seems to have evolved shrunken eyes as small as blind pinhole slits, while developing its sense of sound to better perceive its flowing, billowing world. With its pioneering, species-scale understanding that a reverse pilgrimage back from the sea and into the proto-Ganga might be a cozier evolutionary bet, *Platanista* adapted to the 'shallow' and 'acoustically-cluttered' environs of the Ganga.

After this evolutionary coup, which makes *Platanista* one of India's most ancient living treasures, the river dolphin went on to thrive across South Asia in the Indus, the Karnaphuli-Sangu, the Brahmaputra and Meghna, and, of course, the Ganga. The Fifth Pillar of Buddhist Emperor Ashoka (whose reign lasted from about 273–232 BCE) proclaims that the gangapuputaka (Ganga River dolphin) along with several dozen other animals were to be protected.

Deer are supposed to have been the first creatures who heard the Buddha expound upon enlightenment, but, given the fact that his awakening took place near the Ganga, it's tempting to imagine the dolphins deploying biosonar to interpret his sermons, which critiqued the Hindu belief that the river in which they lived their entire lives could wash away human sins. *Platanista* also pops up in the *Baburnama*, the chronicles of India's first Mughal emperor, in which, perhaps anticipating by several centuries the scientific discovery that dolphins are descended from an ancestral pig, the shushuk is known as the 'water-hog'. It may have contributed to the appearance of the Ganga's mythological mount, the Makara, whose hybrid terrestrial and aquatic nature at least aligns with the dolphin's evolutionary history.

If you look closely, you can see it gracing the lintels of Hindu and Buddhist temples, a sleek, knobby-headed doorstop. Statues and paintings depict a creature whose front half is that of a deer, crocodile, or elephant but whose rear half bears a fish or seal tail. A famous painting shows the creature bearing the Goddess Ganga, with a very human-looking moustache flourishing over its mouth.

As recently as 1982, a naturalist named S. Jones conducted the first survey of the Ganga River dolphin and found it flourishing up and down the length of the Ganga, but that was more than fifty dams ago. As the natural habitat for dolphins, otters, crocodiles, fish, and other creatures became partitioned, the number of dolphins in the river declined. Today, *Platanista*'s upper limit is the Bijnor barrage in Uttar Pradesh.

For the most part, *Platanista* avoided barrages, and remained under the radar, growing increasingly endangered. Few Indians knew about the species, though many worshipped Gangaji and the creature she sat upon. In 2009, the 1,800 remaining members of the species living within India, along with the 800 that live in Nepal, Bangladesh and Pakistan, received the designation of India's national aquatic animal.

The river dolphin's body evolved in response to millions of years and billions of metric tonnes of Himalayan sediment. Its body is soft, grey, and vulnerable to nylon fishing nets, which absorb the clicks the dolphin makes instead of reflecting the sound back. Its more cosmopolitan cousin, the Irrawady River dolphin, can live in both oceans and rivers, but the Ganga River dolphin feels at home only in freshwater, though it can tolerate brackish water. When pulled out of the water, *P. gangetica* is breathtakingly vulnerable, as Dr Behera had said. According to a Japanese team that airlifted four of these dolphins from Bangladesh to Tokyo's Seaworld around 1971, the creature very occasionally mews like a cat. And yet the shushuk's endurance over so many millennia underscores its resilience. Its skeleton has a bony, armour-like head; the long teeth lining its rapier-like mouth make short work of the Ganga's choicest fish.

ON SHAMBHU'S BOAT

Despite the copious amounts of pollution upstream—a seemingly unchangeable feature of how the river is managed—the Ganga River dolphin appeared to be thriving on the day I visited the Vikramshila

Gangetic Dolphin Sanctuary, which spans approximately 65 kilometres from Sultanganj to Kahalgaon. This was not what I expected from a sanctuary downstream from the profane amounts of toxic waste I'd seen enter the river in Kanpur.

Vikramshila is named after an ancient and venerable Buddhist university that once flourished in the area, second only to Nalanda, half a day's journey away. Dharampal, a Bengali ruler, founded the university, and many Tantric texts were taught there. The Ganga here, known as the Uttarvahini Ganga, is considered especially sacred because it flows north.

Shortly after noon on 30 December 2015, I stepped onto Shambhu Lal's wooden boat from Barari on the Ganga's northern shore at Bhagalpur, Bihar. The river was calm, and despite the amount of local mafia activity, both of us were unarmed.

I had met Shambhu, twenty-nine, and his friend Bhuvan the previous day through Dr Sunil Chaudhary, the dolphin expert at Bhagalpur University who created the pioneering, and now-defunct, Dolphin Mitra programme, which paid Shambhu, Bhuvan, and five other fishermen about ₹2,000 per month for two years to educate their peers about the laws against killing river dolphins. Mitra means friend, and Shambhu takes his friendship with the river dolphin very seriously.

'Ten years ago, many people would kill dolphins. We ourselves would kill them. Slowly, that's changing,' he said.

Certainly, as ecologist Nachiket Kelkar recounts, the friendship between traditional fishermen and river dolphins is a competitive one. Both favour the same spots along the river, where fish tend to be most abundant—either shallow areas with muddy, rocky bottoms or deep mid-channel waters. Dolphins and fishermen like the same kinds of fish: catfish like *Pangasius pangasius,* ponga in Bangla, jellum in Hindi; *Mystus seenghala* which is known as ari in Hindi and Ayoyeer in Bangla; *Salmostoma bacaila*, a large razor-belly minnow; *Mastacembelus armatus*, a spiny eel; and *Cirrhinus reba*, a carp known as raichang in Bangla, mrigal in Nepali.

But the friendship can still turn into a horror story. Dolphin oil, which is used for joint pain in traditional medicine, can be lucrative. In the past year, three or four dolphins were killed within the sanctuary. The culprits remain unknown. But killings of this kind have decreased considerably since the Dolphin Mitra programme began, according to Dr Chaudhary. Shambhu, who has been working with Dr Chaudhary for fifteen years, is convinced that there are synergies underlying the friendship between fishermen and dolphins. 'The dolphin cleans the Ganga. It doesn't hurt fishermen,' he said. Shambhu explained that everyone now knows about the ban on killing dolphins, as well as the costly fines for getting caught (he does not think the newly synergistic friendship is any less genuine for being partly court-ordered). He once cut his own costly net to release an entangled dolphin, which exhaled with relief as it swam away.

I had approached Shambhu's boat from Barari, walking downhill from the red-and-gold spangled flag beside the tiny, informal shrine to Ardhanarishwar, the image of god as half male and half female. I walked past the man in the white lungi who was meticulously washing his motorcycle in the holy water, along with a small group of people bathing in the river. To my left loomed the dome of the broken electric crematorium.

Shambhu's crude country boat was docked at a ghat a few hundred metres beyond the confluence of the Chanak and the Ganga. I lifted my foot and placed it on the sandy, purple blanket atop the boat. Shambhu dipped his bamboo pole in the water, and we were off.

Any book on the Ganga would be incomplete without a description of its erosion and deposition. The previous day, winding our way to a settlement on the southern shore about 5 kilometers upstream from Bhagalpur, we had navigated past an eroding island within the sanctuary that was being worked by people who had less land to cultivate with every passing year. Of course, the river both takes and gives; when the time is right, these farmers hope to move to new land laid down by the intermingling of the Ganga and the Chanak.

The Chanak has sixteen offshoots and originates in the hills of Bihar. Both the Ganga and the Chanak shift their course from year to year, creating small islands in their floodplain. We set out for the Diyara, the collective term for islands of newly deposited alluvial land. Alluvium, from the Latin *alluere*, 'to wash against', is loose soil or sediment eroded and reshaped by water and left behind on land that was once flooded or where a river once flowed. In other words, the new land was the latest incarnation of soil that had once lodged itself in the Himalayan mountain range, only to be dislodged by wind, ice, time, and rivers.

This was the first time I'd ventured so far away from shore upon the Ganga. I settled onto the royal purple blanket patterned with pink flowers, and marvelled at how different the river looked and felt from our vantage on its surface. Shambhu rowed at the prow, alert and grounded, as the deep waters swirled below us. About 2 kilometres from the northern shore, we stepped onto an island in the Diyara. Shambhu anchored the boat with a sharp iron spike tied to a rope; the mud was just pliant enough to hold it.

This island was so raw that no one had settled it yet—a rarity in India. We stepped ashore onto silt that crumbled underfoot into a mush. We were only a few kilometres away from the nerve-jangling chaos of Bhagalpur with its eardrum-splitting horns and traffic jams. I hadn't expected the feeling of discovery, isolation, and wilderness.

Shambhu walked barefoot. As soon as his feet touched the edge of the shore, his soles picked up the imprint of paw prints that I, in my sandals, had walked past. 'Udbilao,' he said. Smooth-coated otter.

I took my sandals off, inviting the wonder and fragility of this alluvium to seep into my pores. The mud was glorious underfoot and it came in at least seven different shades of orange.

'The udbilao like to play here,' Shambhu said. As we walked, we saw the otter tracks over and over, with five small toe-dimples surrounding a larger foot-pad dimple. Each print looked like a large and confident flower.

Shambhu has observed the otters swimming in this area for years, including the previous year, when this island was still underwater. There are four of them—two adults and two young ones. They live 18 kilometres upstream, in the jungle. He guessed that the tracks we were seeing were five or six days old. They were mingled with the tracks of birds. In the distance we saw four hawks. I rested my own foot on the otter's paw print. 'They are very powerful. They can cut through any net, including mosquito nets,' Shambhu said. That struck me as odd and when I pressed him, he explained that mosquito nets were a high-tech (albeit illegal) alternative to the intricate traditional fishing nets that could take months to weave.

I touched the riverside grass. It looked bright and new. I collected two shells on the river bank. One shell was brown and shaped like a cyclone; the other was iridescent and fragile, like polythene made by snails. Shambhu brought me shells with no inhabitants and then one that was occupied by a snail.

Everywhere we walked, we saw shiny tracks that looked like garbled infinity symbols. They stretched out on top of each other, like figures-of-eight stretched here and there, repeating endlessly, like tiny slick dunes.

'Setu,' Shambhu said. Snail. The bent-out-of-shape infinity signs reminded me of the snakes worshipped all along the river, including at the Manasa Temple in Barari, only a few hundred metres from where I had met Shambhu. And the snakes reminded me of the snaky hand gestures that a mountaineer I once met used to describe the river winding its way out of the glacier. Try to perceive the river whole, and you might glimpse infinity—or a twisted rubber band that breaks when you pull it.

Infinity implies limitlessness. And limitless is what we used to think the river was. But the heavily engineered, rectilinear canals upstream, placed against the snail tracks, the hidden, poorly understood dramas both above and below the waters, and the endless snaky hand gestures, seemed to bind the fragile edges of resilience.

'Let's go to a new island,' Shambhu said. So we got back into the wooden boat. Shambhu rowed a few hundred metres west, and manoeuvered us onto a smaller patch of land near one of the columns of the Vikramshila Bridge, a massive grey concrete structure that looms above this entire stretch of river.

Shambhu seemed calm, unruffled. But as soon as we stepped onto the new island, he told me something that broke my reverie. 'You see, on paper, the Forest Department claims this land.' But, in reality, according to Shambhu, the mafia does.

As I was still swallowing Shambhu's news, we glimpsed a river dolphin as it inhaled the sweet river air. I blinked as its gleaming, sword-like snout pierced the water's surface and arced above the river. I had spent ten years trying to see a Ganga River dolphin. Yet my response was muted. I didn't hear any cherubim sing and no nature documentary theme songs started to play. I didn't allow my heart to leap—that would have been too risky.

When I'd left the shore, I didn't grasp the twin risks I was taking. Above these waters, there were threatening humans. And below, there were 'non-human persons', creatures who had swum in these waters before humans had left the continent of Africa. Now, their quality of life, and chance of survival, seemed far from assured. I was not afraid of the dolphins, of course. I was afraid for them. It was caring about these gentle, childlike beings that was risky.

I could have listened to the lulling, peaceful slosh of Shambhu's bamboo oars on the water for hours. But I didn't have much time left on the water.

The boat's oars slapping rhythmically against the waves made me remember a passing comment I'd heard the previous day from the seventy-year-old Mangaldeb Mandal. He had lived beside the river all his life and seen it go through many changes. The literacy rates have increased and tractors, fertilizers and insecticides have improved their quality of life. His village of 10,000 voters has a female MLA. The present ruling party's great achievement was making electricity available twenty hours per day. But the fish population has dwindled. In the past twenty years, the river has moved 10 kilometres from north to south. The riparian zones alongside the village were on the verge of erosion, a heap of gunny sacks barely holding it all together. 'The river was so deep and the flow so adequate that in the middle of the night, we could hear the sound of the Ganga from the village. It sounded like an echo. These days, we are not hearing that sound,' Mandal had said.

I don't know why, but I kept my ear out for it. My desire to spot the river dolphin had led me to this sanctuary, filled with sounds I longed to hear but couldn't: from the large, resonant echo of the Ganga booming against the shore of the village to the underwater echoes emitted by dolphins fishing alone in the daytime or in small groups late at night.

Platanista means oar-shaped, I remembered, as I sank into the womb-like sound of the water. I imagined the unseen presence underwater of so many flat, broad, oars—*Platanista*. After hearing so many people speak about managing the river, and suspecting that their approach was more like waiting for a living person to die than appreciating the functional integrity of her circulatory system and organs, it was a real relief to spend a few minutes with Shambhu, whose focus was larger than anyone's eyes could manage. He seemed to feel all that was still intact within the river, and willing to guide others to feel it too.

Maybe one way to be superhuman is to respect the unquantifiable: Shambhu's ability to drink the faecal-coliform-filled Ganga water every day, and live; his skill at patiently disentangling the shushuk, the sos (dolphin) whose saas (breath) you can hear in the water by the tide at full moon, less than 5 kilometres from the malls of Bhagalpur, dense with the extended arms of shoppers taking selfies.

I soaked up the cool, hypnotic peace of the river, rich with its biodiversity; its mud; its fine-grained, wind-tossed Aeolian sand, bhur, its quartz-laden clayey sand dotted with mica; khader, its sparkling alluvium, containing the purest water straight from the Himalayan glaciers. The river dolphin seemed, miraculously, at home here—not yet a fugitive.

But there are fugitives here, who walk on two legs, and they too enjoy a sort of sanctuary, at least for now.

THE MAFIA

Stepping back onto the riverbank, my boat ride over, I paid Shambhu for taking me out on the water and spending half a day with me. The life-changing experience cost less than what I would have spent on a nice dinner for two in Kolkata. I asked Shambhu to join me for lunch back at my hotel, so that I could learn more about him.

He did not attend a formal school; since 1994, when he first went out on his father's boat, his school has been the river. As a child he liked fishing a lot. Now, he makes up to ₹6,000 a month on the Ganga. He is married, with four children, and fervently hopes his children don't follow in his footsteps. The Ganga river dolphin's survival is intimately intertwined with the livelihood of those who know it best. Yet experts like Shambhu are grossly undervalued by our current economy.

Shambhu sleeps on the boat at night. He catches between zero and ten kilograms of fish per expedition. Ten years ago, they could catch up to twenty or twenty-five kilograms of fish per night; now, the average is four or five. Shambhu blames the rise of nylon nets, many of which are made of ordinary mosquito netting, available in any store. Although they are forbidden, poachers prefer them to chati jaal, the traditional cloth nets. Shambhu makes his own chati jaal by hand, attaching long pieces of iron to the bottom. The process can take up to a month.

'Fishing is our only business. There is no other work for us, up above,' he said. He recently acquired an assistant.

To him the little islands we saw were like open books. Like an economist reading graphs and charts, Shambhu could read scratch-marks amidst the green algae slime, infer bricks hidden in the water, and discern the type of net that had recently been used nearby. I had encountered so many people focused on mapping and modelling the river during my journey, but his facility reminded me that the map must never be confused with the territory.

Shambhu alleged that Forest Department officials only patrol the river for two or three hours every few weeks. They call ahead and let the mafia know that they are coming.... Those who are forewarned remove their illegal nets. The police look the other way.

Two or three days earlier, Shambhu had had an encounter with the mafia. It was 12.30 a.m. He was fishing on the southern shore of the river on his small wooden boat when the mafia came; they were riding a big motorboat. They forced him to go ashore. Forty people emerged out of the darkness. Five of them had sticks. Thirty-five had guns. They took all the fish, about 800 rupees' worth, and his net, which was worth 8,000 rupees.

Shambhu didn't have a mobile phone with him, and he didn't file a police report because he said the police would only jail the perpetrators for a few days, after which he would live in fear of the repercussions. In 2010, the mafia killed a fisherman, whose body was found fourteen days later. The killer spent one year in jail. Now he's allegedly back to stealing fish and nets from people. The mafia operates in the open, with encampments on the riverbank. Shambhu does not have insurance. 'What's gone is gone,' Shambhu said.

I asked Shambhu to tell me more about the 'ruler' of the island where we stood. It turns out that he is far from an elected official. He rose to power, Shambhu explained, when his brother died. 'The badmash log change. But new ones arise to take their place. It's endless.... The police capture them for one month and then let them go scot-free. They roam around in groups of thirty or forty people.'

Many people with the last name 'Mandal' identify as part of the Gangota caste. Shambhu's friend Bhuvan, a fisherman and fellow Dolphin Mitra, is a member of this caste. As he describes it: 'There are three types of Gangota: Koiri Mandal, Kurmi Mandal, and Dhanak Mandal. We are pure Gangota Mandal. We are Delphora Mandal. We write Mandal, but we are Gangota.'

Bhuvan defines Gangota as 'Wo jo Ganga se juda hua tha' (those who were entwined with the Ganga). Their reputation is as terrific swimmers who used to work both on the river and the shore. The Gangotas trace their origins back to Jahnu Muni who was born from dust and who may have re-birthed the Ganga from his ear or his thigh after Bhagirath worshipped him. There is a small temple dedicated to him farther upstream.

Despite the illustriousness of his mythical ancestor, Bhuvan says, 'We don't want our children to do paani-ki-kaam (water work).' Echoing Shambhu, he says, 'Let them ply a broom. Our work is very dangerous.' Bhuvan goes to list some of his recent occupational hazards. The day that we went to Choti Alalpur, on the southern shore, he returned to the same spot in the evening to fish. 'That evening, [mafia] bosses approached us with guns. They demand ransom, rides to Kehelgaon, and so forth. On 18 November, four guns were fired at my boat by old men.' He fasts every Tuesday, praying for respite from the mafia. He was not alone in his concern; during my stay at the sanctuary, every fisherman and fisherwoman I spoke with seemed similarly fearful. I had got a taste of this myself: At one point, when I was sitting with my notebook at Barari Ghat, a shifty-eyed man approached me and asked me if I worked for the government. I said 'No,' and he gave me a long look. Luckily, he left soon after.

One afternoon, I sat under a peepal tree near the Visahara Manasa snake temple a few hundred metres from the river with eighteen fisherwomen. They sang lovely, ancient Bhojpuri songs about the Ganga—songs the younger generation didn't have time to learn, because they were too busy studying.

The first song they sang was about the Ganga and her seven sister streams. 'During monsoon, all seven sisters are united,' said one of the older fisherwomen. 'They come to their mothers' home just like sisters coming together for a wedding. Then, they go away to their in-laws when the flood dries. Gangamayi is the oldest. Then Kosi, Ghaghra. They have one brother, Bhaironath, Shiva, Shankar. Ganga is the mother of us all, and of Manasa, the snake-goddess.'

The second song is about Ganga's daughter, who was on her way to her in-laws' when her boat capsized. The parents cry because their daughter drowned. But the sister-in-law is happy. The daughter was never found.

All the fisherwomen too alleged that it is the mafia, not the Ganga, which actually captures boats. They usually extort money and beat the boatmen for good measure.

Bhishm Sani, a fisherman who lives in Kehelgaon, told the same story. 'We are fish, they are gharials [crocodiles]. If we try to shoot them, they will come after us with three more men, and more guns. Who makes the sarkar [government]—we do. But the sarkar is exploiting us. We only know about law and order from TV shows. We've never seen due process here in Bhagalpur. If you pay ₹500, you can get released from jail. Bribery is continuing. Poor people are suffering. Even though it's the time of computers. If we kill them, what will be the difference between them and us? Why don't they earn a living without guns?'

Charan are side-channels of the river, cut off from the main channel. Some are present throughout the year, while others only appear during the rains. In March and April, they tend to be flooded. They are very important for fish because there is a lot of food there; the slower channels grow rich in plankton. When cordoned off with a fishing net, charan are known as koldhabs. The Fisheries Department owns the koldhabs. Today, according to the fishermen I spoke with, between two and four mafia members control the leases on these side-channels.

Ashok Sani explained, 'After the monsoon, the fish suck the grasses in the floodplains. They don't live in the main current. At this time, mosquito net barricades block the ephemeral pools and are leased to people from criminal backgrounds from their own caste. We protest, but nothing happens. Money talks. The full-pantwallahs who don't get down in the water shouldn't make the decisions.... Our complaints never reach the sarkar. Information on government schemes, meetings and decisions only goes to those who pay revenue [through the leases].'

When I pressed him, Subhasis Dey, a naturalist and key member of the Vikramshila Gangetic Dolphin Sanctuary's team, admitted his conflicted feelings about the rule of law on the river: 'I know who is converting from traditional to mosquito nets... [But] we warn the poor fishermen when patrols happen. [M]orally, ethically, it's the right thing to do. I know it's wrong, even from my side.' But my hosts might be safer on a river where the laws were strictly enforced. He claimed that a few months back, the mafia shot at them when they were on a boat tracking dolphins. Dey said, 'Either they confused us with the administration, or a rival gang.'

Chaudhary and his friend, Rai Pravir Kumar, a cultural activist and sitar player, explained their understanding of local history and the murky role the sanctuary designation had played in it. Since the Mughal era, feudal water-lords, known as panidars, ruled the 80-kilometre stretch of the river from Pirpainti to Sultanganj. While panidari was modelled after zamindari (the Indian system of feudal land-holding), it was unique in India because the panidars leased water-rights to fishermen.

After India gained independence in 1947, two water-lords, Mahasey Ghosh and Musarraf Hussein, leased the stretch from the government and sublet it. They employed largely Muslims. 'Each type of net had a different tax associated with it,' says Kumar. 'You had to show your receipt for using each type of net, and woe upon you if you couldn't produce it.... Even swimming was taxed.'

As Chaudhary sees it, protests against taxes were the origin of the Ganga Mukti Andolan (Free Ganga Insurrection). 'The Ganga Mukti Andolan started in 1982 as a movement against tax, but grew to include many other aspects. There was extortion and exploitation. Weak and illiterate fishermen couldn't do anything.' Persecution also increased. False cases were instituted against the fishermen, but their aggressive protests continued. There were a hundred boat rallies upstream. Each family hosted one out-of-state delegate. It was well-organized, and women and kids were involved.

Chaudhary described the protests as a 'people's movement to liberate the river from the landlords'. Finally, in 1990, the lease system was abolished; for Chaudhary, the movement was comparable to the Chipko Movement which fought against deforestation in Uttarakhand. 'All credit,' Chaudhary concluded, goes to the poor people, resourceless but powerful. 'The GMA won, but it was a short-lived victory because, immediately afterwards, the area was declared a sanctuary.'

Kumar continued, 'Laluji [Bihar's first scheduled caste chief minister, Lalu Prasad Yadav] came to power in 1990. He made the Ganga tax-free in 1991, and it became a free-for-all. The same year, the sanctuary suddenly appeared. We agitated against it because we were in the movement on behalf of fishermen. Ganga free hone ke bad, criminal bhi free ho gaya' (After the Ganga was free, criminals became free too). Due to caste politics, traditional livelihoods ended. So that today, the sons of the

Gangota fishermen hate fishing and prefer to go to factories despite the illnesses they pick up there. Ganga bhi samapt ho gayi aur machhwara bhi' (Both the Ganga and the fishermen are done for).

After much dialogue with Dr Chaudhary, Kumar and the fishermen activists changed their minds about the sanctuary. According to Chaudhary, they realized that it benefited their livelihoods, because a thriving dolphin population means a thriving fish population. But that same year, the ecological crisis started. The fish population started diminishing in spite of the sanctuary's benefits. 'Just like a fish dies when it is removed from the water,' Kumar said, 'if a fisherman is removed from the Ganga, his whole identity and existence will be destroyed.'

A few years ago, Chaudhary and Kumar had spent three days collaborating with a local drama troupe on a conservation-oriented street theatre project written in Angika, the local dialect. 'I didn't want to say yeh mat karo, who mat karo. But the message was very clear: why our positions have changed. Why no one is happy,' Chaudhary explained. The play was performed over a hundred times. 'In it, everyone was happy. The dolphins, the turtles, the crocodiles. There was enough food. It was the song of life.'

I was surprised to hear him endorse such an idyllic view of the circle of life, one that stops just short of every species holding hands; after all, as an expert on ecosystems, he had to know that the many different species in a food web are connected via hierarchies of need, distributed throughout. Ancient Hindu scriptures express the point of view that the whole world is a family, or nest—Vasudeva kutumbhakam. Dr Chaudhary echoed this ancient perspective.

But nests are loved by predators. And, in this world, predators can come from within the nest. How to perch between doom-and-gloom and the circle of life? Better yet, how to dive deep underneath this polarity, finding the fast-running riffle-pools where the river can still lull us until we intuitively find a balanced relationship with non-human persons? Until we discover the collective strength to throw off strait-jacketed engineering systems dreamed of in other countries and in other centuries?

Chaudhary delivered a brief history of the attempt to protect the species within Vikramshila: 'In 1991, Vikramshila was declared a sanctuary. Although the gazetteers note a 50-kilometre stretch, its boundary changes year to year, and the real sanctuary is about 65 kilometres. The gazetteer needs amendment.'

While the acreage in question spans about twenty-five football fields, a river sanctuary is different from a land sanctuary. 'On land, there are markers. But the markers need to be flexible in the river. The Write Wildlife Act 1972 didn't consider this. It needs amendment.' Chaudhary explained that fishermen prefer to fish inside the sanctuary because of its deep waters but they have to get permission from the Wildlife Authority to fish there. Therefore, much of the fishing that happens is illegal.

He explained that the declaration of the sanctuary for the dolphins did not ultimately lead to any positive changes for the fishermen, who came to see the government officials, some of whom had no training or qualification, as oppressive heirs to the landlords they had fought against before the sanctuary was created. The circumstances were ripe for crime. Those who used to work for the landlords now became the mafia; they divided the river up and began their extortion racket, terrorizing the fishermen. This meant that the fishermen had to fish more, since they were not able to keep their whole catch. This, in turn, led fishermen to start using contraband nets (such as mosquito nets), which are banned because they net so many fish that they deplete the dolphins' food supply.

As I listened to my hosts narrate the history of the sanctuary, I suddenly realized that all the fishing I'd witnessed, including everything Shambhu did, was illegal. If his children, and the children of his colleagues, led the onshore, upwardly mobile life that their parents imagined for them, would this be better for the dolphins? Would they have more fish to themselves, and fewer moonlit shoot-outs to be startled by?

GANGA KI GARBH MEIN (IN THE WOMB OF THE GANGA)
Out on Shambhu's boat, I had started to care, against my will, about both the fishermen and the river dolphin, but the two seemed to be on a collision course, worsened by environmental stressors that were harming both sides. I decided to spend more time with the scientists at Bhagalpur University, hoping that they could help me understand how optimistic I should feel about the river dolphin's future.

The Bhagalpur University botany department, which Chaudhary heads, seems to exist in many time periods at once. Less than a century ago, the river used to be several hundred metres closer. There is a building named after Tagore, who visited Bhagalpur once, back when it was a bustling metropolis invigorated by business-minded Bengalis. There were langurs in the trees, and many species of euphorbs, zamia, and bamboo, along with petrified trees from the Jurassic period and a pool with multicoloured tuberoses around it. Bhagalpur also boasts of donkeys, open sewers and the aforementioned men with guns.

Chaudhary's office bore evidence of his unflagging dedication to river dolphins. A poster documenting the first dolphin research that he and Dey published hangs on the wall. Under the glass on his desk, there are photographs of the shushuk taken by Dey's brother, also a naturalist. And behind Chaudhary's chair is a poster about ethical leadership handed out by the Rotary Club and a framed letter documenting the Fulbright scholarship that enabled Chaudhary to study with some of the world's leading dolphin experts.

But it's the unbounded versatility in Chaudhary and Dey's exploration that most reminds me of Victorian-era science. Dey does not have a PhD, but he has been Chaudhary's closest collaborator since the 1980s, when the two of them participated in the Mandar Nature Club. Together, they got the local district magistrate, who was initially not well disposed to the idea, to protect a nearby lake that serves as an important sanctuary for both the Greater and the Lesser Adjutant Stork. Bhagalpur is one of the rare spots where both the endangered bird species can be found. The scientists gave me a circular bumper sticker featuring the Lesser Adjutant, but the sticker had faded and gone grey in the office's sunlight.

Before migrating from botany to cetology, like a proto-whale leaving land for water, Chaudhary studied aquatic plants and the Ganga's water quality within the sanctuary. Brian Smith, then at the UK's Whale and Dolphin Conservation Society, had encouraged and supported him to study dolphins (indeed, it was Brian who first told him that the shushuk *was* a dolphin).

Chaudhary is proud of using jugaad to do cutting edge research. 'We have contributed a lot to science in this boat for fifteen years,' he says, speaking of his wooden boat and its modified, sputtering diesel engine. 'In the US, one can't think of doing research in this country boat.' It's on the flimsy bamboo platforms of this very boat that he will undertake research on dolphin acoustics in partnership with a Japanese scientist. And it's on this boat that Chaudhary, Dey, and the rest of their team created a double-observer monitoring method for river dolphins, one that improved upon the existing single-observer dolphin monitoring methods approved by the International Union for Conservation of Nature (IUCN).

Chaudhary and his team's innovative method involves two teams of observers on the same boat with two separate GPS trackers separated by a bamboo hut so that they cannot see each other.

In 1998, Chaudhary told me, ninety-five to ninety-eight dolphins were observed in the sanctuary. By 2015, that number had more than doubled, to about 207 (as of July 2018, however, it had gone down to 154). I heard his figures with my heart in my mouth. Should I rejoice? I'd come prepared to practise detachment with regard to the river dolphin, so that I wouldn't be too disappointed by its inevitable extinction in my lifetime. Chaudhary's response was sober. It's possible that the number of dolphins had initially doubled due to conservation and local awareness. But given the later discovery that the number had gone down, it's also possible that conservation practices need to be improved.

'The Ganges River dolphin is the most mysterious creature on earth,' Dey said.

The Vikramshila dolphin team was quick to note that it's important to consider not just the river dolphin, but also its whole ecosystem. 'The dolphin is an icon. For us the whole river is very important. In toto, in integrity,' says Chaudhary. He and his colleagues emphasized the unusually democratic, teamwork oriented nature of their group, and their multi-year collaboration with the fishermen. But I kept pressing them about the question that haunted me: how optimistic should we feel about the future of the river dolphin?

Unfortunately, the scientists couldn't tell me. But Chaudhary did tell me that, at Barari, where Shambhu and I had entered the river, the Ganga's average depth is 7–8 metres. Under a particular mid-column of Vikramshila Bridge, the river can run up to 33 metres deep—as deep as it's thought to be anywhere along its length. That's where the dolphins love to hang out. There, in the cross-currents, is what you might call their sweet spot. 'The dolphin encounter rate is two or three per kilometre. You don't find this encounter rate in the Karnauli, Padma, or Brahmaputra,' Chaudhary says. 'Volunteers from Alaska, from Israel, from Karnataka are coming. For me, that is a great achievement.'

I remembered my cousin, who hails from Allahabad and lives in Delhi. She had never heard of a dolphin sanctuary downstream. 'Bahar se log aate hein, hum nahi jate hain (there are so many places in India that people come from outside the country to see, but we don't go),' she said.

When the bridge was built in 2001, engineers drilled 53 metres down. 'Fossils of all different species, so many things were coming up,' Chaudhary told me. 'From mammals to fishes, freshwater to swampy, five million-year-old elephant teeth. Such a perfect assemblage was found nowhere else.' He says the fossils are in Geological Survey of India, Kolkata and in Mandar Nature Club, and admits that some are in private collections. 'You know, human weakness,' he says. 'Ganga ki garbh me kitni cheezein hein jisko hum jaan nahi payenge (within Ganga's womb there are so many things which we will never be able to know),' he says. 'So many stories of civilizations past which we cannot know. All vertebrates, many land mammals.' I asked him where these animals came from. 'One possibility is they drifted down from the Nepal hills. You won't find this at Varanasi, at Patna, at Kanpur,' he replied.

'Ganga's proper faunal assemblage is found here,' Dr Chaudhary says, offering me a cardamom biscuit during our final trip on his boat. 'This stretch should be conserved for posterity so people can see what was the real Ganga.' As we rowed past, an Asian open-billed stork flew off. They breed and nest here.

In fact, more than 200 bird species come to this stretch of the river, including migrants from Eastern Europe and Central Asia. No other portion has as much biodiversity as these 65 to 70 kilometres, according to Chaudhary and Dey. I saw the black ibis and the insectivorous red-naped ibis. I saw golden Brahminy ducks, also known as ruddy shelducks, from Kashmir and Tibet. In Hindi and Urdu they are called chakwa, chakwi, or 'laal surkhab'. They mate for life; it is said that one starves to death without the other. The story of the chakwa and chakwi is enough to make me cry. It reminds me of my father-in-law, who left his job for a year and a half while he nursed my mother-in-law, his wife of forty-five years, through blood cancer. She didn't make it. It reminds me of those I know and love, now living alone.

We need animals to think, says philosopher Paul Shepherd. Do the chakwa and chakwi have anything in common with the way my parents-in-law felt about each other? I couldn't say. But, by blending with the myth surrounding the ruddy shelduck, their individual story starts to shade into a universal story about heartbreak and loss, a story so heart-rending that the human species is alone not large enough to hold it.

The shelducks' story is a place where I briefly rest my heartbreak from the losses in my family and the conflicts in the sanctuary. For a moment, as I watch them fly, the sky around them seems spacious enough to hold both purity and pollution, mafia and fishermen, history and the future, governments both central and local, a few decades of profit versus millions of years of evolutionary wisdom, coal versus dolphins, and silence versus noise. Soon enough, the shelducks disappear into the horizon. Their species is healthy—their status is of 'least concern', in the language of international conservation biology. But if, somehow, they were lost to the earth, then we would have one less way to understand love, commitment, and loss. The loss of a species as mysterious, as complicated and beautiful as the shushuk—the loss to *us*, to our ability to understand the world—would be incalculable.

Ganga River dolphins appeared at my wedding in 2013. I did not see them; I was looking toward the shore of my birthplace, Kolkata. The photo from our boat on the Hooghly, a tributary of the Ganga, shows only the awe on the faces of my wedding guests. They look as if they had just seen a fugitive. I didn't mind that I was looking away; I was happy. Later, a friend from China mentioned that the Yangtze dolphin had gone extinct after thirty years of debate between bureaucrats and conservationists about how to save it.

In *Witness to Extinction*, Dr Simon Turvey, a naturalist who teaches at Oxford, speaks about his first-hand experience of failing to conserve the shushuk's enigmatic cousin, the Yangtze River dolphin in China, which was officially declared extinct in 2007. Turvey condemns the conservation community for spending thirty years deliberating whether the best way to conserve the species was to keep it in the rapidly degrading river, or to take it out. He founded the organization called Edge of Existence to raise awareness about evolutionarily unique species on the brink of extinction. *Platanista gangetica* is featured in their database.

In Nepal, according to Chaudhary, tourists pay top dollar to see a single river dolphin in the Karnali River. Later, he explained why. There are no agreed-upon regulations to manage tourism with its possible impacts of heavier traffic—vibrations, oil spills—on the dolphins' 'hearing, their foraging, even their reproductive behaviours'. But the fragility of this entire sanctuary is thrown into high relief when one considers the dredging operations already underway within the sanctuary. In 2013, the minister of shipping at the time, G. K. Vasan, launched a movement to transport coal along 'National Waterway 1'. In order to transport coal, the river has to be dredged. Reports from 2018 cite Chaudhary saying that the recent decline in the shushuk population could be due to 'the movement of big cargo vessels in the river and dredging activities [that] have impacted the number of dolphins'.

'For plying these big vessels, the river needs to be at least 5 metres deep. Dredging hurts the river's ecology,' said Chaudhary. Our hunger for fossil-fuel-driven growth may end up wiping out the river dolphins en route to degrading the global climate.

'Climate change of late has affected Bihar rampantly,' Abinash Mohanty told me during the monsoon of 2017, almost two years after my visit to the dolphin sanctuary. Drought-prone areas are now becoming flood-prone. Last year, the Falgu, which is a dry river, and a tributary of the Ganga, was flooded due to flash floods in Jharkhand while Gaya, the major city that the river flows through, was suffering drought.

Mohanty is completing his PhD in environmental science while patenting a teabag-like filter that cleanses fluorides and boron from water. He has been based in Patna for three-and-a-half years and is now a project director at the Asian Development Research Institute's newly-minted Centre for Energy, Environment, and Climate Change, a research/policy think tank based in Patna and Ranchi, accredited (and funded) by the Ministry of Environment.

However, the width of the Ganga at Patna has decreased by 5 kilometres, which has also affected people's ability to hold traditional funeral rites. When I spoke to him, he was in the thick of testing the silt in the river at Patna in order to analyse how well it could hold water. If it could hold a healthy amount, then his team could greenlight a commercial bamboo plantation on the river's edge in order to prevent erosion. The bamboo grows fast, is lucrative, and, Mohanty insists, could (and should) be managed by a community living nearby. If bamboo wouldn't work, then paddy, which would strengthen the soil due to the way its roots channel water, might be more appropriate.

Mohanty is part of a new breed of Gangaji's stewards; grounded in integrated community management of environmental resources, deeply versed in tradition, yet quick to debunk stories, like that of the Akash Ganga, in the Vishnupath Temple in Bodhgaya, the ancient Bihari city where people come to pay homage to their ancestors along the Falgu (and where detailed records of pilgrims and their localities are kept up to several generations back). At the temple, it is believed that if you are pure of heart, water drips on you from the black stone above. Mohanty spent eight or nine hours in the temple with a gauge meter, studying the black stone rocks. The water drips because of condensation due to the moisture difference, he says. Nonetheless, the mystery of the Ganga seemed very present for him. 'You'll feel joy, sorrow, hope, everything there,' he says.

'No one in government understands climate change or integrated environmental resources management. We need to do capacity-building for government officials,' said Mohanty, whose centre is embarking on an eighteen-month-long effort to help civil servants learn about the interconnected nature of managing the river. To balance this perspective, he spoke about the resilience of Bihar. Farmers' suicides are unknown there, in part because of state assistance, and in part because farmers plant three different crops per year so that one bad season can't undo them.

Mohanty envisions a future where traditional water conservation strategies are revived. He notes that the Falgu is a subsurface river in Bihar (though, according to him, it has plenty of surface water upstream in U.P. before entering Bihar). He points out that there are eighteen interconnected ponds in and around the Falgu; twelve are now abandoned, while six are important in key religious rituals like Chhat. During these rituals, water is pumped from the underground river to the ponds that are still in use. 'We can use these ponds for water harvesting,' he adds.

'We respect the Ganga, we personify the Ganga, but we do not understand integrated management,' he concluded, pointing to the need for working on impurities at their source, and for changing behaviour while yet understanding belief systems. Twenty years from now, Abinash dreams of a continuous flow in the river, with no contamination. Like Dr Chaudhary and his team, Abinash has felt personally threatened as a result of a community-based social change he has been involved in. Just like Dr Chaudhary, he is patient and committed to teaching others about the patterns that connect humans and the more-than-human world in a web of interdependence: 'When flash floods came, if the Falgu hadn't been there as a dry subsurface river, the whole of Gaya would have been gone.'

Unfortunately for the shushuk, this vision of free, continuous flow is under new threat. In 'Digging Our Rivers' Graves', a February 2016 blog post published by the South Asian Network on Dams, Rivers, and People, Nachiket Kelkar, a PhD student who works under Dr Chaudhary and has co-authored several papers with him, warned against the potentially dire consequences of the National Waterways Act (approved by Parliament in April 2016), which proposed to transform 111 Indian rivers and creeks into canals for cheap, efficient, and allegedly 'eco-friendly' transport of cargo, coal, and industrial raw materials. While the Allahabad-Haldia stretch of the Ganga–Bhagirathi–Hooghly was declared National Waterway 1 in 1986, the new Act proposes to make further changes in order to make this stretch navigable by large barges. Indeed, the World Bank has pledged $375 million for this purpose.

Kelkar, who is affiliated with Ashoka Trust for Research in Ecology and Environment, points out that the Waterways Act 'envisions the centralized, unitary control of rivers by the government of India', which would conduct regular high-intensity dredging of riverbeds. This would dislodge sediment and destroy fish breeding grounds, threatening habitat for endangered freshwater turtles, fishes, invertebrates, birds, and others. Indeed, tiny fish that breed in riverbeds might become locally extinct, with potentially catastrophic consequences for the bulk of fisheries, which depend on these bottom-dwellers for food. Moreover, the Act would convert floodplains and riverbanks to concrete embankments, with no consideration for local rights to use water for diverse social and ecological needs that go beyond fuel-efficient transportation for fossil fuels.

And what of the river dolphins? Kelkar documented the dredging already occurring within Vikramshila Gangetic Dolphin Sanctuary. It's not a pretty sight. A dredging rig looks a little like an oil rig. As the rig's motor churns up a vast black cloud of sediment from the river bed, and spews it into the air, it's hard not to think about the cloud of black smoke hanging in the air above the Ganga in the eighteenth-century portrait commemorating Robert Clive's conquest of Bengal for the British East India Company.

At least Clive left the river dolphin alone, as far as we know. According to Kelkar's research, 'Dredging for waterways at the scale envisaged by the Act will further endanger the river dolphin.'

Local extinction has already occurred from riverwater unavailability, for example in the Son River, the second largest tributary of the Ganga after the Yamuna. Scientists believe that the dolphins' powers of echolocation, used to navigate and feed, might be disturbed by the sounds of engines and the raising of sediment caused by the dredging seems to harm the dolphins as well. During a week in May 2014 when the river experienced intense dredging from the Inland Waterways Authority, Kelkar and his team observed the following changes, which should have raised a red-flag alert: dolphins of Bhagalpur began moving 2 kilometres downstream of their preferred hotspot near Barari where Shambhu and I had rowed; they began surfacing three times less often—a clear sign of stress, especially given that they need to surface to breathe; they also vocalized a lot less than normal. Most alarmingly, propellers from tourist cruise ships in the new stretch of river claimed the lives of some dolphins, presumably unused to encountering such ships (steered by ignorant pilots who may not have been used to encountering river dolphins).

This pattern of envisioning massively ambitious new infrastructure while yesterday's grand schemes flounder is unconscionably common. For example, Chaudhary criticized the National Mission for Clean Ganga, which focuses only on minimum ecological flow, without taking adequate measures to change people's mindsets, or to provide sewage treatment or electricity generation options that are consistent with the needs of the land. 'Our question is, who will decide the minimum? The minimum for dolphins is not the minimum for otters. It should be *adequate*. You are interrupting the river. That changes the entire biodiversity composition and the course of the channel.'

In defence of the NMCG, it's worth noting that the 2015 Ganga River Basin Management Plan strongly discourages dredging and sandmining on the Ganga. Even Bihar's then chief minister, Nitish Kumar, opposed it.

In an April 2017 opinion piece published in the *Indian Express*, Kelkar weighed in on the National Waterways Bill after it officially became an Act, one month after the river was granted human status by the state of Uttarakhand: 'Despite the diverse geographies and ecologies along its course, the essence of the Ganga is undeniably a singular idea; it is a wholesome individual being.'

He predicted that the Namami Gange initiative would split the Ganga between the water resource ministry, which would market the river as a destination for spiritual tourism, and the transport and shipping ministry, which would alter the river to expedite passage of coal and goods. Noting that the river upstream of Varanasi would not be affected by the Act, Kelkar writes: '[D]ownstream of Varanasi, river dredging is rampant and ongoing despite a stay order last year by the National Green Tribunal.' One back-of-the-envelope estimate suggests that by 2020, approximately twenty-eight ships will traverse the river within an hour at any given point.

Hearing these figures, and shutting my eyes, I also heard sounds and saw images from the past: hands pouring water back and forth from one vessel to another; time moving slowly, gurgling like water in a water clock; fisher families pausing to look up at a duck racing from water to land, its wings beating like feathery propellers. Then the clock turned digital; the human hands disappeared from view, and the peaceful sanctuary was disrupted by riverine congestion nearly as hectic as the inland traffic in Delhi. The sound of dredging overpowered everything else. Slowly, fewer and fewer dolphins broke the surface of the water, and, when they did surface, they were resigned to a silence without breath.

I remembered what Dr Dhruv Kazi had said about accountable re-enchantment when I'd grilled him about the Kumbh Mela. Kazi had emphasized that, if only we taught people to imagine their way out of the traps in the status quo, they could innovate respectful solutions to the challenges faced by the river, and hold political leaders accountable as they did so. Nachiket Kelkar's conclusion was pretty much the same:

'If we really wish to heal its wounds and restore the river's personhood,' he suggested, 'we have to do more than clean a part of it. It is evident that no more development of the proposed scale (for waterways or for river linking) should be allowed in the future.'

An analogy may drive this point home. Our differing national plans fragmenting the river remind me of the surrealist party game Exquisite Corpse. One person draws a head, then folds the paper so that the head disappears, leaving only a brief trace of neck; the next person draws a torso and arms coming from the neck, and then folds the paper over at the waist for a third person to draw the legs and feet. Then the piece of paper is unfolded, and the absurdity of the sketched body is celebrated.

This aspect of Gangaji—her disintegrated, disintegrating corpse—is visible from the holistic perspectives of ecology, systems theory, and integrated environmental management—all disciplines that challenge the foundation of India's education system, which is focused on producing a workforce skilled enough to build the bridges and operate the levers of commerce that are the outgrowths of the British empire's need for more revenue, which led to Cautley building the first Ganges Canal.

Kelkar embodies a commitment to holistic thinking. In August 2017, I had a chance to speak with him. In conversation, he appeared much more balanced than I'd expected him to be, given how radical his writing on the river was.

I was eager to talk with Kelkar because he seems much more comfortable than the previous generation was with critiquing political and economic trends that may adversely affect the ecosystems he studies. Like a true social ecologist, Kelkar is at ease with straddling disciplinary boundaries. Grounded in history and social science, he is equally comfortable tracking dolphins on Bihar's wild Kosi River, empathizing with the condition of the fishermen who live side-by-side with them, and analysing his dolphin sightings using Bayesian statistics (a powerful approach to modelling which focuses on knowledge, observation, and belief).

This approach, which relies on continuously updating statistical analyses based on the most current data available, is appropriate for a system as fluid and dynamic as the Ganga. It has led Kelkar to critique the Dolphin Action Plan 2020's vision for conservation of the shushuk, written by three venerable dolphin researchers whom Kelkar hails as 'pioneers'. They include Sandeep Behera, whom I interviewed at the National Mission for Clean Ganga's office in Delhi and Dr R. K. Sinha, who was awarded a Padma Shri in 2016 and is known as the 'Dolphin

Man' of Bihar. Nonetheless, Kelkar believes that the report is flawed for a number of reasons. 'It's very, very disappointing. It doesn't go beyond rhetoric and idealism. There's a huge chasm between knowing about the number of dolphins and the volume of water and doing conservation. It's troubling when conservation reports look like government reports,' he said. I did not point out that, technically, the Action Plan, though written by conservationists, is a government report or ask Kelkar if he believed conservationists simply shouldn't work for the government.

In any case, Kelkar's research, which established a robust method for estimating the dolphin population by accounting for common errors, shows that, between 2008 and 2015, when I visited Vikramshila, the dolphin population was stable. But in 2016 and 2017, the population declined. Seven years is too short a time period to spot a significant trend, Kelkar emphasized, especially given that dolphins only give birth once every two to three years. Nonetheless, he was confident that the supposed increase in the number of dolphins that Dr Chaudhary had told me about was in fact because volunteers had got better at spotting dolphins, not because the actual number of dolphins in the sanctuary had increased.

According to Kelkar, this finding raises important questions. 'Is the protected area doing anything?' There are the same number of dolphins inside as outside. The sanctuary has a symbolic value for the fishermen, who see that conservation does bring in some money for them. 'Let us not assume that investment in awareness leads to protection.' He notes the complex, desperate situation faced by the fishing community, many of whom are to migrating to Delhi and Punjab in search of jobs.

This is why he is critical of Dolphin Action Plan, 2020, which tends to see fishermen and dolphins as two static groups with stable interests, and which ignores threats like irrigation pumps, which decrease water levels. The DAP contradicts itself by calling for a ban on nets of a certain size, while simultaneously emphasizing the need to work in partnership with fishing communities. Kelkar questions whether awareness programmes like Dolphin Mitra result in increasing the number of dolphins and frowns upon the DAP's tendency to showcase photos of fisherfolk holding Save the Dolphin posters as though everyone were on the same, simple side. Their on-the-ground reality is far more complex (as my own encounters with the fishing communities had revealed).

'Most people only know the Haridwar to Varanasi pilgrimage,' Kelkar said. His 'wishful thinking and hope' is that city-dwellers would come to have empathy with the fishermen who know the dolphin best. In other words, the best way to know the dolphin is to know the people who know the dolphin. Trying to break out of my own tendency to focus on the Haridwar–Varanasi stretch, I asked him about the reach of the river from Narora to Bijnor, where the shushuk also lives. The Edge of Existence website credits the World Wide Fund for Nature (WWF) India's good work, in conjunction with local communities along the upper Ganga, for increasing the number of river dolphins locally; the area has also been declared a Ramsar site—a wetland of international significance—which affords it special protections that the Vikramshila sanctuary does not yet enjoy.

'There is no water there because of barrages. In the dry season, dolphins frequently get trapped in the canals,' said Kelkar. Although the Uttar Pradesh officials and the WWF are doing a good job of catching and releasing the trapped creatures who frequent the Narora-to-Bijnor stretch, the dolphin can hardly flourish in that reach because of the low water levels.

When I asked if he thinks that the shushuk will go the way of the Yangtze's baiji—the Chinese river dolphin—and if so, by when, he finally gave me the optimistic answer I had been seeking. He expressed confidence that 'India's river dolphin won't go the way of the baiji very soon.'

He grounded this in the fact that the river dolphins are found in four countries, including Pakistan, where fifteen hundred *Platanista* (albeit belonging to a different subspecies) still live even though the Indus has seven barrages on it. 'There is something about this animal that is remarkably adaptable and resilient,' he says. 'Research, including ours, shows that it can withstand quite a lot of human pressure.' In addition, 'India is different from China, and I hope it remains so,' he said. 'We are a secular democracy. We still have individual agency which people in China lost long ago.'

The details also differ, as he sees it. Citing *Witness to Extinction*, he notes that the extinction of the baiji happened in two separate stages. First, in the 1950s, Chairman Mao cleared the Yangtze for navigation which led to the baiji being killed by the propellers on boats. Over time, the baiji's mortality increased due to pollution. After the Three Gorges Dam was built in 2006, the Chinese alligator became 'critically endangered' (meaning 'facing an extremely high risk of extinction in the wild'), along with the sturgeon and several other species of fish. Those who depended on the river became more and more desperate, and started fishing with electric rolling hooks, which led to the baiji's demise in 2006.

When I heard this, I felt torn between two poles: the feeling of affectionate awe stirred up by the river dolphin and the cautious detachment that arose when I explored the scientific and historical evidence.

Kelkar made me want to believe in the future of the Ganga River dolphin because of his optimism, but, to me, his account of what had happened in China sounded alarmingly like what was happening in India. I asked Kelkar whether the Waterways Act wouldn't simply exacerbate the pressures that Kelkar himself had noticed in the sanctuary. After all, his research has shown increased dolphin mortality in Vikramshila due to propeller hits from tourist boats. He has also documented that Kahalgaon, the deepest point of the river until it met the Brahmaputra, has seen a marked decrease in depth. It used to be up to 60 metres in the dry season but, over the past ten years in the same season, Kelkar and others have recorded depths of 35–40 metres. He attributes this to the NTPC (the largest power company in India) withdrawing water, as well as to small-scale irrigation pumps. The shushuk has less room to move about, and its home has become fragmented as a result of this reduction. Moreover, as I had witnessed during my visit, overfishing, and the pressure on fishing communities which causes it, seems to be increasing inexorably in and around Vikramshila.

I asked Kelkar why so few people had spoken out against the Waterways Act. He said he thought it was because they were still waiting and watching to understand its implications. He agrees that, if India's proposed river-interlinking projects ever come to fruition (both economists and bureaucrats, he notes, have long suggested that interlinking won't be economically feasible), and if the Waterways Act is implemented as proposed, both would pose grave threats to the dolphin's future (I touch on environmentalist critiques of proposed river-linking schemes further downstream, near Farakka).

'The Waterways Act is not going to be the last nail in the coffin,' he says. 'But it's a bigger scale of transformation than anything in the last thirty years'—that is, since the government went on a dam-building spree in the 1960s and 70s. 'We need to work both with and against this massive transformation,' he said.

But historically the roots of the hard infrastructure ideals underpinning the Waterways Act go much deeper. If implemented as proposed, Kelkar suggests, the Act would fulfil a dream of the British East India Company, which wanted navigation to be stabilized along a Ganga rendered dynamic by the Himalaya's relative youth and high levels of tectonic activity. The only reason the British didn't turn the Ganga into more of a canal is that riverine navigation fell out of style, except for local boat traffic, after the advent of the railways.

According to a 2018 Rajya Sabha Standing Committee report about the National Waterways Act, 5.5 million metric tonnes (MT) are currently transported along the Ganga every year. The Act plans to scale this up to 21.89 MT by 2021, and twelve times by 2050. The primary beneficiary of the Act would be the NTPC, because the increased number of ships on the river would be transporting coal, oil, and hazardous waste. Moreover, building the waterways would reduce the cost of transporting coal by up to 25 per cent.

However, according to a report on the National Waterways Act issued by Manthan, a civil society organization based in Delhi, NTPC is the primary user of the Allahabad–Haldia stretch of the Ganga known as National Waterway 1. It uses the waterway to transport coal to its powerplant at Farakka. It told a parliamentary standing committee that '…the transport cost through waterway is only slightly lesser compared to the railways right now, since the cargo is transported one way only'.

I asked Kelkar about how the proposed changes would affect the shushuk and the fishing communities I had met. 'The waterways issue is like a chameleon,' he said, insisting that he wasn't claiming that India shouldn't want or need waterways, but that there are many unknowns about the Waterways Act that need further attention. For starters, we don't know how dredging on the proposed scale will affect humans, dolphins, and other species. However, there are some well-grounded hypotheses. For example, dredging could undo the river's self-purifying capacity by unleashing arsenic on the river, which would endanger human health. 'We need to respect the ecological limits. This is not currently being done on any of the waterways,' he said. 'You can build another road, but not another river. It's irreplaceable.'

The week before I spoke with Kelkar, the Ministry of Environment and Forests (MOEF) had said that the Waterways Act should not be implemented without environmental clearances. Kelkar was feeling optimistic about the possibility of a bureaucratic turf war between the MOEF and the Ministry of Shipping. 'There is still room to navigate, with checks and balances,' he said.

My memories of kinship amongst the non-human persons who live in Vikramshila had left me with a question: Surely this bureaucratic turf war necessitated more public debate about the modifications needed to the Waterways Act, not less?

Kelkar noted that the Act centralizes decision-making regarding not just the Ganga, but 105 other water bodies, taking authority away from local decision makers. I asked if centralized decision-making could increase integrated management of the river; he responded that it is 'thought to be clean, more efficient, and corruption-free'. I wasn't sure if he was supportive of this centralization, and I wondered if he was trying to be diplomatic. For my part, I firmly believe that, given the central government's track record on Ganga issues so far, it should empower local decision makers more, and build their capacity to ensure that the river dolphin and the fishing communities not just survive but thrive.

But the bottom line on the National Waterways Act, as far as Kelkar is concerned, is that it cannot be implemented as proposed for a very simple reason: 'There is not enough water in the river.' If this is a known fact, I asked him, why are government agencies debating about the best way to implement the Act? He pointed out that bureaucrats are incentivized to create construction jobs, but are not held accountable if the project doesn't work on the ground as it is supposed to.

He suggests that an approach that respects the limits of nature would encourage us to ask new questions. For example, can a waterway be run without dredging? How much human pressure can the river dolphin withstand? How does the cost of dredging get accounted for? Where do we draw the line?

To me, Kelkar's answer felt surprisingly diplomatic, offered up by a brilliant ecologist who may have received pushback from the Ministry of Inland Waterways for his fiery blog posts. What troubled me is that few people in India currently are asking the questions Kelkar raised. In 2015, the central government cracked down on more than 1,000 civil society organizations, including Greenpeace, 350.org, and the Ford Foundation, accusing them of receiving foreign funds and focusing on 'ways to create obstacles in India's energy plans'. In October 2018 *India Today*'s Anand Patel reported, 'In four years, Modi govt released only one-third of pledged amount for cleaning up Ganga: RTI disclosure.'

In the midst of so many questions and so much change, I remember something Chaudhary told me—a finding he hasn't published yet. 'The river has shifted course over the centuries. But there are certain spots that the dolphins keep returning to, year after year. Those hotspots haven't changed.'

◆

Back at Barari Ghat, under a chalky drawing of Shiva on a bridge column anchored on land, the National Mission for Clean Ganga's hand-painted sign in Hindi forbids people from spitting or soaping in the river.

A young man approached me thinking I worked for the government. He wanted me to find him a job. He'd already been cleaning the riverside, for free, he said, out of devotion—but also out of boredom.

Sona went to the local college but dropped out due to lack of funds. He didn't have his own mobile phone; instead, he gave me his uncle's number. 'Maiya hai to humlog hain; wo chali jayengi to hum kaise rehenge?' (as long as Mother Ganga is here, we are here; if she goes away, how will we remain?). He makes 50 to 100 rupees per day doing petty jobs.

He was critical of the current central government. Whatever they are claiming, the opposite is happening on the ground, he said, echoing most people I encountered. 'If they say don't wash your mouth in the river, more people wash. This is Bihar. This is Bhagalpur.'

But Sona was more entrepreneurial when confronted with Gangaji's problems than most people I had talked to. 'Give me one chance,' he kept repeating. 'I'll show you how much I can clean the riverside. Now I want benefits. The Swachh Ganga people won't listen to me. Give me one chance and, Ganga kasam, Chhakka maar dunga, Munger se yiha tak' (I swear on Ganga, I'll hit a sixer, from here to Munger).

As odd as it seems, I found something of myself in him. The intensity of his distress with the status quo brought out my own conflicted feelings about economic growth, and about warming up to caring for a species that science cannot guarantee will continue to endure.

As I left Bhagalpur, a photo of a dead dolphin I'd seen in Dr Chaudhary's office haunted me. It was trapped by an illegal nylon fishing net. It looked small and awkward on the ground, fallen out of the Ganga's lap. Next to it, on Dr Chaudhary's wall, a poster brimmed with pride: our national aquatic animal.

PART III
DELTA

CHAPTER 7

TRIANGULATING THE BENGAL DELTA:
FALLING OFF THE MAP (BANGLADESH)

The unknown Bird in the cage...
how does it fly in and out?

—Lalon's verse 'Unknown Bird'
Translated by Carol Solomon

PROFANE GANGA

I travelled to Bangladesh after two incidents made it imperative for
me to travel there. First, in an Indian village, I bought a VCD that
promised to deliver Bangladeshi folk songs, and so it did—sung by a
procession of dancing women. They oddly looked a lot like me. Then,
during my trip to the Gangotri glacier, I got into an argument about
whether the Ganga flows in other countries besides India. I pulled out
an atlas to prove that it didn't, but the neat lines on the map failed to
convince my venerable trekking guide, who insisted that twenty years
ago he had carried research equipment for some Germans down the
length of the Ganga—and into Bangladesh!

My great-grandparents were born in present-day Bangladesh, but
my family in India has lost all ties to the new country. When I visited
in 2010, Bangladesh was thirty-nine years old, exactly a decade older
than I was. My relatives, who are Hindus, were thrilled but apprehensive
about my trip. 'Muslims,' they said, by way of explanation. My father
was a little more nuanced: 'Dhaka is okay. But don't go to the border
areas. Don't get involved with infiltrators, drug dealers, smugglers.' I was
curious to know more about his take on Bangladesh. Growing up, I'd
heard a lot from my mother's side of the family, about how their ways
of speaking and cooking marked them as ghotis (with long-standing
roots in West Bengal), whereas my father's family were bangals (recent
immigrants to West Bengal from what used to be called East Bengal). I

was fascinated by this culture that seemed so different and yet so close to the one I grew up in, and I wondered how the Ganga had influenced these distinctions. I also had a cartographic fight to win.

Map after map had bolstered the claim I'd made to my trekking guide: that the Ganga flows only through India. In 2007, a correspondent for National Public Radio in the US published six dispatches from his trip down 'India's holiest river', during which he asked a lot of Hindus why the river was sacred to *them*. In the accompanying map, the Ganga had one beginning and one end, draped across India like a demure sari—and what proper Hindu wants to imagine India's holiest sari cut in two and partially wrapped around a Muslim neighbour? An Indian river cruise company's website, which has since been taken offline, put it as directly as possible: 'The Ganga flows through India only. It flows through no other countries.'

But just when I was convinced I could prove my old trekking guide wrong, I came across a second kind of map which showed the Ganga breaking in half near the border and flowing through both India and Bangladesh, occasionally meeting other rivers, sometimes layering on new names, and eventually fragmenting into smaller and smaller channels until all the waterways reached the Bay of Bengal, forming what are sometimes called 'the mouths of the Ganges'. Only a few of these mouths emerged in the Indian half, which geologists have labelled a 'moribund delta' because it is older, less fertile, and less influenced by shifting rivers than the 'active' delta on the Bangladeshi side.

Only three friends of mine had ever been to Bangladesh. All of them had visited in 2007, when the country began its most recent military dictatorship. Their anecdotes were not calculated to reassure. 'Someone high up in the military warned us about the coup beforehand,' two of them said. 'We were told to stockpile food and stay in our apartment for two weeks. We barely ventured outside the capital.' The third friend told me, 'Don't believe anything they tell you about Bangladesh. You're going to love it.'

I had to see for myself. So I bought a seat on a train heading from Kolkata to Dhaka, the capital city, approximately 320 kilometres away. The Bangladesh Railways train, after a multi-decade gap in cross-border train service, has travelled between the two countries twice a week since 2008. With its plastic interiors and tiny compartments, it looked like a toy train. The twelve-hour train journey between India and Bangladesh takes about five hours longer than it should because both countries subject passengers to a series of customs checks. As I waited, the compartment door swung open, revealing a vast river swirling below.

After a few minutes, which seemed like a few hours, the train was still crossing the river. Everything about the waterway—its disorienting enormousness, a grey flatness dotted with invasive Brazilian water hyacinths and forlorn wooden boats—resembled India's Ganga River. But all those reputable maps had insisted that the Ganga does not flow through Bangladesh! Had the train passed through a spatial wormhole while I was reading? Were we somehow back in India? I asked a woman who had asked me to stand guard at the door while she used the toilet. 'It's the Padma,' she said, as if her casual revelation were the most self-evident thing in the world: 'You know, it's a branch of the Ganga.' I knew that the British East India Company had sailed into Calcutta, my birth-city, via the Ganga and made it the capital of their empire. I knew that they had floated logs, opium, and indentured slaves back down the river. I knew that Bengal got its name—Vanga, Vangal, Bangal, Bengal—from the Ganga. I knew what it was like to bathe in the Ganga at Varanasi—India's holiest city—during a total solar eclipse. I knew that the Ganga had received the ashes of my great-great-grandmother and millions of others. I knew what it was like to wake up from a dazzling dream at the foot of the rapidly-melting Gangotri glacier.

But, as I crossed this other Ganga, I realized how little I knew of the delta that it formed—the world's largest delta, the Bengal Delta. Its nature had been, to me, as unknown, as half-hidden yet oddly familiar as those Bangladeshi women lip-syncing to folk songs. As the train travelled over the waterscape, I admitted to myself that I had lost the map-war.

SINUOUS, SHIFTING, MISMAPPED DELTA

I didn't straighten out the exact details of how the Ganga morphed into the Padma until weeks later. I couldn't help wondering why so many of the maps contradicted each other. So, in Dhaka, I ended up peering over the shoulder of the hydrological engineer Maminul Haque Sarker as he possessively looked through rare, old maps of Bengal on his computer. Sarker's office is in the campus of the Centre for Environmental and Geographic Information Systems (CEGIS) in Gulshan One, a Dhaka suburb that none of the city's quarter-million rickshaws is allowed to enter. Sarker is the Centre's deputy executive director, which makes him Bangladesh's deputy chief mapmaker.

Hesitantly, I asked Sarker whether the Ganga flowed through Bangladesh. I felt slightly foolish, like a Mexican asking whether the Gulf of Mexico is American.

Sarker's response was as shifty and meandering as the river in question. 'The Ganga doesn't flow through Bangladesh,' he said. 'But the Ganges does'. He explained that technical literature uses 'Ganges' for the stretch of river between the village of Khejurtala in West Bengal, near the Bangladeshi border, to Aricha, about 72 kilometres inside Bangladesh. 'It's been that way since 1776, when James Rennell first surveyed the river. But Rennell also recorded another name—the Padma' (padma means 'lotus' in many Indian languages with a Sanskrit root and 'aricha' was the name of the leaf I ate near Gangotri when I felt nauseous).

'Locally, the river is known as the Padma from the point where the Ganga forks in two. And, unlike the Ganga, the Padma is not considered holy,' Sarkar continued. The forking point he was referring to lies in Giria, Murshidabad, in West Bengal, where the Ganga splits into the Hoogly–Bhagirathi and the Padma. The river Padma enters Bangladesh at Shibganj in Chapai Nababganj District.

So my trekking guide and I were both right? I made one last stab at total victory. 'How much of the Ganga's water flows into the Padma?' Sarker smiled. I shouldn't have asked. 'During the monsoon, between June and October, 98 per cent of the Ganga flows into the Padma, and only 2 per cent flows into the Bhagirathi–Hooghly, which Indians call the Ganga. In the dry season, the division is more like fifty-fifty.'

The numbers seemed controversial. During the wet season—four months of every year—India's holiest river flows almost entirely through Bangladesh, but somehow sheds its name—and its holiness—in Murshidabad, West Bengal (I explore the history of the Padma in the next chapter). During the dry season, a man-made feeder canal diverts water from the Padma into the Bhagirathi–Hooghly, which is also known as the Adi Ganga, or Original Ganga. Without human intervention, this 'original' Ganga would be dead already. Nevertheless, the true Ganga, carrying sanctified human ashes mixed with sewage and industrial waste, does flow through Bangladesh—but neither Indians nor Bangladeshis acknowledge it as such, and their maps reflect this reluctance. Indeed, this reluctance is reflected not only in maps, but also in the ways of thinking we have inherited from colonial times.

As I learned while visiting the Upper Ganga Canal in Haridwar, and painfully re-learned while sneaking into the disued Ganga model in Varanasi, colonial engineers thought in terms of straight lines and clean edges. But this reductive geometry is at odds with the river's preferred shapes, which take the form of meanders and oxbows, tributaries (which feed a stream or lake), and distributaries (which leave the main stream).

I delighted in the simple fact that a distributary can grow to dwarf the main stream as the Padma does the Hoogly–Bhagirathi. In a journey filled with questions about how we can learn more effectively from the more-than-human world, one of the most liberating insights was that the main stream might peter out and be trumped by its distributaries.

Sarkar was happy to learn that I was descended (albeit distantly) from the author of *Boatman of the River Padma*, and shared this fact with his colleagues. 'If Manik saw the Padma today he would [suffer a] heart-fail immediately,' one of them told me. The Padma is silt-ridden and drying up, thanks to India's controversial Farakka Barrage, which is deplored by fishermen as far upstream as Bihar. I had many more questions for him, but Sarker shoved aside the stack of river maps on his desk, and offered me a ride home.

What else might the maps leave out? I had always taken the headlines about Bangladesh with a grain of river-salt. After my conversation with Sarker, I couldn't consult a unified map or model of the region without noticing how significantly it tended to mislead. I also observed how learning about new shapes like tributaries and distributaries enriched my sense of the possibility of boundaries being flexible, accommodating, even unbound. So I started visiting the river, and constructing my own, unofficial mental map—sinuous, incomplete, and oscillating between boundaries that did not reveal themselves until long after they were crossed.

RUFFLED DELTA

Bangladesh is pockmarked with shallow tube wells that draw groundwater up to the surface. Dr Jessica Dittmar did her PhD at the Swiss Federal Institute of Technology (ETH) in Zurich in 2011 on the arsenic contamination in the water used to irrigate Bangladeshi paddy fields in Sreenagar village, Munshiganj district, about an hour's drive south of Dhaka. She told me that the landscape of tube wells plunged into the Gangetic plains in Bangladesh is 'like spaghetti…so many holes in the ground, so many people drawing water'.

In 1975, the United Nations Children's Fund (UNICEF) started digging thousands of such wells across the country. They believed that Bangladesh's abysmally high infant mortality rates were being caused due to the unawareness among the people that their myriad rivers, streams, and ponds were teeming with invisible bacteria that would curlicue into the intestines of their children, speeding them to early deaths. Once mapped by superior European microscopes, these translucent wrigglers required action: drilling 10 to 70 metres, and sometimes as deep as 150 metres below the earth, in search of ancient sandpits which stored water a century old. For twenty years or so, these tube wells—which countered invisible bacteria with invisible sources of water—were credited as lifesavers. Bangladesh's infant mortality rate plummeted. Foreign funders approved.

Then, in the mid-90s, rural patients in Bangladesh started showing up in clinics with boils on their hands and feet, along with formerly rare forms of skin cancer. When tested, the well water in sixty-one out of sixty-four districts revealed contamination and up to 77 million people were at risk of arsenic poisoning, if not poisoned already. Despite its good intentions, UNICEF had neglected to check the groundwater for arsenic, which occurs naturally in the Ganga and Brahmaputra deltas due to the 15 billion metric tonnes of sediment flowing downstream from the Himalaya. As groundwater overuse increased, so did arsenic poisoning.

In June 2010, *The Lancet*, a British medical journal, reported a decade-long study that suggests that one in five deaths in affected areas were directly caused by arsenic poisoning. In other words, a reduction in infant mortality was won at a cost of conferring a slow, painful death, decades in the making, upon a whole generation (and their parents, and their children). It has been called the worst case of mass poisoning in history: larger than Chernobyl, larger than Bhopal, and still unfolding.

The aquifers in Bangladesh have been mapped into three categories so simple they verge on imbecility: Upper, Main, and Deep. The Upper (or 10–70 metres deep) and Main (70–150 metres deep) aquifers contain the poisoned water. When arsenic accumulated in the upper layers a hundred years ago, the British empire, always eyeing new sources of revenue, was actively offering land grants to those who would settle Bangladesh's constantly shifting delta, where the arsenic contamination is now at its worst. When present-day Bangladeshis drink the poisoned water, they taste the colonial era. After Independence, development specialists, stuck in imperial footprints, decided that the people living in that area needed better water supplies, and chose to reclassify the categories on the basis of shallow, deep, and deeper.

But Bangladesh's underground aquifers aren't shallow, deep, and deeper. They don't even run from side to side. Mohammad Nehal Uddin, Deputy Director of the Bangladesh Geological Survey, explains that when the Indian plate slammed into the Eurasian plate at least 50 million years ago, forming the Himalaya, and parts of Bangladesh started to rise up in response to the shock while other parts began to sink downwards. This push-and-pull has made the ground beneath Bangladesh an uneven swirl of different geological eras—more like wildly disarrayed neck-ruffles crushed together than the straight-and-narrow fairways that the well-diggers imagined.

Bangladesh's few highland areas are relatively impervious, but the arsenic is spread across both sides of the Ganga Delta. Uddin believes that the older underground ruffles—dating from the early Holocene and the Pleistocene—have contained safe drinking water for tens of thousands of years, since the Ganga was the proto-Ganges (Bangladeshi geologists are guerilla rangers in the map-wars: they refer to the whole river as the Ganges, even eschewing the term 'Padma'). But even geology, which often seems stable is hard to pin down in Bangladesh. Uddin emphasizes that the Bengal Delta, disrupted so long ago, is still tilting downwards faster than almost any other region of the world, which makes any map a moving target.

◆

About 60 kilometres past the Padma, near the India–Bangladesh border, I visited a man who had made significant strides in solving the arsenic crisis in Bangladesh.

'The donors get crazy ideas sometimes. At one point they wanted us to filter the water of the Padma River and drink it,' said Dr A. K. M. Munir as he shut the faux-Pharaonic door to his house. Dr Munir, a practising physician with a doctorate in chemistry, remodelled his house after winning the US-based Grainger Challenge for Sustainability, beating heavyweight competitors like Proctor and Gamble. Munir and his brother invented the SONO filter, a household arsenic-removal method that, under controlled conditions, appears to pull arsenic out of drinking water for eight years. Their house is right next to a large shed-cum-warehouse, where Munir's staff hand-assembles hundreds of filters per year. The filters are cheap because they are made from locally sourced materials: plastic buckets, charcoal, iron filings, and sand.

Munir claims that after arsenic-laced water has passed through this mixture, the remaining amount of arsenic is 'non-detectable and non-hazardous'. But he also emphasizes that no one understands exactly how it works. He hands it over to anyone who asks—including the US EPA, which apparently verified his results—but no one can figure out how the porous iron bonds to the arsenic, or what exactly happens to it during the bonding process. 'We can't find the arsenic anywhere. Certainly it must be in there, but we can't find it,' says Munir, joking that I can quote him when he wins the Nobel Prize.

However, two Bangladeshi geologists based at Kansas State University do not believe the hype. They have carried out an internet campaign against Munir, claiming that he refuses to allow independent verification, and worrying that the used filters could re-release arsenic to the water supply. Another study by UNICEF in 2018 suggested that the SONO filter had a much shorter lifespan under actual conditions than under controlled conditions.

In 2017 I had the chance to ask Dr Jessica Dittmar, the aforementioned expert on arsenic contamination via irrigation water, about Munir's claims. She had not only heard of Munir's SONO filter, but was also familiar with efforts to test it under different conditions. 'It worked in most cases, but not all,' she said, noting that in situations where the water has high levels of phosphate, or is too acidic, the SONO filter tends to fail. Dittmar thinks that Munir does, in fact, know how the filter works, but doesn't want to reveal his trade secrets. She doesn't believe that the SONO filter is an appropriate solution, however, because, no matter how effectively it filters, it results in waste that contains arsenic. 'What do you do with the waste?' she asks. 'Arsenic is not like bacteria you can kill. It's an element. It will always be there. If you put the waste behind your house, it will eventually find its way back into the system.'

'The second Green Revolution was great in theory, not in practice,' says Dittmar, who now advises Catholic Relief Services on climate-smart agriculture in Mali. Her research predicted that, by 2050, more arsenic would accumulate in Bangladesh soil, causing lower crop yields (although the monsoon washes the arsenic out into the rivers, it still builds up over time). Given the thousands of litres of arsenic-contaminated tube well water used to irrigate paddy fields, the idea of filtering out arsenic from aquifer water seems absurd to Dittmar. Her proposed solution is the one Munir dismissed: filter surface water and drink it, because that water contains only living things, which can be killed, but not a chemical element which simply moves from water to filter and, eventually, back into water. Even if households filtered and drank surface water, that still leaves the problem of using arsenic-laced tube well water for irrigating paddy fields.

The 2018 UNICEF study addresses these challenges. It advocates for a more holistic approach to drinking water that includes water treatment, safe storage practices supported by annual regeneration and daily water delivery. And it suggests several options for addressing contaminated paddy fields. The first, and the most drastic one, is to change people's diets en masse, from rice to another type of grain that is less susceptible to arsenic poisoning. The second is to introduce more oxygen into the soil in rice paddies by changing cultivation practices.

After speaking with her, I researched Munshiganj district, where Dittmar had done her research on paddy fields. I was shocked to realize that this was the same area known as Bikrampur—the place my great-great-grandfather and his brother, Manik, hailed from. Fourteen rivers passed through it, including the Padma and the Meghna (both Gangetic tributaries). I never made it to Bikrampur, but I heard a lot about its legendary mishti doi (sweet yogurt), which offsets its spicy preparations of bottle gourd, and its place in Bangladeshi history as an ancient cultural capital. Four generations after my great-great-grandparents had lived there, feeling connected to the rivers and the aquifers of that land seemed mentally and physically laborious. Why hold on to a sense of identification with this land steeped in poison? Did I have a choice?

THE ENCHANTED DELTA OF DR KABIR

'Antara is incommunicado. No one knows how to get in touch with her except her gardener and her dog groomer, and they're not answering their mobiles,' said physicist Rohini Kamal, more amused than annoyed as she settled back onto the cushions of her parents' beautiful Dhaka apartment. Bangladeshi folk music and the Padma, my twin obsessions, had led me to Rohini, along with her two cousins: Ananya Jahanara Kabir, an English professor at Leeds University, and Antara Kabir, whose first name means 'interiority'.

I hadn't met Antara yet, but I was a little jealous of her supreme indifference to time and space. Reputedly, she frequently disappeared into the solitude of her family's guest cottage, only to re-emerge weeks later, walking barefoot through the streets of Dhaka in the company of a holy man. I was charmed by Antara's outlier reputation, because it reminded me of a poem by Dombipada, a medieval Buddhist from the region:

The boat sails on/between the Ganges and the Jumna,
The Lady brings her children/to the other shore.

Dombipada belonged to the Sahajiya sect of Buddhism, which challenged the difference between opposites, and often celebrated unions with outcaste women.

Antara had promised to meet us at a music festival honouring one of Dombipada's spiritual heirs, Fakir Lalon Shah. Vanishingly few Dhaka elites make it to Lalon Utsav, one of Bangladesh's largest folk music festivals, which commemorates Lalon, an eighteenth-century mystic whose songs invoke a numinous divinity through paradox, blasphemy, and gender-fluidity, all the while lovingly mocking the rituals of both Hinduism and Islam. Lalon was born in Nadia, a district now split by the border. He is remembered on the Indian side as well, but Bangladesh has embraced him as a national icon.

It is often claimed that Lalon was a Hindu who married a Muslim. Some people consider him a Sufi, but others contend that Lalon refused to affiliate himself with any school. Those who insist on pinning mystics to particular traditions have had better success arguing that Lalon, who celebrated the sacredness of the body and overrode distinctions between the Quran and the Bhagavad Gita, belonged to a Bengali folk religion known as Baul. Nomadic folk musicians converge near Lalon's grave in the spirit of Baul, twice a year, to commemorate his birth and death with their music. Here is one of many Lalon poems about the Ganga. It encapsulates the traditional understanding that the human body is a microcosm of the universal macrocosm:

Man is as deep as the Ganges.
Only love can enter there.
Lalon says: 'I drowned to reach the depths.'

In Lalon's poem, the Ganga is no longer a goddess. Lalon encourages each one of us to envision our own bodies as vast enough to contain the mighty Ganga. For Lalon, reaching God was as easy plumbing the depths of his own Ganga-body in order to pierce the god-fish who swam within. I liked to imagine that my body was as rippling and all-powerful as the Ganga. But then I started envisioning the canals that have strangled my body, the toxic waste that has poisoned it and the massive cement barrages that have dammed it. I couldn't picture the god-fish. It was hard to imagine that it could have remained alive inside my body. More than likely it had drifted to the bottom of one of my canals, knocked out by a toxic cocktail of tannery chemicals. Or maybe its gills had been split apart by pustules full of arsenic. Or perhaps its entrails had been gutted on one of the Farakka Barrage's 109 main gates. Forget the god-fish—visualizing that my body was vast enough to contain the Ganga suddenly became too much like conceiving a slow and gruesome death for myself. Lalon's song began to ring hollow, as if it was too innocent for our time.

Joking around as if we'd known each other for a long time, Rohini, Ananya, and I left Dhaka for Lalon Utsav in a cushy SUV. As our rented SUV yielded to the city's jammed roads, my companions and I discovered that we were all descended from river-writers. Ananya's grandfather, Humayun Kabir, an eminent Muslim politician, left his extended family in Bangladesh, moved his immediate family to India, where he wrote a book in English called *Men and Rivers*, published in 1945. Ananya was still trying to figure out why. A few years earlier, in 1942, Manik Bandhopadhyay, an atheist, was drawing out his childhood memories of the eastern delta into *Boatman of the River Padma*, documenting the eponymous boatmen's precarious lives with an anthropologist's ear and Maxim Gorky's flair. West Bengal's Communist government, catapulted to power partly by an influx of Bangladeshi refugees, would eventually celebrate his proletarian chronicle by giving his son a job in a bank.

Manik wrote about Hussein, a charismatic money lender whose power stems in part from the maps and sextants which let him navigate past the Padma River into the Bay of Bengal, there to trade in goods that the boatmen could barely imagine. In the novel, a boatman, who 'needed no pieces of paper to guide his boat over the broad river', stares at Hussein's maps, 'unable to understand by what witchery these markings indicated the position of the islands and the divisions of land and water'.

Near dusk, an immense multistoreyed ferry carried us over the Padma. Ananya and I traded stories about our riverine patriarchs. 'Getting over our post-Partition amnesia feels good, doesn't it?' she said. Even though both of us were from West Bengal, we would likely never have discovered our common heritage if we hadn't chosen to cross the Padma together.

I remembered her telling me, on our way to Lalonpalooza (as one of my travelling companions insisted on calling it), that she'd become fascinated, after some difficult years, by the ability of music and collective movement to heal trauma. But when I read her work, what struck me was how often the word 'enchantment' occurred. She speaks about the disenchantment that occurs with modernity, and contrasts that with the legendary enchantment attributed to both Kashmir (where she had done research) and the Bengal Delta. In the years that followed, we kept in touch. In 2013 she mentioned our meeting in *Partition's Post-Amnesias: 1947, 1971 and Modern South Asia*, in which she recounted how the grandchildren of Partition, like us, strove to make sense of the traumatic wounds of partition. Her bold fusion of family stories with history and culture suggests new possibilities for how a cross-border narrative about the Ganga might be told.

GANGETIC DELTA BLUES

Through deep darkness, my companions and I walked towards Lalon Shah's grave, past a seemingly endless stream of men, some dancing to Western techno by the light of crude fires, and others, farther in, sitting in informal circles, as if expecting a hidden core of singers to be moved by the spirit any moment now. We circumambulated Lalon's grave, clinging to each other inside the immense crowd. Many devotees had camped out nearby, as if there for the long haul.

Real Baul music has what the Spanish poet Federico Garcia Lorca called 'duende'—raw and wild soul. Lalon's term for soul was Auchin Pakhi, the unknown bird flitting about in a cage. The music we heard was too smooth, too practised, too groomed for the cameras, to feel truly Baul. Two or three picturesque dervishes in long woollen coats whirled in front of the singers, carefully shepherded within the TV frame. Still, Lalon's words rang through us. Even if Lalon's view of the Ganga still felt dated to me, the rest of his oeuvre delighted us with its confounding paradoxes and its unabashed inversion of propriety.

Rakesh Kamath, a renowned Indian filmmaker who teaches street theatre, said that Baul songs are the 'blues of Bengal'. This made me want to explore the connection between the Mississippi Delta, where the blues flourished in the nineteenth and early twentieth centuries, and the Bengal Delta, where Baul music flourished during the same time though it originated several centuries prior. After all, the Mississippi's twists and turns might rival the Ganga's; both rivers have changed course countless times, bringing now fertile floodplains, now calamitous flooding, all the while dealing ceaselessly in life and death.

Less than 8 kilometres from the banks of the Padma, everywhere along the edges of the Lalon festival, in the informal moonlit jam circles, people were belting out songs that challenged the divisions between Hinduism and Islam, men and women, rich and poor. Lalon's words were an upside-down orthodoxy here. Lalonpalooza unfolds over three days and three nights. We returned to the festival grounds in the morning, when many more women were around. Celebrants were jammed together in informal circles, drawing sound from any available surface. At the centre of one circle, a blind bare-chested boy was ecstatically fingering a one-stringed lute.

And when a Baul singer opened his or her mouth, and let the unknown bird sing, the notes were so raw and beautiful that they blurred the distinction between the audience and performer. Everyone in the jam circles was transfixed, and pitched in however they could—some kept time by banging on a pot. Others played the one-stringed ektara, an instrument made from a single piece of wood (and not unlike the home-made Diddley Bow that Missippi Delta Bluesmen favour), or the xalam or khomsa, the simple lute, ancestor of the banjo.

I decided to talk to several rural women who had left their homes and families in order to travel from one Baul festival to another, singing. The presence of these laughing older women, clad in white saris, dignified despite their wild hair, seemed to be easily accepted by the men at the Lalon festival. The women I spoke with had shed their family names and adopted the last name Puglee: madwoman. Because Lalon is so celebrated here, these women were not dismissed as outcastes; they had a stable identity reserved for them in Bengali society, which was capacious enough to accommodate their nomadic tendencies and their strange ideas about god and their own bodies. 'What should I do if I want to understand Lalon's power?' I asked them. 'Look inside yourself,' Mahima Puglee told me, tapping her chest and smiling as if she knew what she was talking about.

Instead, I purchased a curved tree-branch which, I was convinced by a purveyor, would 'ensure harmony' in my household. Over the years, it followed me across the seas and to my current home in California, serving as a curvilinear reminder of the interconnection between outer landscape and inner peace.

◆

In 2008, the hard-line Islamic opposition party, the BNP (Bangladesh Nationalist Party), came to power in Bangladesh and threatened to demolish statues celebrating Lalon and the Bauls. Naturally, protests erupted. The progressive rallying cry was, 'Fascist forces be warned, we are all Bengalis, we are united.' When I mentioned this to the writer and artist Naeem Mohaiemen, he hammered the slogan apart. '*We?*' he asks. 'Left anti-fascists replicate fascism, in oblivion of people other than Bengalis.' As he sees it, Bangladesh's indigenous people, many of whom are Buddhist or Hindu, 'have been force-fed a diet of 'Be Bengali" since Bangladeshi independence.'

If Lalon walked the earth today, would he identify with the Bangladeshis who are so eager to claim him? With the Indians who cautiously preserve his memory? Would he have better luck finding his Auchin Pakhi, his unknown bird, in the hills? Probably not. In her journal, Kalpana Chakma, an indigenous hill-tribe Bangladeshi who disappeared after criticizing the government, wrote, 'When a caged bird wants to be free, does it mean she wants freedom for herself alone?… I think if she understands that she has been imprisoned…then she has every right to claim the freedom of the skies.'

THE WEAVER BIRD'S NEST

The final leg of Bangladesh journey took me to Salban Vihara, the ruined monastic dormitory of the last great Buddhist university in the subcontinent, which would have been well known to the students at Vikramshila and Nalanda universities in Bihar. Its vast red-brick complex shimmered in the high noon. A small boy walked by. When he saw me looking at the weaver bird's nest in his hand, he offered it to me.

I stuck my fist into the thatched ovoid. It was as warm and snug as a mitten. The weaver bird gathers unruly tufts from here and there and binds them together into a uniform nest snug as a sock. Supposedly, it hangs glow-worms inside, for light. When I looked inside, points of sunlight poked through the date palm thatching and into the dark hollow like tiny stars. I'd seen these nests and coveted them in West Bengal.

The boy walked with me through the ruins as if he owned them. He insisted that I walk through the endless monastery cells to see the monumental gateway embellished with reliefs of fantastic animals and flying women. For some reason, I tried to bully him a little, asking whether he had displaced any birds when grabbing the nest. Amused, he glanced up at an impossibly high date palm tree nearby, where eight other nests still dangled.

The mouths of the Bengal Delta flow into the ocean. And there begins the delta's hidden obverse—the Bengal Fan, the largest in the world, created from a billion metric tonnes of Himalayan sediment brought annually by the Ganga and Brahmaputra. Science has recently discovered that the fan and the Bengal delta are governed by 'scale-free mathematics', in which the pressures, patterns, and forces which apply to the most delicate root-like rivulets work in much the same way on the mighty, forking rivers. The smallest thread mirrors the biggest structure. From the outside, I could see the triangle on the map, the hollow inside the weaver bird's nest. What was it like to be the weaver bird?

I held on to the nest. My father assured me it would disintegrate if I tried to transport it. But it made it back to West Bengal, and then over the ocean; I still have it with me, here in California. I hold on to it like a talisman against the distance between where I live now and where my ancestors lived. The nest is woven too tightly to fall apart.

The boy ran off before I could get his name.

CHAPTER 8

GRAVES OF THE GANGA
(GAUR, FARAKKA, AND SAGAR ISLAND)

O, parrot dear, fly away to the other bank of the Ganga
Please put the Devi to sleep.

—translated by Shakuntala Varma in
An Anthology of Writings on the Ganga

JOURNEY

In late 2010, after I returned to West Bengal from Bangladesh, I decided to visit four parts of the moribund delta—so called, as I mentioned earlier, because it is older, less fertile, and less influenced by shifting rivers than the 'active' delta on the Bangladeshi side. I headed to Gaur, Murshidabad, Farakka, and Sagar Island to discover what the river's sloughed-off channels could teach me about its future.

Here's what I knew before I went: The bulk of the Ganga, which may have given Bengal its name—Ganga-Vanga-Banga—abandoned modern-day West Bengal 400 years ago, when it switched course and started flowing through what is now Bangladesh. The river's departure left sweeping changes behind. Plague and death, caused partly by malarial mosquitoes rising out of the stagnant, abandoned river channels, were the Ganga's parting gift to Gaur, once the thriving capital of this region, now a ruined city. As I travelled into the moribund delta, I was alarmed to discover that the river's death-giving tendencies were still fresh.

After my recent journey to Bangladesh, the taste of Bangladeshi cooking still clung to my tongue: jackfruit seed bharta; thankuni (centella leaves, garlic, cumin seeds, onion, tossed in hot oil); kathbel, or wood apple chutney; and fish galore (batashi, kakle, pangash, ilish, mola, shingh, kolshey, taki, shol). Not just fish but the stories of fish: Jahannath, a refugee from Bhola Island, which is falling into the sea, told me about how people go fishing in the rice fields using their bare hands as nets and how abundant the fish still are—they swim into one's hands. When water floods their houses, they crawl up to safety onto mud benches. Her brother told her she would grow hair on her palms, catching fish like that. In reply, she quickly caught a lot of fish and emptied them all on him.

I closed my eyes again and let myself follow in my mind's eye the most delicate root-like rivulets of the Ganga downstream from the point where the river's last muddy threads stretched into the salty Bay of Bengal. When clumps of riverbank fell into my path, I ducked. When I hungered, I benefited from one of the woven-bamboo traps staked into the riverbed and feasted on the silvery fish swimming in frantic circles inside. At night, I tried blowing out the stars with a harmonica. When I tired, I exfoliated my feet upon the billion metric tonnes of Himalayan sediment that the river moves through the world's largest delta each year. It was winter, so my imagination could pause upon one of the shifting sandbar islands and rest awhile on its bone-white silt.

Soon, the river broadened and I saw that the smallest rivulet patterns echo the river's larger meander. I left the mangrove swamps behind. My heartbeat slowed. I had seen no border, but from here on as I travelled upstream along the villages beside the Ganga, the living delta flows into the moribund delta as Bangladesh flows into India, as the Ganga's waters are inexorably clamped and redirected by the Farakka Barrage.

I hugged my disorientation close, wrapping it around myself. Then I sloughed it off bit by bit, like a snake. I was in the moribund delta of the great Ganga, which is home to over ten million Indians and Bangladeshis.

Death floats up immediately from this delta. A book about the challenges of sustainable development puts it best: 'It is a land of dead and decaying rivers.' For the 80 million Bengalis who have suffered arsenic poisoning on both sides of the border, the moribund delta is also a land of dead and decaying persons whose untimely demise can be blamed on a mixture of geology and politics.

Although I was born in the mature delta, in Kolkata, I was delta-illiterate until I followed the Ganga into Bangladesh. I knew that the state of West Bengal lies in the Bengal Delta, the world's largest. But if I am asked to describe the entire life cycle of the delta—what the geologists call its subaqueous, tidally active, mature, active, and moribund stages—I would probably have shifted uncomfortably and looked away.

But there was really no need to do that. The decaying maturity and loss of vitality surrounding me were, in fact, the climax of an astonishing geological story in which hundreds of millions of years of riverine history show something of themselves, but only to an aerial eye, through different colors. As millions of metric tonnes of Himalayan sediment have poured into the Bay of Bengal over time, they have formed an underwater (or subaqueous) fan that is about 12.5 million cubic kilometres—a still-forming delta underwater vastly larger than the delta above sea level. It includes a horn-shaped submerged canyon, some 500 metres deep, known as the Swatch of No Ground. A few hundred million years in the future, this subaqueous delta will rise above sea level and become new land. The part of the delta called tidally active is where land and water meet; from a satellite image, this area looks like a dense green cluster veined with silvery riverine inlets. Here, of course, lie the mangrove forests of the Sundarbans. Upstream is the active delta—still influenced by tides, but further removed from the Bay. Then there is the moribund delta, often difficult to distinguish, as Kalyan Rudra points out, from the mature stage. The moribund delta refers to about 30,000 square kilometers in Bangladesh and a good portion of northern Bengal where eight out of fifteen rivers are dead and the rest seem to be dying.

Who can blame me for not wanting to admit that the land of my birth is partly moribund? By some accounts, the Ganga in West Bengal has been on its deathbed for two centuries or more. If one of my goals in tracing the river's course was to witness its formation and history as a whole, I would not be able to avoid the final stages. And here they were.

HOW A MEANDER CHANGED HISTORY

The shifting channels of the Ganga and the Brahmaputra had once made Bengal one of the richest places on earth—so rich that strangers had flocked there, determined to make their mark on the marshy floodplain. The earliest inhabitants of the delta, which has been continuously settled since the fifth century BCE, likely practised shifting cultivation and spoke an Austroasiatic language called Munda, which might have been intelligible to the Maoris and the Polynesians who settled Hawaii. The relationship between Hinduism and Buddhism also had its shifting channels. Between the eighth to the twelfth centuries CE, for example, Bengal was the last stronghold of Buddhism in the subcontinent under the Pala dynasty. But Buddhism was an isolated palace cult; outside the palace, Hindu priests officiated over most marriages, births, and deaths. By the twelfth century CE, the Hindu Sena dynasty had replaced the Palas, only to be replaced by a tribe of nomadic Turkic Muslims under Muhammad bin Bakhtiar Khilji—the military general of Qutb al-Din Aibak—who conquered northwest Bengal, but didn't know what to do with it. North Indian rulers had always imagined Bengal to be a thickly forested, inaccessible backwater, populated by a multitude of tribes. These changes also shaped what counted as successful human strategies to influence the superhuman world.

In this long accommodation of originally contrasting traditions, one belief seems to have been constant—that Bengal itself seems inhospitable to Muslims, who continue to see it as a backwater. And yet, somehow, the first British census of India (conducted in 1871–72) found that the regions with the highest percentages of Muslims in the population were the eastern Bengal delta and western Punjab. At first glance, this geographical division seems enigmatic; most of India's Muslim conquerors had entered from the Central Asian steppes in the far west. How did they manage to convert so many people in the country's far east, without first winning the hearts and minds of those who lived in the middle of the subcontinent?

Here is where the Ganga decodes the enigma. Although the Ganga had shifted course thousands of times in the Bengal Delta, one of these meanders changed the course of history. According to historian Richard Eaton, the Ganga left behind its western and southern channels in order to unite with the Padma River, at the very point in the late sixteenth century when the subcontinent's Mughal rulers were looking to expand into the eastern frontier.

As the Ganga's nutrient-rich sediments started building up in the eastern delta, it became much easier to grow rice, cotton, and silk there, and the life-giving confluence made it much easier and cheaper to transport these commodities up north, into Mughal territory. Soon, Muslim warriors looking to become rulers, and charismatic Sufis, who attracted devotees, arrived in Bengal to claim land and offer it to peasants in exchange for settling the thick Bengali rainforest. Put simply, the union of the Ganga and the Padma helped turn Bengal into a mix of Hindu, Muslim, and indigenous religion and culture.

During this time, Eaton explains, the lines between 'Hindu' and 'Muslim' were often quite permeable. Strict Brahminical Hinduism had not penetrated the delta as deeply as it had the Upper and Middle Gangetic plains. While many popular accounts claim that the living delta became predominantly Muslim in order to escape the hierarchical Hindu caste system, more recent scholarship suggests that the area was mostly populated at that time by tribes who were not yet Hindu.

Sufis were intrigued by the spiritual practices indigenous to the Ganges–Brahmaputra delta. Shortly after Bakhtiar Khilji, an Afghani Turk conquered Bengal and Bihar around the end of the twelfth century, the *Amrtakunda* (Pool of Nectar, also translated as 'The Water of Life'), a tantric yoga manual, was translated from Sanskrit into Arabic and Persian. Kamrup, an Assamese Brahmin who converted to Islam, is credited with authorship. Although the original is lost, the translations circulated throughout the Muslim world for the next five centuries and were integrated into Indian Sufism. The text hails forty of the sixty-four yoginis (Ganga Mati amongst them) who were worshipped by Nath yogis for their power to confer immortality and control.

Eaton traces the *Amrtakunda*'s placement within a Sufi narrative called the *Bahr al-hayāt* which describes a covenant between a journeyman and a king who promises that the two will meet at the end of the journey; the journeyman undertakes a perilous voyage through metaphorical and literal seas and mountains. At the end, he meets a sheikh who duplicates his every word and gesture. An aha moment follows as he proclaims that: 'I found the king and minister in myself.'

While Sufi scholars emphasized the similarities between the Sufi legend and the yogic manual, Eaton argues that in the *Amrtakunda* and *Bahr al-hayāt* 'yoga and Sufi ideas resisted true fusion', and are 'two independent and self-contained world views placed alongside one another'. For example, he notes that Sufis interpreted a yogic breathing technique that describes how a foetus breathes in the mother's womb by referencing Kwaja Khizr, the Iranian saint who is believed to have walked on water atop a giant fish. Al-Khizr is celebrated during the

Bhera Bhasan festival upon the Ganga in and around Murshidabad by both Hindus and Muslims to this day.

Even if syncretism seems idealistic in the political reality we live in and even if metaphysics is a consolation for an out-of-control world, if we are to change our relationship with the rivers, we must look for hope in unexpected places. Learning that people of disparate faiths and religions have bowed to the transformative power of breath, of water and of interlinking stories gives me hope.

Despite this rich and complex history, as I learned more about the delta, I realized that the Ganga's union with the Padma had, in some ways, tilted the economic balance from the western towards the eastern delta. As the Ganga brought more alluvial sediment to the eastern delta, rice cultivation skyrocketed, and population density in the region shot up.

British policy had certainly accentuated the divide between Hindus and Muslims. Religious affiliation, or so I grew up thinking, became a critical means of attaining political power. Moreover, because the British rulers played one group off against the other, the divides between both the communities deepened further.

The Muslims supported Bengal's first partition, which separated the Muslim eastern areas from the Hindu western areas, in 1905, in the hope that it would grant the eastern delta's Muslim elite more political power. But popular Hindu sentiment against the partition was so strong that it catapulted the Indian independence movement to a much higher key. In face of continued protests, Lord Curzon annulled the first partition in 1911.

To placate the Dhaka Muslims after the annulment, the British built them Dhaka University. The apex of its hybrid Mughal-colonial architecture is the physics building, Curzon Hall, where rambling, crimson-flowered vines twist palm trees into the building's red-brick minarets. In 1924, despite the political upheaval, and even though he had limited access to academic journals, it was here that Satyendra Nath Bose made one of the greatest discoveries in quantum physics of the twentieth century. His statistical innovation and collaboration with Albert Einstein would later lead a quantum particle, the boson, to be named after him. In 2012, the Higgs boson, aka 'the god particle', was discovered. It is significant because it provides support for the theoretical existence of an invisible energy field that 'imbues other particles with mass'.

In a delta with so much past, present, and potential upheaval, I find it reassuring that the Higgs-boson boasts just the right properties 'needed to keep the universe on the brink of instability'. Even though the Bengal Delta may feel chaotic, it, and the rest of the known world possess just the right amount of chaos at the quantum level.

In the decades to come, the British policy of divide and conquer continued. In two controversial books, Cambridge historian Joya Chatterji has argued that by the time Bengal was decisively partitioned in 1947, both the Hindu and Muslim elite had actively worked towards this decision in the hope of gaining more influence for their respective blocs. Chatterji shows how the Bengali Hindu zamindars, or landed gentry, focused on drawing a border that would maximize their own influence. Further, these politicians assumed there would be no major movements of people or loss of livelihood following partition.

This relatively new dichotomy between Hindus and Muslims, which culminated in the creation of an international boundary, helped entrench West Bengal's economic stagnancy. The Partition in 1947 was particularly problematic regarding two key watersheds that had nourished the subcontinent's civilizations for millennia: the Indus Valley and the Ganga Delta. Building dams in order to hold back the water that gave life to the territories of East Pakistan (later Bangladesh), which they no longer controlled governmentally but whose water they could cut off physically, became a key project in newly independent India.

Remember Arthur Cotton, Proby Cautley's school friend-turned-enemy because of his criticism of the way Cautley built the Ganges Canal? Cotton had floated the idea of a dam that would maintain the health of the Kolkata port in the 1850s. A century later, D. W. Hensen, a British technocrat in newly independent India gave the green light to Cotton's proposal. The Chief Engineer of West Bengal at the time opposed the barrage, saying it wouldn't work. He was fired. In order to ensure the navigability of the Port of Kolkata, India gently told Pakistan that it had started constructing the Farakka Barrage in 1961. The Farakka Barrage, which started operating in 1975, is amongst the world's largest of its kind. It is a complex dam with 109 main gates straddling the Ganga.

The Farakka Barrage forcibly collects half of the Ganga's dry season flow in India. The Indo-Bangladesh Joint River Commission's

Bangladesh Chapter estimates that, between 1976 and 1993, Farakka caused damages of up to 3 billion USD for Bangladesh. India and Bangladesh signed a thirty-year water-sharing agreement in 1996; it recognized Bangladesh's right to have 52 per cent of the Ganga's water in the dry season. But Bangladesh still suffered because the treaty ignored recent data suggesting that the total amount of water available in the dry season had considerably decreased because of withdrawals in North India. Bangladesh's Dr Ainun Nishat told the journalist Cheryl Colopy that Farakka's diversion of water disrupted the economy of southwest Bangladesh; as land there (and in the Bangladeshi Sundarbans) became saline, about 20 million Bangladeshi environmental refugees, mostly from Kushtia, Jessore, and Khulna (the districts impacted by the Ganga's flow) flocked to India to work as cleaners and prostitutes.

Plenty of people attest that the Farakka Barrage has been disastrous for both Bihar and Bangladesh without having any positive impact on Kolkata's port or West Bengal. In *Dirty, Sacred Rivers*, Cheryl Colopy cites experts who continue to disagree about the physics behind why the net impact of the barrage has been so negative. She notes that the shape of the dying Gorai River—whose decline some, but not all, attribute to Farakka—and all the water that is withdrawn for irrigation upstream, most likely also contributed to the negative impact. With regard to the Gorai, Colopy concludes: 'The river may have been shifting and silting up anyway, as a number of experts maintain. But its demise was hastened by an intervention: a barrage that failed to accomplish its central purpose for India and did damage to Bangladesh. There was a disturbance in the system; the engineers made it worse.'

'The growing demand for irrigation water in both India and Bangladesh would have led to conflict eventually,' Ben Crow, a professor of sociology at the University of Southern California who has studied the issue for decades, suggested to Colopy. He believes that the barrage hastened this conflict by a few decades. As Colopy points out, following Crow, 'The fact that the tussle focused on Farakka, not on broader issues of watershed management, may have limited later discussions to arguments over cusecs during the dry season instead of opening up an exploration of the two nations' irrigation needs, a discussion so badly needed now.' Crow's perspective reminded me of what Dr Ananya Jahanara Kabir had taught me to recognize as post-Partition amnesia. Crow claims that, while the Indian negotiating position was hardly blameless, 'the tendency to replay the scene of the Farakka loss, hoping that repetition will lead to a different outcome has not helped Bangladesh'.

What can be inferred clearly is how little we understand the complexity of the river system—which is why making massive interventions seems foolish. Based on the past forty years, it also seems clear that people whose lives have been badly affected will understandably blame the dam, if not the state, in the absence of scientific consensus on the broader picture, or any definitive answers. As Colopy notes, India and Bangladesh share fifty-four rivers, which means they have plenty of issues about rights and precedents to negotiate; she claims that sharing the Brahmaputra may become a bigger issue in this century. If China intensifies diversion of the Yarlung Tsangpo, which runs through the Tibetan plateau and forms the Brahmaputra's upper reaches, then India and Bangladesh may have stronger reason to increase their allyship. Greater regional cooperation, and recognition that the river basin system is a regional treasure, will be even more important in the future.

The barrage's upstream effects are grave too.

Fluvial geomorphologists—people who study the shape and flow of rivers—refer to the 'neck cut-offs' of the Ganga—the moments when the river decisively shifts from one channel to another, leaving the moribund channel to become 'fossilized'. For example, E. A. Addink and Martin Kleinhans, two Dutchmen studying satellite images taken over the last three decades of the Ganga's Hooghly and Gorai channels in West Bengal found that, 'The lack of small meanders in the present residual channels indicates that both were abandoned so suddenly that meander geometry could not adjust to the waning discharge…. In the process of meander formation and displacement, neck cut-offs take place so that meander beds are abandoned.' But these were geologically-ordained neck cut-offs, while the Farakka is a political guillotine. The Farakka increased freshwater in the Hooghly, and made the Kolkata port more navigable—consequently salinity levels fell throughout the river, which decreased plankton, which in turn decreased the population of fish who used to eat the plankton. On my travels, I witnessed how fisheries have been devastated upriver in Allahabad and Bhagalpur, where (ilish) hilsa and other species once flourished. (Downstream of the barrage, however, the hilsa population increased.)

Clearly, evidence suggests that when monolithic human designs work against the superhuman Ganga River system's fluid designs, the results will clumsily backfire with dire consequences for the most vulnerable. Nonetheless, interlinking India's rivers, a fantasy first dreamed of in the nineteenth century, when such evidence was not readily available, is still being considered seriously today.

It was none other than the infamous Arthur Cotton who first conceived of interlinking rivers in the nineteenth-century British India. In newly independent India in the 1960s, technocrat K. L. Rao revisited Cotton's dream in hopes that interlinking might address the paradox of simultaneous flood and famine in India. Interlinking was given the green-light by the Supreme Court in the early 2000s and embraced by the current prime minister, Narendra Modi, who aspires to complete the project during his tenure. Yet, Colopy, who visited the effort to link the Ken and the Betwa in Bundelkhand in 2008, notes that the link hasn't been completed yet because of inter-state disagreements. She cautions against using the term 'interlinking', noting that it makes a grandiose and unfeasible set of proposals seem real in a way that is anti-reality.

'Every thirty years somebody comes along and says there's a lot of drought in this area and a lot of water in that area, why don't we join them up? Pretty logical,' Ashok Khosla, India's first environment minister, the former head of UNEP, and the founder of Development Alternatives, told Colopy. 'It has come up over the past 150 years on a regular basis. In my lifetime it's come up three times. It will be a bubble and then they'll find out it doesn't make any sense—that the cost is greater than the benefits. It slows down and then nothing is done and it becomes dormant. Like a virus, it just stays in the system and then blows up again.'

Given Bangladesh's aversion to Farakka, Colopy thinks it's extremely unlikely that Bangladesh would allow India to interlink the waters of the Brahmaputra with Indian waters. (This would be considerably cheaper than proposals to bring the Brahmaputra's water through the 'chicken neck' in Assam into India.) She concludes her book by underscoring the need for better regional cooperation and water sharing between China, Nepal, Bangladesh, and India. She also highlights experts who propose alternatives to interlinking proposals such as rainwater harvesting and reverting to traditional water management methods.

Bidisha Banerjee

♦

Neck cut-offs are nothing new in the Bengal Delta, where the Ganga has many mouths and thus many serpentine heads.

The *Manasa Mangal Kavya*, a collection of late fifteenth-century Bengali epic poems in praise of the indigenous snake-goddess Manasa, pits the goddess against an influential merchant. According to historian Swati Chattopadhyay, Manasa murders the merchant's sons and destroys his ships until he agrees to add her to his pantheon of upper-caste deities. Chattopadhyay notes that the 'merchant-hero' of these epic poems sails down the Hooghly, disembarking at port towns near present-day Kolkata—Saptagram, Tribeni, Kumarhatta, and many more—whose ports have long since 'dried up'.

The reverse, of course, happens as well. Three centuries later, Robert Hyde Colebrooke, a British surveyor, was dispatched to map the Ganga in 1795 in order to gauge its suitability for canal building. Colebrooke immediately noticed the havoc the river wreaked along its banks:

> I have seen whole villages thus deserted, the inhabitants of which had rebuilt their huts on safer spots inland, or had removed entirely to some neighbouring village or town. The Topography, I might almost say Geography, of a large portion of the country, will be liable to perpetual fluctuation from this cause; as the face of the country is not only altered by the rivers, but the villages are removed from one side to the other; some are completely destroyed, and new villages are continually rising up in other spots.

Colebrooke 'became obsessed with documenting these changes along the river and encouraged others to do so', writes Swati Chattopadhyay. She marvels at Colebrooke's habit of sketching tiger-tracks, boatmen, and pastoral scenes in the margins of his maps even though Colebrooke must have known full well how impermanent these landscapes were. In 1807, Colebrooke revisited the Ganga in the Sundarbans: 'Having surveyed this part of the Ganga in 1797 I was astonished to observe the alterations in the formation of the sand which had taken place... Several islands raised considerably above the surface of the water, upon which cattle graze and corn is sown, now occupy the space of the river... which earlier was at least 30 feet deep.'

Even though accurately mapping the Ganga was impossible, these maps were in high demand as the British sought to extract revenue from their new dominion. Within a century, however, Bengal's colonial rulers came to believe that, even if surveyors could not perfectly map the Ganga, statisticians could understand it mathematically, using trigonometric surveys. Chattopadhyay quotes an architectural historian named James Fergusson. In his 1863 essay, 'On Recent Changes in the Delta of the Ganga', Fergusson acknowledged that the river was still as unpredictable as ever: 'The city of Serajgunge—the largest and most important mart in that part of the country—is somewhere in the neighbourhood now, but not where marked on the map, of course, and it is annually obliged to accommodate itself of the vagaries of the stream, and change its locality. It may be ten miles up the stream, or ten miles further down, or five miles further east and west, but is somewhere thereabout.'

An archaeology enthusiast, Fergusson was fascinated by the 'rise and fall of towns' in the Gangetic plains. But Fergusson had his limitations, and Chattopadhyay calls them out. Unsettled by the Ganga's unpredictability, he turned to questionable mathematical models of how rivers around the world behaved. 'The larger geographical or geological history was a hovering presence in his surveys', Chattopadhyay writes. In other words, Fergusson had learned to look past the buildings right before him and see the implicit history of the delta.

Despite massive advances in remote sensing, aspects of the river's behaviour remain mysterious. The two Dutch scientists mentioned earlier, Addink and Kleinhans, who study the Ganga's past and present meanders in order to predict flooding risks and viable shipping routes downstream, found maps and aerial photographs unsuitable for their task and turned to satellite imagery. But the river's complexity remained. In a 2008 paper, Addink and Kleinhans note that meanders which are clearly visible to the eye cannot always be distinguished by automated analysis. The scientists conclude their paper on a wistful note: '[V]isual comparison of the channel map with the satellite image reveals that not all channels are detected, yet.'

Between geological neck cut-offs, political guillotines, and unknowable meanders, the Ganga has changed course countless times in the past. What could my own human vision pick out if I visited the graves of the Ganga—the river's scarred, abandoned channels?

Bidisha Banerjee

By chasing after ghosts, I hoped that I too, like Colebrooke, might be able to see not just the current shifting delta and those who lived upon it, but also the delta that had existed in the past, supporting those who had come before us. With the climate changing faster than predicted, could the ghosts teach me something about coping with the changes to come along the Gangetic delta? How much closer to the future could I get?

GAUR AND ITS GODDESSES

After travelling more than 300 kilometres north from Kolkata, in the 'mature delta', to Gaur, in the moribund delta, I realized that Gaur exists in two different states at once since it spans over 32 square kilometres across the India–Bangladesh border. To reach that border, I had to walk through the thatched roofs of the Indian village of Ram Kelli, which is separated from the ruins of Gaur by a low barbed wire fence. Although it was once the capital of medieval Bengal, today it is easy to miss the fact that you have reached Gaur—and even easier to miss the terrifying stories that cling to the edges of the ruins.

Gaur is believed to have a long and glorious history; its documented history begins around 1198 CE when it was reportedly captured. If I had visited it during the sixteenth century, I would have found a bustling metropolis of 40,000 people who walked on brick-paved streets and shopped at ample markets supplied by Arab, Iranian, and Abyssinian shopkeepers. According to historian Richard Eaton, the Portuguese merchant Ludovico di Varthema, who visited Gaur in its heyday, called it 'one of the best [cities] that I had hitherto seen', home to 'the richest merchants I have ever met'. If di Varthema can be trusted, Gaur's crowded streets were not too different from the streets of a modern Indian town. 'The market is everywhere and everything—food and other goods alike—is in plentiful supply and very cheap,' he wrote. 'The streets and cross-lanes are so full of people that [it] is impossible to move and it has reached the point where the high noblemen have taken to being preceded along the road to the palace by men carrying bamboo sticks to push people out of the way.'

Contemporaries of di Varthema also described Gaur's great opulence— the sultan's polo matches in the inner courtyard, the silk scarves and bathing tanks all around, the provisions of food and money thrown from a platform into a crowd of 4,000–5,000 people. Yet all these luxuries came to naught. By the end of the sixteenth century, Gaur was a wasteland; the Ganga had shifted course, moving several kilometers east, and as freshwater disappeared, plague and malaria spread. Soon, Gaur became a dead city.

I went to Gaur to discover stories from the past. I knew I'd reached my destination when I saw the long barbed-wire fence, the manicured lawns and the brick-walled structures, their crumbling surface knobbly like the trunks of the date palms growing nearby.

I walked into Gaur's Baraduari Mosque, which has a doubly inaccurate name. Baraduari means twelve-doored, but the mosque has only eleven. It is also known as the Great Golden Mosque—although the gilding fell off long ago. Parts of its doorways, built during the city's early days as a Hindu and Buddhist stronghold, were firm basalt, the colour of a cloudy full-moon night. Other parts were crumbling brick, built during Gaur's later years as a Muslim citadel. Two or three thin, hard-working masons moved silently from sunlight to shadow, repairing the terracotta bricks. The mosque had stone lotuses stamped above the arches, which cast beautiful, dizzying shadows on the ground at high noon. From one end of the mosque's eleven arches, the site of a former ladies' gallery, the banana leaves on the other end glowed brightly in the relative darkness.

Gaur is a ghostly interplay of geometry, shade, and light. But as I walked out of Baraduari, I caught a glimpse of something more surreal.

Under a banyan tree just outside the ruined complex was a small, boxy room closed off by an iron grille—a temple less than five feet from one of the entrances to Gaur, so small it may have been nameless, at least I have not found its name. The temple contained one of the bloodiest idols I have ever seen—an image of the Tantric goddess Chinnamasta, an incarnation of Shakti, after she had cut her own neck off.

Legend has it that Chinnamasta was obliged to behead herself when her handmaidens begged for food. She held her detached head aloft in one hand while directing the jets of blood spurting from her neck at her hungry hand-maidens' mouths; at her feet, half-hidden by her sari's folds, a couple copulated. In her other hand, she carried a scimitar and wore a string of other people's heads attached to a serpent that doubled as her garland. Next to her was an image of the snake goddess Manasa, cradling a small child in her arms. Behind the two goddesses hung, unaccountably, various old clocks with their hands frozen in many positions. Above Chinnamasta, Shiva's head gleamed, small and easy to miss. And, down below, someone had made sure to place golden marigolds and blood-red hibiscus flowers.

The temple captured my imagination immediately—in all my travels through rural India, I'd never seen anything like it. Chinnamasta's form was so riveting that I was almost paralysed. The second site, an arched gateway a quarter of a mile up the road, was filled with bats. But I was still haunted by Chinnamasta's cut-off neck. This goddess emblematized the fierce, dangerous Shakti who rarely appeared in the glossy idealized renditions of the goddess Ganga. Seeing Ma Manasa and Chinnamasta together, I felt moved by the indigenous wisdom that knew how to transform anger and bloodthirst into objects of devotion. Growing up, I'd never known how to be present with my own anger. But receiving darshan from these ancient idols, so far off the beaten track, made me determined to contact my own anger and use it as fuel for new possibilities in service of telling Gangaji's stories. In the future, climate change is expected to intensify the number of vector-borne diseases. Gaur gave me a taste of how quickly plague can devastate a seemingly opulent capital city.

'Please take us back to Baraduari,' I asked the rental car's driver, a whip-thin man in tight trousers who never took off his sun-glasses. At first, he refused to turn around, even though Baraduari was less than a quarter mile behind us. He wouldn't explain his reluctance, but I was dead set and eventually convinced him to retrace our steps.

Our driver took us back to the village of Ram Kelli, close to Baraduari. I asked around about the temple and its headless idol. And that is how I met Radharani Ghosh, the priestess who built the Chinnamasta Temple after the goddess had come to her in a dream decades ago.

A small, formidable woman in her sixties, Radharani wore a faded lime-green sari with white, serpentine patterns. On her wrinkled right wrist, I saw black ink tattoos of a grain of rice, a rice-husker, and the puffy kodom flower (bur-flower), which signals the arrival of the monsoon. Radharani is a power to reckon with: she owns cattle, the village sweet-shop, and some land, which her son tills for her.

She told me that the goddess at her temple is very jagrat—awake. 'A girl came here once, and immediately went into a trance,' Radharani said. 'She stayed here for two years, often falling into a trance and dancing in front of Ma.' She also told me about a tantric holy man who came to the temple. Radharani shunned him, but he lured away a widow from across the road, convincing her to leave her children, and travel with him. Radharani told me this story by way of emphasizing that even though Chinnamasta is considered a tantric deity, Radharani herself didn't indulge in tantric practices. She wasn't inclined to lounge beside corpses in charnel grounds, meditating on death, and transgressive sex wasn't her chosen path towards union with the divine.

I asked Radharani about Manasa, the snake-goddess indigenous to the delta. Her response hinted that the balance of power between the human and non-human worlds remained alive and well in her part of the river. 'Husband-and-wife snakes used to stay here, under this tree,' she told me. 'They never harmed anyone. Often I'd be sleeping and wake up to see a giant snake on the box near my bed or on the bricks. No one kills snakes here even though there are so many poisonous snakes around. We believe they are the spirits of old people. They come here, drink milk and go away.'

As we spoke further, I started to realize that Radharani was a trove of Gaur's recent history. She had lived through a very dark time in the delta's past: the massacre of over a million Bangladeshi civilians by the Pakistani soldiers between 1971, when Bangladesh's first prime minister, Mujibar Rahman, declared the nation's independence from Pakistan, and 1974, when Mujibar was assassinated. Radharani was born in Kanshat, Bangladesh, around 1955, when Bangladesh was still considered East Pakistan. 'We came to India in 1970, returned to Bangladesh in 1971, then came back after Mujibar was killed,' she said.

'Gaur was filled with refugee camps when I first came here,' Radharani said, looking past me over the long barbed-wire fence beside the temple. Bengali-speaking Hindus and Muslims from what was then East Pakistan took refuge in the camps, hiding out from Urdu-speaking West Pakistani soldiers, who were attempting to put down a Bengali language movement in the east. Under the lead of the then Prime Minister Indira Gandhi, India stepped in and aided Bangladesh in its battle against West Pakistan. Many Bangladeshi soldiers received training, shelter, and food in India. 'All the children had diarrhoea and cried all night. Indira Gandhi took good care of us. She gave us food, and even sindur boxes so that married Hindu women could apply vermilion paste on their foreheads… The Pakistanis would have finished us,' Radharani added matter-of-factly.

A small boy who had been sitting on a rusted rice husker nearby crept closer to listen. Radharani started recalling how Pakistanis would tell Hindu Bangladeshis to 'Line up, Line up. They shot people, threw them into graves in the ground, speaking Urdu all the while,' she said, using the term 'Pathan' (Pashtun) to refer to the Pakistanis. The Pakistani Muslims from the northwest treated Radharani very differently from the Muslims of her village, who, she says, saved her and her family. 'We had a shop by the roadside. The Pathans came in six cars. My father-in-law said, "I won't leave. I was born here." Then the Pathans killed our priest.'

The priestess associates her Muslim neighbours with the compassion of God: 'Our Muslim neighbours gave my father-in-law a Muslim loincloth to wear,' she told me. 'Goats saved our lives too. The Pathans were distracted by the goats and started eating. Later, they burned our house with petrol. God saved us. I would rather die than go back to Bangladesh,' she said, referring to the country five miles away.

Shaken, I thanked Radharani for her story and took my leave. She invited me to come back during the monsoon festival to sing snake-songs to the snake goddess. It wasn't until I was a few miles away that I realized that we had barely talked about Chinnamasta, perpetually balanced in the act of taking her own life in order to sustain her hungry hand-maidens. But I felt a glimmer of understanding about why this goddess, in this particular form, was alive and well in this border town whose fortunes had been defined by a river that gave life and death and life and death, over and over.

Until I'd seen the Chinnamasta idol and felt Radharani's quiet confidence and high status in the village, I had never felt the power that came from worshipping death as a goddess. Despite Radharani's clarification that she wasn't a tantric priestess, after my encounter with the goddess on that blood-soaked soil, the tantric practice of meditating on corpses inside charnel grounds made visceral sense to me for the first time. The strangled, poisoned, and dammed corpse of the Ganga began to haunt me.

Once I left Radharani's village, I assumed that I wouldn't run into the snake goddess again unless I came back for the monsoon. Yet less than a mile away, at another one of Gaur's ruins, I came across an abandoned Manasa idol, already faded to show the straw beneath, propped up next to a banyan tree. I leaned on the tree too. The snake-goddess kept me company as I peered through a frame of fleshy leaves at a squat, three-storeyed tower—the Firoz Minar. The land nearby was filled with ponds. A small girl was washing dishes in one of them. The featureless straw image of another idol—Gaur Nitai, a local man who had turned into an incarnation of Krishna—was partly submerged and floating in the water next to her, slowly dissolving into biomass. As I stared up at the sand-coloured tower, I recalled the story of one of Bengal's many multicultural past lives.

The Firoz Minar was built by the first Ethiopian ruler of Bengal, Firoz Shah, after he wrested control of the land from Barbak Shahzada. For a few brief years—1487 to 1493—Ethiopian warrior-slaves, many of whom played a powerful role in the Mughal empire, ruled Bengal. Some historians refer to this period as the 'Abyssinian Interlude'. Within a relatively brief time, however, the Ethiopians were chased out of Bengal and found a warmer reception in other parts of the subcontinent. To this day, Ethiopian food, with its richly spiced lentils, curries, and clarified butter bears the imprints of the interlude with India.

KISA GOTAMI

On my way to the stagnant, once plague-ridden backwaters of Gaur and the vast Farakka Barrage, I had followed the narrow Hooghly–Bhagirathi towards Murshidabad, past Plassey (now Palasi), where the British, in 1757, had vanquished Bengal's rulers once and for all. Just south of Murshidabad, an enormous frieze, ashen and blue-grey, compelled me to stop at the river's edge.

The figure of a girl, her turbulent, flowing hair frozen in stone, had placed a stiff, pallid lump near the Buddha's feet. Her hands were folded in prayer; with every bone of her body she seemed to be beseeching the Buddha—who was avoiding eye contact with her, looking inwards, one hand touching the earth as he meditated under a thick-leaved banyan tree whose aerial roots snaked around tiny embossed birds, a miniature elephant, and the Buddha's serene halo.

The frieze led to a second storey: a tall pink building streaked with grime and mildew. Three pyramidal spires were stacked atop the roof, above small, steamy glass windows lined with ashen blue rims. The walls were palimpsests—their present dirty pinkness obscured Bengali letters that had faded to faint ultramarine. The only legible words were 'electric crematorium'.

If there was an entrance, it lay behind the conical deodar trees, whose serrated, unruly leaves all pointed down—except on one tree, where they inexplicably bristled upwards. We climbed up some stairs to find ourselves facing a dark passage. As we stood there, the crematorium operator, Tapan Saha, a trim, middle-aged man with well-oiled hair, emerged.

Saha was polite, but impatient to go back inside, where I was not permitted; his job required him to burn ten bodies every day. Saha has worked here, at the Khagra Ghat electric crematorium, since its construction in 1997. Before it was built, wooden pyres were the norm in Khagra Ghat. 'Wood was more polluting for the river,' Saha assured me, waving towards the thin ribbon of Ganga flowing behind us. 'Now there is less pollution of air, and less pollution of the river.'

Electricity has even diminished the remains from each human body. 'Earlier, there were 5 to 10 kilograms of ash per person,' Saha said proudly. 'Now, we only get about 500 grams.'

I asked Saha whether electricity shortages interrupted his labours. 'Absolutely not,' he said. 'We always have current.'

'Who is that woman?' I asked Saha, pointing to the frieze.

'You don't know the story of Kisa Gotami?' Saha asked impatiently, eager to return to his kilns.

'I know the story. I'll tell her,' my uncle Ponku, who had accompanied me, said. And there, at the river's edge, Ponku told me about Kisa Gotami. She was a woman who went mad after her son died. She roamed from house to house, asking for a potion that would cure him. She was told to consult the Buddha. He agreed to bring her the potion she asked for, on one condition: that she brings him a mustard seed from a family that has never known death. Kisa Gotami wandered from home to home asking her mad question until finally her madness gave way to clarity. She returned to the Buddha and became one of his disciples. Near the end of her life, it is said, she attained enlightenment, perhaps an indirect expression for saying that she accepted her loss.

Much later, I heard a different telling of Kisa Gotami's story—one where the flood of death is literal and the riverbanks hold poisonous snakes and funeral pyres. In this version, Kisa Gotami loses even more, all at once—her husband dies of snakebite, leaving her to cross a swollen river with two young children. A hawk carries off one child, while the flooded river drowns the other. As Kisa Gotami stumbles alone to her parents' house, she sees her mother, her father, and her brother being cremated on a single pyre. She says as related in the *Kisagotami Theri*, 'Then I saw/ In the midst of the charnel ground/ the muscles of sons being chewed/ with family killed/ Despised by all/ My husband dead/ I reached the Deathless.'

It's hard to reconcile the story of the stone girl on the wall of the Khagra Ghat crematorium with the sanitized electric kilns inside, which Saha spoke about so proudly but wouldn't let me see. Kisa Gotami's story, like Chinnamasta's, is preoccupied with the balance of life and death. In her story, I also hear the suggestion that, in a region prone to flooding, one good response may be to stop fighting the flood. As these morbid, wild aspects of the Ganga retreat into myth, the literal importance of being cremated on her banks is also receding. The funeral pyres have retreated indoors.

THE FARAKKA BARRAGE

'Nothing below us but shunya—zero, emptiness,' Saumya Mallick, the owner of an internet café in North Bengal, whispered into my freezing ear on a December night. The two of us were dangling from the open door of a night train speeding over the 2.25 kilometre-long span of the Farakka Barrage, which lies upon the Ganga like a gigantic many-pronged belt. 'If the train weren't so loud you could hear the river's garjan—its roar,' Mallick said, as we raced past the coal-fired power plant next to the dam. In the attendant darkness, the sound of priests blowing conchshells and the smell of roasted peanuts mingled with the train's whistle and the stench of the urinal. One of our berth-mates insisted that the great barrage had 108 sluice gates—the number of names of deities in the Hindu tradition. 'I always count them when I'm on this train,' she announced with quiet pride, as if she knew how to string a massive rosary out of the concrete structures looming in our wake. The barrage may be a mystical entity, but it has come unmoored from our traditions. There is at least one more gate, a 109th, on land in Malda.

I didn't dare try to count the gates when I visited the dam the following afternoon, since I didn't want to attract undue attention from the two paunchy border guards in khaki uniform who patrolled the dam. Still, I couldn't help myself entirely. Perhaps confirming their suspicion that we were spies, or weirdos, my uncle and I ran along the high wall above the half-open sluice gates that raked into the grey, roiling Ganga like the teeth of a gigantic comb. My father followed alongside in a cab, fretting. Above, electric wires partitioned the slate-coloured sky; the sun was almost absent, a clouded smear. Below us, the river foamed, trapped, agitated by the gates, which directed the bulk of its water via feeder canal towards Kolkata and away from Bangladesh, sixteen kilometres distant.

As I raced across the dam, camera out, I saw no land—only a bone-white sandbank sporting a metallic electrical tower. So far as I could see, there were no functioning fish ladders either—that part of a dam that allows fish to pass through. In the decades since the Farakka was built, the coal-fired power plant next to it has brought intermittent electricity to the region, but there has been a 92 per cent decline in the amount of hilsa and other economically important fish caught upstream. Like salmon in the US, the silvery-green hilsa, a large fish rich in tasty, complex oils, is born in freshwater, swims out to sea, and then heads 1,200 miles back upstream, to spawn and die in its natal waters. In February 2019, the government announced that the navigation lock at Farakka will be redesigned. A tiny 8 metre pass will allow a fraction of the hilsa to swim upstream.

I turned around to find out that one of the border guards had been chasing us and had finally caught up. 'Give me your memory card,' he said. I eyed him, eyed the distance to the main road, eyed his old-fashioned but well-oiled rifle, and reluctantly handed him my memory card, sacrificing the few photos I had taken.

Is environment versus development really a binary choice? If the Ganga is the symbol, memory, and pehchaan of India, as Nehru had it, what aspects of our identity did we lose when we lost the river's integrity? As I looked upstream from Farakka, I reflected on the places where the goddess Ganga—revered for millennia as an all-forgiving mother who cleans up her children's messes—had been gradually guillotined.

I recalled some ripples of hope: the Himalayan villagers who picked trash out of the river every day, the proposed algal waste water ponds in Varanasi. One day, these tiny ripples might gather force and buck the stagnating status quo. Individuals with a strongly developed sense of spirituality and solidarity had mounted these efforts. They didn't look to the Ganga to cleanse their sins, or reset their bad karma. Instead, they dared to intervene in the river's fate, to clean the nation's sins, despite the bad faith and oligarchical politics that had ensured the river's decline.

'What a gorgeous dam—it makes me proud to be an Indian,' said my father, who had spent most of his working life abroad, as my uncle and I scrambled into the cab next to him. I rolled my eyes and bit my tongue.

Near Farakka, I had crossed the artificial, constricted Hooghly–Bhagirathi feeder canal on a rickety barge. Its floor was made of bamboo poles blackened with soot from the old diesel engine which powered it. About fifteen people crossed the river with me, all of us standing and swaying back and forth. It was the only way to reach their village on the opposite shore. As we got off the boat, two men awaited. Next to them, a framed image of Kali, goddess of death and destruction, beloved of bandits, wearing a necklace of skulls-and-bones, tongue dripping with blood, sword held aloft, reminded us to pay, or else. They didn't need to say anything. I tentatively put down a coin or two.

Because evening was approaching, I could not explore the village on the other side. So I turned around and took the next barge back to the shore I had come from. Such pockets of isolation still exist in our moribund delta.

SAGAR ISLAND

Ganga Sagar on Sagar Island became popular as a site of mass pilgrimage a few hundred years after the Ganga stopped meeting the ocean there. While Gaur, Farakka, and Murshidabad, like many other once flourishing centres, are hardly tourist hotspots today, Sagar Island draws close to 500,000 visitors every 14th January, on Makar Sankranti, when the sun transitions into Capricorn and days start becoming warmer and longer. Throughout India, people celebrate an end-of-winter harvest festival during this time. In Tamil Nadu, for example, virgins, cows, and cooked rice are all venerated. But at Sagar Island, the proximate goddess is the Ganga, and people worship her by bathing at the confluence of the Hooghly and the ocean.

As I learned during my journey to Farakka, the Hooghly is a dead arm of the Ganga, kept alive by artificial resuscitation in the form of the Hooghly–Bhagirathi feeder canal, built in 1972. Did it matter that half a million people were flocking to a grave of the Ganga each year? At Ganga Sagar, the goddess was worshipped more directly than anywhere else I had seen, not as a river but in the form of the goddess, perched atop her mythical mount, Makara, which looks to me like a mix of crocodile, deer, elephant, dolphin, fish, and seal. Did this elide the knowledge that the Ganga was not a living river here?

The crocodile aspect of the Makara is testament to the Bengal delta's rapaciousness, writes historian Steven G. Darian, noting that the creature is considered much gentler upstream. In Bengal, babies shaped out of clay are placed near the statues of the Makara to placate its hungry jaws. Darian quotes the *Calcutta Review* from 1859 regarding the underlying threat: 'A young Hindu girl about 14 years old came to get a pitcher of water, and had hardly put her feet into the water, when the crocodile, who had been lying in wait inside the enclosure, rushed at the poor girl, seized her in his formidable jaws, scrambled up the banks of the river, holding the shrieking, struggling girl well up in the air by the middle of her body, and plunged heavily into the river outside the stake. A smothered scream, a ripple upon the water, a few bubbles, and the frightful scene was closed.' Darian also writes about how, on nearby islands, the crocodile is sometimes pictured as a shark, for sharks are common near the dying Hooghly's mouth. During the Makar Sankranti festival, according to Darian, people occasionally enter the water hoping to sacrifice themselves to sharks in order to gain good karma; they walk away disappointed and weeping if the sharks ignore them.

Sagar Island has signs of human habitation dating back to the third century BCE. It is here that King Sagara's horse was said to be hidden by Indra from the King's 60,000 sons, prompting the ecocide that blighted the earth until Bhagirath brought the goddess Ganga down from heaven with his 1,000-year-long tapasya. Sagar Island has been a sacred pilgrimage spot for Hindus ever since, but until the British began settling Burmese subjects there in the nineteenth century, it was always remote and mythical—a mouth of the Ganga, intimately caught up in the story of how the river began, and as remote and mythical as Gangotri, the source of the Ganga. To get there, travellers had to hack through the mangrove forests of the Sundarbans, avoid the attentions of

Bengal tigers and poisonous snakes and undertake a dangerous ocean-crossing journey to the southern tip of the island itself. No wonder people were considered enlightened if they made it there. The Bengali writer Bankim Chandra Chatterjee, in 1890, put it on the map with his novel *Sagar Sangame Nabakumar*, a stirring description of standing at the confluence of the Ganga and the ocean.

Bankim hoped to spark a Bengali renaissance with his writing, and he had a measure of popular success too: his song Vande Mataram became a rallying cry for Indian freedom fighters. I had been raised to view Bankim as a giant of Bengali literature, but when I finally read him, he seemed like yet another victim of the divide-and-conquer politics that had split Bengal, Gaur and the Ganga.

Today, Bankim's rhapsody about the sacred and natural purity of Sagar Island is prescribed reading for West Bengal's tenth grade state board exam. 'People read his work, and flock here en masse,' said Shirshendu, a young naturalist I met on the island. He gave me a VCD of the Ganga Sagar pilgrimage: hundreds of women carrying heavy bundles on their heads flocking to the island via bus, then train, then ferry and then foot. Men are arriving en masse too, many of them sitting atop buses. The VCD had image after image of ash-smeared ascetics, the temple of Kapil Muni, sparkling shots of river water, 'bazaar art' images of the god Shiva, coconuts, marigolds, thousands of people bathing on the beach at sunrise and, of course, the image of the Ganga as a female goddess, sitting atop a Makara that looks particularly like a hungry crocodile.

Something about Sagar Island made me crave the experience of revering the river alone, rather than in a crowd.

After taking a commuter train 128 kilometres south of Kolkata, then a cycle-cart to the ferry at Namkhana, I crossed the salty waters separating the mainland from Sagar Island. By now it was night, and the island, home to 160,000 people, was almost entirely dark. The few lights I saw came from solar panels attached to thatched huts. My host, Kirti Chowdhury, received me warmly and showed me to my bedroom, a one-room schoolhouse. Kirti works for PUPA (Paribesh Unnayan Parishad), an NGO which disseminates environmental education throughout the island.

In the morning, Kirti and his colleagues took me on a walk around the island. They pointed out the mangrove buffers planted by the shore ten years ago, proudly telling me about the different species of mangrove on the island and the various chutneys that can be made from sour mangrove fruit. As we walked by, a few people emerged from the mangrove thickets with pilfered sticks for kindling. Overall, though, Kirti said, the island's mangroves were doing well. He pointed out Ghoramara ('Dead Horse'), the next island, which was being carved up by the water, forcing many inhabitants to flee. As we walked, I saw the riprap, or stone wall, that holds the eastern edge of the island together; without it, it would crumble into the sea. Sagar Island is one of the places in the world most vulnerable to climate change.

Despite living so close to death, Kirti and his colleagues are trying to forge a way of living on the island that is simultaneously modern and in greater harmony with its ecosystem than the last century's practices were. Two of Kirti's colleagues, Anima and Shirshendu, told me they are reintroducing native fishes to the local ponds, are actively supporting farmers' collectives on the island, and have established flourishing vermicompost piles. The vermicompost has proved a boon, especially for growing betel nut leaves, which are shipped from Sagar Island to cities throughout the country. Many of the richest farmers on the island grow betel nut; it's immediately obvious who they are because almost all of them have installed solar panels atop their thatched huts.

But betel nut was only one of many plants whose properties Kirti and his colleagues were eager to tap. They showed me dozens of medicinal plants and smiled indulgently at a golden snake sunning itself on a haystack. 'It's not poisonous,' Kirti said with an unworried smile. As we continued our walk around the perimeter of the island, Anima pointed out snakeroot, or *Rauwolfia serpentina*, a flowering plant in the milkweed family, a traditional antidote to snake-bite and a widely used Ayurvedic medicine in India.

When I pronounced *Rauwolfia*'s Latin name aloud, Anima and Kirti exchanged a meaningful look and they told me about another of their colleagues, Sahiba Khatun, a twenty-one-year-old woman from an indigent Muslim family which would have married her off years ago if she hadn't shown a fierce talent for conservation. Sahiba has identified and recorded the names of over 300 species of birds, animals, and plants for the People's Biodiversity Register, sponsored by the Government of India. She has also started eco-clubs throughout the island. When I met her later that day, she had just saved a jungle cat, *Felis chaus* (also known as the 'swamp lynx'), from being shot and was rearing it in her house on a diet of milk and chapattis. Meanwhile, she'd called the WWF headquarters in Kolkata, where she works part-time, and was waiting for a scientist to come see the cat and help her make make plans to conserve the species on the island. I was moved by Sahiba, Kirti, Shirshendu, and all their colleagues who were attempting to conserve life on an island that may well die at the hands of the sea within our lifetime.

Shirshendu took me on his motorbike to Ganga Sagar via the island's single main road. As we sped along, I saw what I thought for a moment was a ghost—a blank-faced female doll in a red dress, wrapped in garlands, propped up on a chair facing the water, looking dreamily out to the spot where pilgrims would come to bathe in a month's time. 'That's the goddess Ganga,' Shirsendu explained.

I inquired after Kapil Muni's ashram and was told that the original ashram had long since been lost to the ocean—as had its second and third iterations. The current ashram was the fourth one to be built. The island's lighthouse had met a similar fate; its rotting remnants haunted an eroding cliff-face on the western edge of the island, bolstered with yet more mesh-bound riprap.

I asked everyone I met where the Hooghly met the sea, but no one could answer my question. 'It meets the sea all around us,' said the man who had served as caretaker of the Kapil Muni temple for four decades. 'You can't see a difference in the colour of the water, as in Allahabad.' The pilgrims bathe directly in front of the fourth version of the temple, which is half a mile from where the first one was built. Half a million people come here from all over India to bathe at one particular spot in one particular beach—but no one seemed to know where the artificially resuscitated Hooghly meets the Bay of Bengal.

We need the real river, and we need the goddess who is the river, but we no longer care if the two are not one and the same. That's what it means to be moribund, isn't it? To be exhausted on the verge of death, decay, stagnation? Death always forces us to separate the memory of the beloved from the body of the beloved.

I had glimpsed many Gangas during my travels—the imperilled-but-still-magnificent Padma in Bangladesh; the object of fascination that sells thousands of pilgrimage DVDs in Haridwar; the goddess whom the faithful will always be able to see in their mind's eye, whether she exists or not. Maharaj, the sage in the Himalaya, had told me that the Ganga would disappear within our lifetimes, but that she would still be visible to those who truly loved her. I was less sure that any connection would remain if the river disappeared.

So I stepped into its faecal-bacteria-laden waters over and over while it was still here, attempting to open my pores to something beyond nostalgia, beyond toxicity, to the animate ecology that all early humankind had perceived. When I was not near it, I delved deeper into science, deeper into politics, trying to understand how other polluted rivers had been cleaned, how other dams had been dismantled. And, somewhere along the way, I began conducting the daily rituals that my mother, grandmother, and all my ancestors before me had performed. Nothing big. Just a little incense, fresh flowers offered to the goddess, 'Ganga, Ganga,' muttered in the bath, and a little more austerity. These rituals stitch together my days. They remind me that my ancestors bartered daily with the more-than-human world, and took time out to acknowledge the fundamental luxuries of food, drink, and peace. I find peace in knowing that these rituals evolved against the backdrop of the unfathomable otherness which defined my ancestors' sense of what it means to be human—the otherness of golden, tiger-like fish, and snow-white trout, blind dolphins, and long-nosed crocodiles who played in riffle pools that flowed fast enough and free enough to purify my ancestors' sins, fast enough and free enough to let them shatter the monotonous carousel of death and rebirth.

CHAPTER 9

THE WILD WOMAN'S GANGA
(THE SUNDARBANS)

The Anthropocene has forced us to recognize that there are other, fully aware eyes looking over our shoulders.

—Amitav Ghosh,
The Great Derangement: Climate Change and the Unthinkable

JOURNEY TO SATJELIA

One bright morning in mid-January 2016, I began my voyage deep into the Sundarbans—the mangrove-dominated Ganga Delta—spanning India and Bangladesh where the river's mouths merge with the Bay of Bengal and about a hundred Royal Bengal tigers thrive in the border region. I was on my way to Bonbibi Pujo, an obscure local festival honouring an elusive and misunderstood 'goddess' whose name means 'woman of the forest'. Unfortunately, Ballygunge station in Kolkata was so crowded with people that I pushed my way to the train just as it was departing, with hundreds of people hanging off it. The train was already moving so quickly that I felt inadequate to the task of boarding it. I had waited for this day for ten years, ever since I'd read Amitav Ghosh's novel *The Hungry Tide*, which depicts the Sundarbans' devotion to Bonbibi. Still, I almost turned back. So, in order to talk myself into sticking it out on the next train, I struck a deal between my makar mind, my monkey mind, and my Ganga-heart (more on this in a moment).

Later I realized I must have been very afraid of making the journey. But at that time, I didn't know how to recognize the sensations of fear, let alone name the emotion. I had grown up amongst bourgeois Bengali bhadralok for whom fear was largely unacceptable. What exactly was I afraid of? Was it the crowd? Was it the Sundarbans' reputation as the land of pirates, moger muluk? The man-eating tigers, allegedly aggressive due to their diet of saltwater corpses brought to them by the Ganga, and driven mad by frequent cyclones? Maybe cobras and sharks loomed in some hidden corner of my imagination? This wasn't even my first trip to the Sundarbans—I had travelled to a botanical preserve with a group of students in 2007.

Neuroscientists claim that fear lives in our amygdala, which is a part of our reptilian brain: our oldest neurological system, which gets activated under intense pressure. Our emotions live in our mammalian brain, and our rational thinking resides in our neocortex, the most newly evolved part of our brain. Some spiritual teachers claim that many of our problems result not from our fears or emotions but from our thoughts, cooked up by our monkey (mammalian) mind. I remembered that Gangaji's mount, the makara, the creature in whose honour people were celebrating Makar Sankranti that weekend, is sometimes depicted as part-crocodile.

'Bonbibi Pujo only happens one day a year,' I told myself, breathing deeply, shifting from one foot to the other, silently asking Gangaji for the resolution to proceed.

Finally, I called Leeladi, my host-to-be, whom I was supposed to have met in the train I had just missed. 'Don't worry,' she said. 'I will meet you at Canning.' Half an hour later, I stepped on to the next train, leaving the familiar world of Kolkata behind.

For the next few hours, all I could do was breathe, sandwiched in the seat I was very lucky to get. The ladies' compartment was more crowded than anything I'd ever experienced. Two separate fights broke out among the brightly garbed women who were hanging from the handrails.

Leelabati Mondal, my host, met me at Canning. She was in her fifties, with a strong, broad, generous, unlined face.

I found out, as we stopped to buy sweets for her family, that Leeladi had been extraordinarily supportive to my friend Annu, whom we were about to meet. The two had enjoyed a close relationship for almost twenty years, and she had hosted Annu in her mud hut for two years while Annu was researching her thesis. Leeladi now worked in Kolkata, as a nurse's aide at a private nursing home. She was heading back to the islands for Bonbibi Pujo.

Satjelia, Leeladi's marital home, was only 97 kilometres from Kolkata, but it took the better part of the day to make three river-crossings, traversing the Matla, Bidhyahari, and Datta (on increasingly flimsy ferries). Between ferries, we took local transport: a series of buses, followed by alternating bhan-garis, engine-powered carts with room for several passengers, which jerked uncomfortably over the narrow paved brick lanes which ran between the rice fields. I clutched my bottle of water and rested my gaze upon the rolling paddies. At our final bhan-gari stop, I met my friend Annu Jalais and her son Jehan. Annu is an anthropologist who teaches in Singapore. The author of *Forest of Tigers: People, Politics, and Environment in the Sundarbans,* she is one of the world's leading academic experts on Bonbibi. Our paths had crossed at Yale in 2009, when she was an Agrarian Studies Fellow and I was a student at the School of Forestry and Environmental Studies.

'Sundarbans' means beautiful forest in Bengali. The area is home to more than twenty-eight species of mangroves, remarkably adapted to the high tides and salt water thanks to their leathery leaves and breathing-tube-like roots which stick up out of the mud. More than 58 reptile species, 200 bird species, and 50 mammal species can be found here, including the Irawaddy and Ganga River dolphins.

Although Sufi pirs started clearing the forest for agriculture as early as the thirteenth century, humans had a light touch here until relatively recently, when people began to settle the mangrove forests owing to a combination of overpopulation and the imperial need for revenue. This is actually part of the setting of my great-granduncle's novel *Padma Nadir Majhi,* in which Kuber, an indigent fisherman and recent settler in the Sundarbans, tries to resist the capitalist imperialism of Hossein Mia, who lures fishermen into becoming his indentured labourers and helping him settle Moynadeep, a purportedly utopian island where poor people of all regions are welcome, but of which Mia is the sole overlord. Manik Bandhopadhyay was a Communist, but his novel is quite fatalistic: Kuber dies trying to hold true to his identity and traditions.

Satjelia is one of three islands, known as the Gosaba Islands, settled by Sir Daniel Hamilton, a Scottish businessman, in 1903. He advocated for economic independence even before political independence, and set up 33 village cooperative societies that served approximately 10,000 people. He also provided free healthcare, education, and agricultural training. And he discouraged class and religious conflict by banning the buying of land, pork, beef, and alcohol. When Tagore went to visit in

1932, he was both impressed and influenced by what he saw. One of Gandhi's secretaries, too, left with a favourable impression, except that he thought rents should be even lower. After Hamilton's death, though, his Bengali bhadralok trustees allegedly stole the money he had left for the villagers and returned to Kolkata.

In *Forest of Tigers*, Annu recounts how, despite these roguish trustees, the residents attribute the continuing peacefulness of the island to Hamilton's legacy. She mentions that inequality of land ownership actually increased under West Bengal's Communist rule, which persisted for thirty years. However, relative to the state norm, inequality is a little less on the Gosaba Islands, and, thanks to the Ganga's volatile conspiracy with the winds and tides, this is one of the few places in the world where the landless can actually find and settle brand-new land.

Satjelia, shaped like a heart, is among the southernmost of the Sundarban islands. According to Annu, its residents (who predominantly belong to scheduled castes) know it as a low-status 'down' island (compared to higher-status islands which are closer to Kolkata). It was among the most recently inhabited islands, because it's in the Ganga's active delta, which is continuously formed and reformed by the river and its elements. The Pathar River connects the village to the rivers Raymangal, Durgaduani, Bidya, and Matla—all mouths of the Ganga. And it's less than 10 kilometres south of the Sajnekhali Tiger Reserve.

Night had fallen by the time the bhan-gari let us off. We still had more than a kilometre to walk along the embankment, with the river as our constant companion. Most of the houses were still thatched with straw; there was a good smell in the air. As we approached Leeladi's hut in the dark, I tried to practise the centred walking I'd learned in the Himalaya, matching a deep breath to each step. I dragged my heavy luggage and tried to not think about what I'd heard on the way: whispered news that a villager had gone missing the day before. We and our luggage finally made it to the hut that Leeladi shares with her husband, who lives there full-time and whose younger brother, with his wife and child, lives next door.

'Mud compound' is a better term than hut—there was a sleeping hut, an adjoining eating hut, a walled courtyard, with fields out front and a fish-filled pond out back. It was a classic one-acre farm, the kind that permaculturists and organic farmers rhapsodize about because it was sufficiently productive in that it could meet most of the basic needs of a single family. Leeladi was up before anyone else. Her husband caught rui (carp) for us from the pond behind their house. Sitting in the sun, under a coconut tree, I started to relax a little. My fear of the unknown was draining away and I was very glad that I had come. The peace and quiet I had hoped for still proved elusive, though; Hindi songs blared on a loudspeaker, throughout the day.

BONBIBI PUJO

I sensed, behind this cast of characters, the tigers, the Ganga River dolphins (and their cousins, the Irrawady River dolphins, which migrate between freshwater and saltwater), and, behind them, the legendary bhoot and pret (ghosts and spirits).

In the early evening, while the sun was still up, we walked around the village visiting each of the shrines, only a stone's throw away from the muddy embankments guarding against the incursion of river water bolstered by rising seas. The Bonbibi Pujo invokes not just Bonbibi but her brother, Shah Jongoli; Gazi, a Muslim holy man; Dokkhin Rai, a greedy demon who is half-tiger and half-Brahmin; and Dukhe, a humble woodcutter. Annu's son folded his hands and said 'Namo-namo' to each cluster of five figures that we visited, and we followed his lead. But I wasn't yet sure exactly who I was venerating, or why. Each shrine had its own unique flavour; Bonbibi's worshippers included those who hoped to venture into the forest this year, or those who were veterans. Out of respect for the egalitarian custom Bonbibi favours, the shrines were open to all, not enclosed within houses. At each house we visited, we drank tea and ate prasad.

As twilight descended across the soothing smell of haystacks and the lowing of goats, I felt as if I were walking both backwards and forwards in time. The festival celebrated an ancient, traditional wisdom about equitable co-existence with the non-human world. In Leeladi's kitchen, crouching on the earthen floor, ready to eat freshly-caught fish, peeling vegetables while gingerly eyeing the bothi, the traditional floor-mounted knife that is a staple of the Bengali kitchen, I felt unexpectedly at home.

Satjelia is no utopia. Indeed, Satjelia is at the forefront of facing extreme climate events that are expected to become normal for the rest of the world too. But in international and humanitarian terms, it isn't just a 'down island'; it receives the climate damage spilling down from the fossil-fuel-powered global economy that is causing it to slowly crumble into the sea. In 2009, when Cyclone Aila hit, Satjelia was one of the places most affected; embankments were breached, saltwater destroyed farmland, and no pre-alert reached the residents.

But in the moonlight, by the seawall, it was magical to be there, and even the flare of a single match felt monumental and dramatic. As of 2016, people still had limited access to electricity here. Was it a coincidence that people here were amongst the best storytellers I ever met?

As we walked from house to house, Annu and I reminisced about someone we both knew: Dr Pranabes Sanyal, who had once been the head of the Sundarbans Biosphere Reserve. He had been my first guide to the rich mangrove forests of the Sundarbans in 2007. On that trip, I took a short video of a shrimp in the rich estuary mud. He'd congratulated me on discovering a new species of mite that was visible on the shrimp—a tiny red dot, as far as I was concerned. He said that scientists at Jadavpur University would be looking into it, maybe even naming it

Sanyal is the originator of the discredited and deadly mask approach to man–tiger confrontation: he suggested that forest-dwellers don tiger-masks on the backs of their heads to stave off tiger attacks, which kill about twenty-five people on the Indian side per year to this day. The idea was initially well received because a full-grown male Royal Bengal can weigh up to 500 pounds; a master of stealth, it excels at biting into humans' spines. If a person has faces on both the front and back of their head, their spine seems less accessible.

Unfortunately, Sanyal's idea was not a success. Apparently, the tigers were initially fooled, but soon caught up. By the time I visited, no villager would be caught dead wearing a mask on the back of their head. Casualties still abounded, as was painfully evident during my present trip to Satjelia—the disappearance of a villager the day before our arrival. It was suspected that he'd fallen prey to Fokir—a name that locals commonly use to refer to the Royal Bengal.

The Sundarbans is that kind of place. Anything can happen, new discoveries seem to lurk around each corner, and your life hangs uncomfortably in the balance. That's why I was so impressed that Annu had maintained such a close relationship with the area. I was even more impressed that she dared to bring her toddler with her. She managed expertly, and he seemed to be very happy running after chickens and goats.

At each shrine, as dusk fell, people were reading from the *Bonbibi Johuranamah*, written towards the end of the 1800s. The scripture is written in Bengali but it's read back to front and right to left, like Arabic. In Annu's book, she says that the forest fisher-people narrate the story of Bonbibi in order to address 'equitable sharing of food and resources between humans and tigers'. Here is a summary of her account of Bonbibi's scripture:

A forest-dwelling Brahmin sage, Dokkhin Rai ('King of the South'), adopts the form of a tiger and begins to feed on humans. As if that isn't enough to break the bonds of trust between humans and tigers, he also greedily declares that the whole forest and its 370 million spirits, demons, godlings, tigers, crabs, fish, and trees are his private and exclusive property.

Out of compassion for the humans oppressed by Dokkhin Rai, Allah chooses a young girl, Bonbibi, to save them. She too is a forest-dweller, breastfed by a deer after her mother abandoned her. Hearing Allah's call, Bonbibi enlists the help of her brother, Shah Jongoli. They go to Medina for Fatima's blessings, and then bring back some earth from Mecca to the Sundarbans, the land of the eighteen tides, where they mix the holy earth with the soil that Dokkhin Rai has defiled.

Dokkhin Rai tries to intimidate them, but his mother Narayani intervenes, insisting that she, as a woman, should fight Bonbibi instead of Dokkhin Rai. But she sees that Bonbibi will defeat her, and so Narayani calls Bonbibi sai (friend). The young woman accepts Narayani's friendship and an uneasy detente prevails, with Dokkhin Rai unwilling or unable to menace a friend of his mother's.

The story then shifts focus to Dukhe (whose name means 'sadness'), an impoverished young woodcutter who lives with his mother, a widow. His uncle, Dhona (whose name means 'wealth'), convinces Dukhe to venture into the jungle with him and collect honey. In the jungle, Dokkhin Rai persuades Dhona to sell Dukhe to him in exchange for seven boats full of honey and wax.

Just as Dokkhin Rai is about to eat his new purchase, the young woodcutter calls out to Bonbibi to save him. She appears, rescues him, and sends her brother, Shah Jongoli, to admonish Dokkhin Rai. Chastised, the Brahmin tiger runs to his friend Gazi, an Islamic pir, who counsels him to ask Bonbibi's forgiveness and call her 'mother'. Magnanimously, Bonbibi forgives him, and calls him 'son'.

Although its characters are reconciled, the story has one final turn. Dokkhin Rai tells Bonbibi that if humans were left in charge, the forest would soon be destroyed. In response, Bonbibi makes Dukhe, Dokkhin Rai and Gazi promise to treat each other like brothers. She asks Dokkhin Rai and Gazi to give Dukhe some of her wood and gold so that he can return to the village and won't need to cut down the forest anymore. Dukhe's gift does come with a limitation; henceforth, all humans who go into the forest must do so with a 'pure heart-mind', with 'empty hands', and with complete devotion to Bonbibi. The food humans seek (such as fish and crabs) is also the preferred cuisine of tigers. In Bengal, as in much of the world, sharing food creates a sense of family; and sharing the food of the forest connects humans and tigers together—as is made literal in the story through Bonbibi's adoption of Dokkhin Rai.

Annu writes that this portion of the story 'is the 'agreement' between non-humans and humans that permits them both to depend on the forest and yet respect others' needs. This arrangement, they say, can last only as long as those who have enough resources of their own leave the forest and its wealth to those who are in need'. Forest fisherpeople insist that this arrangement is necessary because people from different castes and religions must together reach an agreement on how to deal with the forest commons.

The agreement does not maintain itself as a matter of course; it must be constantly renewed. Superhuman mediators like Bonbibi and Gazi may assist, but keeping such a lofty and idealistic arrangement intact also requires human umpires—those who are both humble and fearless enough to know when to lead others into the jungle, when to confront a tiger, and when to back down.

A TIGER-CHARMER REVEALS HIMSELF

When I set out for Satjelia, I did not expect to meet a bauliya, or tiger-charmer. I knew from Annu's book that tiger-charmers have been despised since the colonial period, and that even now the forest officials tend to mistrust them. Nonetheless, she explains, those who venture into the jungle for wood or honey wouldn't dream of going there unless accompanied by a tiger-charmer—one who has learned how to invoke

Bonbibi for protection by receiving a vision of her in a dream, and then promising to respect animals' needs and enter the forest humbly and generously. Tiger-charmers are bound by strict, largely Muslim, rules. They don't enter the forest on Fridays, touch pork or alcohol, or charge interest on loans. Bonbibi's egalitarian spirit means that the profession is not limited to men; according to Annu, some bauliyas are female.

The tiger-charmers must be exquisitely attuned to timing. Since they are the first to leave the boat and set foot on forest land, sometimes they are unlucky enough to be devoured, their unuttered charms perishing with them. If they survive this first step, they crouch to check the earth (maal dekha) by placing their hands on the ground while reciting invocations to five Muslim holy men and women. If their fingers tremble and refuse to settle on the earth, then the team doesn't disembark but keeps rowing in search of another island. If their hands touch the earth calmly and they sense that it is a good time to enter, they tie a piece of earth to their bodies and their protection spell begins. When the workers are done with their tasks and have safely returned to the boat, the tiger-charmer crouches again to break the spell, unties the piece of earth and returns it to the island, at which point the island's inhabitants resume their normal, uncharmed life. One tiger-charmer told Annu, 'We crouch on the ground to ask for forgiveness from the forest and its inhabitants for barging in on them and upsetting their routine by the charms we use.'

The strongest charms, Annu has learned, are reserved for honey- and wood-collecting, which are the riskiest ventures. A folded leaf might be placed on the ground, as if to hide a lurking tiger. One charm involves 'tying the towel' around the animal, now transformed into a pebble or shell. Other charms can 'shut tigers' mouths', 'make them drowsy', 'force them to run away as if their bodies are on fire', or 'make them ticklish and roll themselves on the ground'.

The violence latent in such charms is acknowledged, and tiger-charmers are not proud of it. Announcing in public that you're a tiger-charmer is, in Annu's words, 'to invite the wrath of the non-humans, as this is seen as arrogance'.

So when Sukumarda fearlessly identified himself as a tiger-charmer as soon as we met, I looked around nervously. Even at first glance, Sukumarda's Bonbibi shrine seemed to stand apart from the others in the village. It was smaller, more private and, therefore, more mysterious. It had a fishing net over it and mangrove leaves that looked freshly picked from the forest. When Annu and I walked up to him, Sukumarda immediately started telling stories. Night had started to fall, so he invited us to come back and visit him after we had toured the rest of the shrines.

Annu accompanied me back to his home, but after a while she had to leave; her son needed to be put to bed. I felt a pang of fear at the thought of being alone and off the grid with this unknown man. I searched my bag, but of course I'd left my mobile phone, switched off, in Leeladi's hut, so that I could conserve its battery for the journey back. Standing alone in the darkness, I experienced fear as a physical chill for the first time. I was shivering, stiff, frozen.

I almost turned and followed Annu back to Leeladi's. But my curiosity and an unexpected greeting from Sukumarda's friend, who was inside, stopped me. Annu had lived here, with these same islanders for two years and she had thrived, I reminded myself. I took my shoes off and stepped into Sukumarda's lamp-lit abode. With its wooden bed, cupboard, and plaster walls that didn't need daily touch-ups with cow dung, his house seemed much more modern than Leeladi's.

What does a tiger-charmer look like? In his traditional long lungi, cotton shirt, and blue-and-white-striped handmade scarf, whose thick purl reminded me of the prowess of Bengali knitters, Sukumarda looked like the wolf playing Little Red Riding Hood's grandma. At sixty-two years old, he was still lean and, if his stories were to be believed, he was able to lead teams of men into the forest and help them survive intense life-and-death encounters with tigers, thanks to Bonbibi's blessings. His friend, a woodcutter and honey-gatherer, backed up the wild stories Sukumarda told me.

'Rikx,' Sukumarda said, summing up his experience of going into the jungle for honey harvesting. It took me a second to realize he meant 'risk'.

'Life rikx,' his friend echoed, explaining that they can earn ₹8,000–10,000 for 5–10 kilograms of honey.

Darkness hung thickly around us, and only the bund separated us from the vast river. Sitting under a mosquito net on Sukumarda's bed, it felt a little like we were camping in the jungle. In his voice you could almost hear the Garal River, which he had swum across in some daring escape from one forest or another. He sounded cautious, though hardly fearless.

Sukumarda's drawl sounded close to Bangladeshi Bengali to me. 'We, three of us, went crab-catching,' so many of his stories began. 'Let's be careful, we told ourselves. Tigers come here. We went into the forest to get kindling to cook with. I noticed a tiger coming towards me. It pulled its nose twice, sniffing the ground. The two other men with me started running away. Sarvanash! Backing away, I climbed onto a tiny tree—you couldn't climb higher than waist height. I had a machete in my hand. Holding the machete, I proceeded to enact a drama with the tiger for fifteen minutes. The tiger was coming at me, almost laughing. Drooling upon the earth. Finally, the other two men came up behind me. They said, don't be afraid, we are here. As soon as they stood beside me, the tiger suddenly crouched on its hind legs and leapt backwards—at least a good six feet. Then it turned around and backed away.'

'Why?' I asked.

'You cannot face a tiger without knowing mantra-tantra. I have the courage to stand up to the tiger,' he answered.

'Do a lot of people know mantra-tantra?' I asked.

'No,' he said. 'One of the men who were with me then is the man who is missing in the jungle now. His son called from the Andamans. He had a dream that his father is still alive in the jungle. That he hasn't been eaten by the tiger. He requested me, as his uncle, to be one of the men to form the search party. His father was brave. He learned mantra-tantra from his uncle.'

'How did you learn mantra-tantra?' I asked.

'Since childhood everyone has sworn that I am a righteous man. I've never harmed anyone. That's why everyone in the village loves me. If you come to the village, and say, show me the way to the zamindar's house, people will point you to my house. I am a landless zamindar. I used to play the role of the zamindar in local dramas.

'I used to call Ma—Bonbibi—in the jungle. Ma came to me in a dream and said, if you say these words, you will be safe in the jungle. In my dream, I saw a childish girl. Jhumjhumjhumjhum—I heard the sound of her anklets. She said, "You always stay on the path of truth. Stay on that path, repeat these words that I will teach you. Mention the names of those who go into the jungle with you. They too will remain safe."

'She identified herself as moner-debi—goddess of my heart. I had this dream at bhor-ratri (dawn-night). My wife was lying wide awake next to me in the bed, not saying a word. I went to the Garal Nadi to catch crabs. Soon after this, I went with two others. There was so much water at the mouth of the khal (creek). I went with Monodeep Burman and Ali. We anchored at the mouth of the khal. We fell asleep by 7 p.m. The boat started drifting into the jungle.

'I woke up and raised Ali, who is a bit deaf, telling him to pull at the anchor while I rowed furiously at the stern. Initially, I had ignored Bonbibi's mantra because I wasn't sure if it was pure or impure. Suddenly, in the midst of all the hubbub, I fell asleep. And, falling asleep, I had a vision of Bonbibi. "Have you uttered the mantra I taught you?" she enquired. "Not yet, Ma." "Not yet?! Say the mantra immediately, after washing your mouth out. After saying these three words, you will set foot on the maal (jungle floor) and, after saying those three words, you will sleep." I said, "Ma, I'm holding my ears and begging your pardon." So, after that, I washed my mouth out and said the words.

'Immediately, Monodeep said, "Do you notice any nadir tufan?" We looked and the storm had abated. "So why are we still alive, sitting in the jungle, in our boat?" we asked ourselves.

'"That's the mark of witchery," Monodeep said. "But as soon as you said those words, the storm dispelled. You should say them."'

Sukumarda's story about the first time he followed the instructions the forest goddess had given him in a dream seemed all the more vivid by the light of the oil-lamp. 'Bonbibi seems very jagrat,' I said, this Bangla word, which means awake, alive, aware, suddenly coming to my lips. True, he didn't tell the story by the book. The storm eased up before I knew there was one. And it was unclear if they got home laden with fish or empty-handed. But telling a story by the book wasn't the point. He included what he thought important. And that's why I have recorded it here just as I heard it.

Sukumarda continued, in his characteristically non sequitur manner, 'To me, taking Ma's name, it doesn't seem like much. Once we went into the jungle to catch fish. Habor. Kan Mach. Jabla—fish bait. You have to spread it in in the water and tie it to a tree on top of a char, a sandy island in the river. Ma appeared to my son. A young girl, wearing a ghaghra. Jhumur jhumur jhumur went her anklets. She told him to tell him to say the mantra.

'Once, nine of us took a boat upon the Tigerkill River, the Baghmara, near Sajnekhali. In the forest, one doesn't say the word "tiger"—only "bondhu" (friend) or "phokir" (fakir).

'I said, wait, let me touch the mal, the jungle earth. Phokir has no choice but to go away once the mantra has been uttered. The mantra made the tiger go away.'

'The tiger is bound to go, baddho hoey jaey,' Sukumarda's friend said. Sukumarda echoed: 'It has to go.'

'Some people's mantras don't work. Many bauliyas have been eaten. Many have done untrue things. Thievery, trickery, asatya.'

Sukumarda said, 'When Ma gave me the mantra, she said, "Don't do wrong to anyone." Since then, I have never wronged anyone.' Later, he told me that the mantra was in 'Muslim language'. Not Urdu, not Arabic, but the dialect that Bengali Muslims speak. For example, they have their own word for blood, Sukumarda, who is Hindu, explained. Earlier, he didn't know this word. But when Bonbibi communicated with his heart-mind, he immediately understood.

His friend gave charming examples of the ways in which Sukumarda helps people out by paying it forward at the market, or helping others during planting season, or healing an eight-year-old boy at death's door. The most prosaic thing about Sukumarda is that his son and daughter-in-law are both high school teachers in Burdwan district. Sukumarda has a high school education himself, but it's clear that his storytelling skills are steeped in vernacular literature and extend back to the oral tradition. He proudly showed me the books on his shelf. Sarat Chandra. Bankim Chandra. Puranas. Mahabharata.

My ears full of long and complicated tales where there was no boundary between magic and daily life, we walked back by moonlight to Leeladi's house, where Sukumarda showed off a maduli he had made: an amulet. It was a silver cylinder, about the size of a big toe. It had a small metal clasp so the wearer could suspend it from around their neck. It was filled with the ground-up leaves, bark and roots of 108 different trees, shrubs, and grasses including durbo, chalti, tulsi (basil) and rarer, more expensive ingredients like mritosanjivani and trees from the mangrove forest.

'It has tiger tongue in it also, right?' Leeladi asked.

'Bones also. I can't tell you everything that's in it,' Sukumarda said. At another time, he said that people do go with guns into the forest. It was late enough that I didn't ask him how he reconciled tiger-charming with guns, or with his access to tiger tongue. 'Chelepuler pissapper jonno debe?' Leeladi enquired. She was asking for an amulet that would prevent her grandchild from wetting the bed.

I had so many questions for him. Did the charms that worked against tigers also work against bed-wetting? How did he trust himself enough to lead men into the jungle? But I held my tongue. I felt oddly exhilarated by my moonlit adventure with the tiger-charmer. Like Manik Bandhopadhyay, I had finally collected a story from someone who was intimate with the river and my heart was sending drumbeats throughout my whole body.

That night, unused to sharing such close quarters with so many people, I lay awake in the pitch-black darkness under the thatched roof, reflecting on the unexpected sense of hope I felt after hearing Sukumarda's stories. Throughout my travels along the Ganga, I had tried to understand how the river might challenge commonplace assumptions about being human. So I was delighted to meet someone who had learned how to mediate between the human and non-human world, who could dream the same supernatural dream as his son. Sukumarda seemed like an outstanding example of someone who knew how to tap into his instinctual self—his felt sense. Indeed, in the forest, his life depended on the ability to navigate with dreams, choose from deep instinct, and know by leaning down and touching the earth. His body was the instrument through which he practised extending his felt instincts outwards to connecting more deeply with the nonhuman world. By cultivating a profound relationship with the uncanny he had put his fear in its right place.

I saw many residents of Satjelia during my short stay there; and, while their lives were difficult, they didn't seem desensitised. On the contrary, the people of Satjelia filled me with hope and admiration. Despite the extreme challenges, there is a lot to like about life in Satjelia. Its residents enjoy not only a unique history, grounded in utopian experimentation (and its limitations), but an intimate connection with nature predicated on respecting the forest as a protected, shared space which rewards both egalitarianism and upholding the rules of kinship with the non-human world.

I stared up into the thatched ceiling wondering how the island will change as global warming makes sea levels rise farther, and as the mainland's culture penetrates deeper into the island. Like the boatmen I'd met at Vikramshila, Leeladi and Sukumarda hoped that their children would live safer and more comfortable lives than their parents. Losing an intimate connection with the non-human world of the river was a trade-off they were willing to make. We don't yet know how to value how much they have to teach those of us who don't live in proximity to the river.

A RIVAL TO BONBIBI?

I woke up refreshed, used the composting toilet, bathed in the pond behind the house, and ate freshly caught fish for breakfast. Leeladi's younger sister-in-law, Notun Bou, with her baby at her hip, told me that she was practising a dance drama with her troupe. They were rehearsing their performance of the story of Bonbibi for tourists. As I watched Notun Bou practise the part of Dokkhin Roy, stalking through the banana trees like an evil man-tiger, I wondered how many tourists apart from me ventured into this remote place.

There certainly were some. A bona fide tourist from Jharkhand greeted me at the eco-lodge that had just been built on the corner of the road that passed by Leeladi's house, bordered by beautiful flowers and thatched huts. One thing was clear: Notun Bou's enactment of the Bonbibi story would have a very different flavour from Sukumarda's blood-curdling tales of the visions of Bonbibi that arose from under his mosquito net. Notun Bou's performance of Bonbibi's story seemed nostalgic—like she was recounting a myth. As a Bengali, nostalgia is like mother's milk for me. Perhaps that's why Sukumarda's direct communication with the woman of the forest left such an impression on me.

Just as I felt my understanding of Bonbibi's story and its significance settling down, Annu told me there are other contenders for Bonbibi's place of honour. Ganga and Kali are the deities favoured by prawn-seed collectors whose lucrative yet dangerous practice threatens to upset the ecology of the Sundarbans. Even though the government has banned the practice, the seed of the tiger-prawn is in such demand that there operates an entire economy in which collectors spread thousands of nets in the estuarine streams of this area. Principally, as prawn-seed collecting becomes more common, other deities such as Ganga and Kali are becoming more popular than Bonbibi. Aren't Bonbibi, Gangaji, and Kali all aspects of the divine feminine? Yes, but Ganga is seen as a greedy goddess, down here in the bottom islands—always grabbing land and homesteads.

A locally popular joke recorded by Annu highlights the grasping nature of the Ganga. A boat taking passengers to the market met with a huge storm, which rocked the boat so threateningly that a scared woman cried out in terror, 'Ma Ganga, please let me cross safely and I shall organize a bhog (ritual feast) in your honour next year.' The weather continued to be rough and the woman now promised to organize this ritual feast each month; she soon extended her promise of devotion to each week, and then every day. The woman invited all her co-passengers to be witness to her promise. Finally, the river calmed down and the boat reached the shore. Upon alighting from the boat, the woman turned to the river and said, 'So, Ma Ganga, you tried to con me through fright, eh? But I appealed to your greed and tricked you!'

Annu notes a sharp contrast between this portrayal of Ganga and the local stories about Bonbibi, in which 'spirits and tigers must be appeased through strict rules highlighting their [humans'] subservience'. As it turns out, Bonbibi, and the tiger-charmers who mediate her laws, along with the Ganga are too peaceful for some. In fact, several female prawn-seed collectors told Annu: 'Ganga is neither strong nor violent enough; besides, she isn't a "world deity" (bishwa debi). Who knows about her? Whereas Kali, with her reputation of being a cut-throat goddess, is perfect for us.'

RETURNING HOME

The next day, at mid-morning, we set out for our return journey to Kolkata. The bhan-gari deposited us back at the mouth of the Datta River, and we crossed it, then the Bidhyahari, then the Matla, in reverse. National Waterway 97, which encompasses the Sundarbans region, is slated for development in the next three years under the National Waterways Act.

As we crossed the Matla I felt both afraid and amazed as I stepped gingerly on the burlap bags that led up to the rickety wooden boat. We sat on its frame—little more than clapboard joined together with rusty nails, with a motor engine at the centre that puffed thick, black clouds of smoke. The river was a smeary grey haze in every direction. For now, though, Satjelia and the islands to the south are blessedly free of smog.

My fears came back to me. Bangladesh and India have proposed to build the Rampal coal plant, 237 kilometres away, across the invisible water border where the Bangladeshi Sundarbans lie. As fossil fuel use increases, it's easy to imagine coal dust covering the Sundari mangrove trees as they drown in the rising ocean. The increased salinity from the eastward shift of the Ganga's mouth will impact cropland while increasing sea levels lead to erosion.

One study predicts that no habitat will be left for Bengal tigers in the Bangladeshi Sundarbans by 2070 due to the combination of climate change and sea level rise. However, Pradeep Vyas, former head of the Indian Sundarbans Biosphere Reserve, contests the veracity of the study. He notes that, in the Sundarbans, even as land is washed away, new land forms due to the silt coming down from the Himalaya. Moreover, he argues, the governments of both India and Bangladesh are committed to protecting the Bengal tiger, and locals are much more educated now; between 2001 and 2019, not even a single tiger who strayed into villages in the Indian Sundarbans was killed, and Bangladesh is striving to emulate this.

While the increased protections for tigers are hopeful, much more will on many fronts is needed. For example, oil spills may severely diminish the number of tigers and rare migratory seabirds in the delta. In fact, according to *The National Geographic*, an 'oil-spill wake-up call apparently went unanswered' in 2015 when a vessel spilled 250,000 tonnes of potash fertilizer into the Bhola River. Only a year before, 94,000 gallons of oil flowed from a tanker into the Shela River, which runs between the two countries. After this incident in 2014, a joint UN and Government of Bangladesh Mission report called for tightening regulations and noted that contingency plans didn't exist. That did not seem to have happened and it's disheartening to hear about the unique waters of the Sundarbans being stained red with harmful chemicals.

In 2016, the year I visited Satjelia, Delhi became the most polluted city in the world. Newspapers announced that each day spent breathing its air was the equivalent of smoking forty cigarettes. The Delhi government ordered vehicles to take to the streets on alternate days, and even forced a power plant to shut down for ten days. It seemed absurd that a coal plant across the border might one day reduce Satjelia, with its tiger-charmers, tasty carp fish, and unique way of life, to a wetter, less populated version of Delhi. It felt even more absurd to think of coal-bearing ships winding their way through the narrow mouths of the Ganga and down the rivers, whose meandering paths have been forced into new configurations to expedite this new metabolism. In light of recent efforts to gag the Ganga further, these fears seem like a real possibility.

But other futures also spread out before me. I imagined the solar lanterns and solar-powered huts I'd seen at Sagar growing to serve the rest of the Sundarbans. I imagined windmills and small-scale hydropower and other, cleaner sources of power growing around the world, and sea-levels rising more slowly. I imagined millions of people joining together to confront their fear of the unknown in order to arrive at this world. And, here, where the ashes of Nirbhaya may have joined the ocean, I imagined millions of men and women reshaping masculinity and femininity in service of a better world. Certainly, the egalitarian history of Satjelia and its continuing devotion to the ideals of Bonbibi had moved me to the core.

After I returned from the Sundarbans, I was surprised by how much more relaxed I felt, even though my tail bone had suffered from the bhan-gari. I had learned so much from the land of the eighteen tides. Islands are great places to understand change and extremes. In one of the most rapidly changing places on earth, I had learned the superhuman power of a simple gesture: grounding by touching the earth. It reminded me of the Buddha statue touching the earth, back in Comilla, but this gesture was alive, available, supercharged. Accessing the ground is something anyone can do anywhere, if they let themselves be comfortable enough to kneel.

CONCLUSION

In the sea is your heart, within the waters; let the plants and the waters enter you.

—Vedic poet, quoted by Darian in
The Ganges in Myth and History

Historian Steven G. Darian notes that the Mahabharata mentions 'several places on the Saraswati where Ganga bathed to wash away the sins accumulated by countless numbers of pilgrims'. Recounting ancient Zoroastrian legends about 'a goddess who descends from heaven, flowing from a mountaintop and bringing life to barren women', he suggests that the nomadic Aryans brought with them memories and symbols of the Arachosia River in southwestern Afghanistan—a possible candidate for the original Saraswati River, though the Ghaggar is also likely. Darian goes on to describe how, in the seventh century CE, the *Harshacharita* describes Emperor Harsha's father's pyre on the Saraswati's banks, even though other lyrics date the practice of throwing the bones of corpses into the Ganga as early as the fourth century. The transfer of the Saraswati's holiness to the Ganga over time poses the question: where will sins be washed when the Ganga is dry? Will any other river be intact enough to receive that burden? And what will the 500 million people who depend on the Ganga not just spiritually but materially do at that point?

Hari Kunzru, in 'Drone', imagines a disembodied India of the future in which a 'cosmic corporate person' named the Seth donates 'sacred weapons' to a 'strategic ashram high in the mountains at Gaumukh, once the source of Holy Mother Ganga'. In this world, 'The rich are fantastical creatures, young gods living in a customized world, generating themselves and their environment out of the stuff of their desires.... Not this, that. Not that, this.' Meanwhile, all that remains of the Ganga at Varanasi is an oily, junk-strewn riverbed.

Our myths might peter out here, in this bereft-of-water riverbed, where the seams between the celestial world, the human world, and the underworld have come undone. It's as if the Himalaya and the rivers therein have been mined and dammed so intensively that they can no longer provide the vertical relief needed for the imaginative leaps that allow cultures to evolve, or the depths needed to buoy us in feeling bodily sensations and emotions fully enough to open our Ganga-hearts to our ancestors, to the common good, and to our descendants. The fluid that fuels our mythic imagination is dry and our tongues are caked with dust. The landscape that once offered psychological healing at no charge come-one-come-all is being transported, sandbag by sandbag, along the national highways.

When I first started travelling along the Ganga, I thought that the challenges that the river faced were technical—for example, due to climate change caused by fossil fuels and other industrial pollutants. Over time though, I came to see that the Ganga's demise has even more to do with greed, apathy, loss of bodily connection to the river, and ignorance about how to transform consciously long-standing mindsets and behaviours. Yet, experiencing the river and its peoples—its next of kin—showed me hope, and how a free-flowing, clean Ganga might be possible.

Thus, I became fascinated by the myth of Bhagirath, who transformed himself over the course of 60,000 years in order to convince the Ganga to descend to earth and purify the sins against ecology and humanity committed by his ancestors. As I continued my journey, and witnessed the river get progressively more polluted and more fettered and as I became more and more open to honouring the spirit of Gangaji, I began to challenge the line drawn by holy men, in charge of orthodox belief systems, between ritual purity and microbial purity. Perhaps Madan Mohan Malaviya's other important contribution to the story of the Ganga—in addition to the coalition he forged at Haridwar which negotiated with the colonial government to protect the river's flow—was his decision to give diksha to Dalits on the river's banks. Reinventing ritual and creating connective tissue between old and new wisdom is more, not less, critical if any significant improvement is to be enacted.

In Kanpur, I was inspired by the commitment shown by Rakesh Jaiswal, the fount of endless knowledge about the drains that spew pollution into the river. Even though he has experienced the river's purity steadily degenerating, by choosing to bear witness, he has transformed himself into a Gangahriday, or Ganga-hearted.

Pilgrims come to the world's largest festival, the Kumbh Mela, on the banks of the river's confluence with the Yamuna at Allahabad. They go there to transform themselves, but the bigger transformation is that of how the state government becomes a paragon, one year out of twelve, in order to enable this collective sacramental celebration. If only such focused action could be the norm rather than the exception.

Both the power and the limitations of transformative collective action were clearly on display in the dolphin sanctuary region in Bhagalpur, Bihar. Fisherfolk were eager to share the story of the Ganga Mukti Andolan. Despite its heady victories, the locals are now stuck with dwindling fish stocks and oppression by the mafia. Meanwhile, in August 2016 another writer who visited the Vikramshila Gangetic Dolphin Sanctuary witnessed no fish in the fish market, and only one dolphin in the stretch of a river where normally fifteen or twenty should have been seen—perhaps due to the dredging that had already begun in preparation for carrying out the mandate laid out by the National Waterways Act, 2016.

Though the river's body is increasingly under siege, in Bangladesh I learned that millions still keep the insights of the Bauls alive: the body is a sacred site for transforming oneself and for communing with the more-than-human world. In Gaur, Murshidabad, Farakka, and Sagar Island, I investigated how identities continue to be transformed on a massive scale along the Ganga's banks where solar-powered thatched huts have now sprung up not far from the site which was once ruled by an Ethiopian king. And finally, in the Sundarbans, I glimpsed how encounters with the more-than-human can create an ethic of deep responsibility that encircles both the world of humans and the world of tigers.

I found no utopia, though Manik Bandhopadhyay's work taught me not to expect it. Instead, I found something more unexpected: a sense of meaning and aliveness. When I started my journey, I didn't know how to pay full attention to the Ganga. Initially, spending a day with the kanwariyas felt overwhelming, and prompted me to escape by reading books set in other countries, in other times. Feeling socially obligated to taste the polluted Gangajal in Kanpur filled me with a heavy blankness. And bearing witness to the Pyrrhic victory of the Ganga Mukti Andolan inspired me to acknowledge and challenge the entitlements that my own privilege brings. One thing is obvious: if I were still stuck in the mental and emotional loops that plagued me when I started my journey, I would still be on the road.

◆

Psychologists call the mental stress caused by holding two contradictory ideas in mind at the same time 'cognitive dissonance'. Generally people feel more at peace when their thoughts and actions are consistent. There are several ways, as social psychologist Leon Festinger has pointed out, to try to re-establish consistency. In addition to denial, here are some of the strategies people commonly adopt: 'Behaviour changes, changes of cognition, and circumspect exposure to new information and new opinions.' In other words, either we seek for facts we lack or views we are able to respect or we deny evidence that contradicts what we believe, or we change how we act or think. Transferred specifically to the stress of seeing the sacred river as deeply polluted and constrained, these responses might be thinking that some pollution and dams are okay here and there, or finding an environmental group to make up for how uncomfortable we feel, or claiming that pollution and dams aren't threatening the river, or deciding that there must be no more pollution or dams on the sacred river—it's important to clean it.

From here, it's only a small step to the viewpoint that our current government advocates—that each person should be responsible for cleaning the Ganga. And yet, as my travels suggested, neither the government's rhetoric nor the pledges of spiritual leaders have increased flow in the river or advanced its clean-up except at a skin-deep level. Yogic breathing might get us some of the way there, but it certainly won't get us all the way there. Will it rid us of our entrenched apathy, greed, and corruption?

Over five years after the BJP-led government launched 'Namami Gange'—its flagship programme for cleaning up and reviving the Ganga—the data paint a dismal picture. As of February 2019, out of 261 projects, only 76 had been completed, with almost 70 per cent of allocated funds lying unutilized. 'Clean Ganga', despite all official claims, remains an elusive dream.

What would the Ganga look like in 2132, I had wondered after witnessing the total solar eclipse in 2009 during which I'd stood immersed in the river with thousands of others. If Gangaji could speak to us from this future, what would she say? Perhaps she would recount the 2020s as the decade of transformative change when cooperative federalism led to perfectly working toilets, sewage and pollution treatment, electricity for crematoria, and renewable energy for industry. In this India, a critical mass of people within India and abroad focused their efforts on protecting both the cultural beliefs and the myriad creatures living in the Ganga's ecosystem. Or perhaps the river would speak about how alternative social, political, and spiritual attitudes led to alterations within India, Bangladesh, and China as nation states, and the formation of new governance units defined by their relationship to waterbodies. In this world, the subcontinent would fully own its competitive advantage in solar-power and 1.3 billion people would be connected to the sense of aliveness, meaning, and purpose inspired by a clean Ganga. Call me a dreamer, but what if disputes could be settled by swimming competitions in a free-flowing Ganga?

I come back to Dr Dhruv Kazi, the public health expert who studied the Kumbh Mela, and who believed that we needed to unleash our imagination about the future of the Ganga. He asked: 'What are the Ganga's pain points?' When he said 'the story has not been communicated very well', he meant the story of how pollutants affect human bodies along the river. Many of the 500 million people who depend on the river are directly affected, but they remain unaware of the actual decision-makers, policymakers, and intermediaries, and how their collusion might lead to devastating impact on their lives.

But Kazi's viewpoint applies to other tales too: tales I've tried to tell in this book but only in passing. For example, there is the story of soft infrastructure. In *Dirty, Sacred Rivers*, Cheryl Colopy explores the legacy of Gandhi's core message, which she characterizes as: 'make everyone responsible for his or her own shit'. The Ganga and Yamuna will not be clean, she suggests, until people tackle sewage 'on a war footing'. This would mean treating sewage at source via septic tanks and biogas digesters, not flushing it out of sight. It would also mean refraining from mixing urine and faeces.

Sheel Raj Shetty, a young architect who works for a Bangalore-based firm focused on ecological architecture, told Colopy: 'All the pathogens are in the faeces. Urine...has nutrients that are being sent to the wrong place; they create algae blooms in water bodies when they could be valuable for agriculture. While those nutrients are being flushed away, Indian farmers buy expensive chemical fertilizers, which pollute rivers and stress soil.' And she describes the wonders of the eco-san toilet, an odourless two-foot by two-foot chamber that produces fertilizer from human waste.

Similarly, the algal ponds that could treat sewage as dreamed up by Varanasi's Veer Bhadra Mishra depart from the traditional (post) colonial norms and blend the needs of the riverscape with human needs. They work—not just in theory, but physically—but they remain unimplemented or fail to yield their full benefits because of failed implementation and unchanging behaviours. Colopy told me about visiting a site in Bihar where these facilities had been built but were lying unused primarily because long-standing Hindu beliefs around sanitation could not be overcome by technology alone. Changing long-standing beliefs that enable inequity is the realm of education at its best. If the Ganga is to be different in the fairly near future, we need a new spirituality, a new politics, and a new set of appropriate technologies which intersect and which must be irrevocably interrelated; these are better approached as I have tried to approach them in this book, not as discrete points in an outline but as a swirling confluence of multiple narratives.

It's worth repeating that our karma from the past several generations comes down to us via our infrastructure. The history of colonial attempts to impose canals upon a region that, for generations, had expected and adjusted to seasonal flooding is admirably told in Colopy's work. So is an account of how people managed to live with floods in precolonial times and how this resilient lifestyle has been challenged by rigid postcolonial embankments and railroads. Notable in this context is the work of Megh Pyne Abhiyan (Cloud's Water Campaign), a grass-roots network which promotes rainwater harvesting and the revival of local water festivals in some of the most inaccessible parts of northern Bihar.

In 2016, as it does each year, Bihar battled both flood and drought. The floods damaged both crops and housing, affecting 88.23 lakh people in 31 out of 38 districts. The state government stepped in amidst splintered roofs, caved-in earthen walls, helter-skelter banana trees, and babies being born on boats. According to Bihar's Disaster Management Department, ministers camped in flooded districts, faced critical press coverage full-on, and prioritized dignity for all. They pre-positioned funds so they could be released quickly, utilized WhatsApp and SMS-based early warning systems, and earned the trust of local responders by strengthening their abilities. The evacuees who were brought to relief camps received cloth, toiletries, and utensils.

But an extensive study by Prof Sanjiv Phansalker and others at Tata Trusts suggests that these 'innovations' failed to address the systemic challenges at the root of the disruption. Moreover, they cite locals who claim that the government relief and rescue process was 'too little, too late'. They note that the majority of people affected by the floods have already changed their cropping patterns (from two to three per season to just one, from vegetables to maize, and begun planting cucumber in riverbeds and dhaincha, a green manure crop, on the areas rendered waste by sand deposition). Phansalker and his associates recommend 'low-hanging fruit' that are more locally adaptive such as elevated platforms and handpumps for drinking water and raised toilets for sanitation, sanitary napkins, floating schools, better accessibility to boats, small irrigation pumps; and creeper gardens. After noting the polarization that comes along with any discussion of embankments in India, they insist upon the need for 'participatory embankment management'.

India's challenge is to stop replicating the monstrous public works of the past, beneath which the Ganga is entombed; instead we must build roads, sewers, buildings, cities, and power sources that prioritize humans working with the intermittency and changeability of natural systems, rather than fighting—and killing—them. River Linking, Highway Golden Quadrilateral, auctioning irreplaceable forestland for mining concessions—these are the catastrophes of our age that we must not numb ourselves against facing.

When the Ganges Canal was built in 1854, it was justified on the grounds that hundreds of thousands were dying of famine. Perhaps the Ganga's fate as a sewage canal was sealed by 1960, when the Green Revolution was funded by the US, at least in part, to win India's sympathies in the Cold War. Anthony Acciavatti recounts how in 1975 Roger Revelle, along with V. Lakshminarayana, coined the phrase 'Ganges Water Machine' in *Science* magazine's 'Food Issue' about the need to increase productivity and management and integrate the Ganga Canal with the tube wells surrounding it in order to sustain the population along the river. 'All of the seemingly disparate and incoherent efforts to transform the basin were finally given a name,' Acciavatti writes in his book. It's tempting to wonder how concerned citizens might effectively organize themselves in order to reform and restore this infrastructural behemoth, with its hundreds of thousands of unlicensed tube wells drawing groundwater out for private use, and its new utility as a waterway.

When will we ever learn? If the 2016 National Waterways Act is implemented as proposed, the subsequent dredging and shipping could drown the river in new hazards and also consign the shushuk, the Ganga River dolphin, to extinction, like so many species in the past few decades. All the while, climate change—accelerated by the burning of the coal which would be ferried down the river—would make the average farmer's life more difficult by shifting weather patterns unpredictably. Some clean energy alternatives do exist, but without a massive shift in policy it's hard for small vendors to compete with the National Thermal Power Plant Company. Most importantly, would centralizing control over the river, as the National Waterways Act proposes to do, truly be a more efficient and corruption-free way to carry out 'integrated management' of the river? Or would seizing power away from local decision-makers sever the relationship communities have with the Ganga and expose the river to venal commercial interests, whereby industry and the government collude with each other, causing long-term ill-health both for the Ganga and the larger environment?

Then there's an emerging story about valuing the services that the Ganga provides economically. The outlines are vague at best because not much initiative has yet been taken on this important topic, despite visionary organizations like the Green India States Trust which values environmental resources held in common. And let's not forget the background antagonists here—laws and policies, whose impacts often take decades to be felt. Given the recent research suggesting that M. C. Mehta's legal actions in the 1980s eventually did benefit human health in Kanpur, perhaps it's not too bold to say that the (pending) 2017 designation of the Ganga as a living human entity, and the 2009 recognition of the river dolphin as a non-human person, could lead to positive changes in the future—if enough people are motivated to transform their own relationship to being human by finding meaning and purpose in navigating our new superhuman ability to impact the planet as if we are a force of nature.

Next, there's the drama of popular movements and the momentum they can generate; for example, the Ganga Mukti Andolan or Save Ganga Insurrection in Bihar resulted in the end of the exploitative landlord regime, but it was immediately replaced by lax state governance and an equally exploitative mafia. And there's the hopeful narrative of how contemplative practices can help deepen the personal and collective transformation that is needed in order to change the story of the Ganga. From the sage Bhagirath's tapasya, which brought the Ganga down to the earth in order to purify the ecocide committed by King Sagar's 60,000 sons, to the body-honouring practices and music of the Bauls, which cuts across orthodox notions of gender, religion, and caste, ancient embodied spiritual practices at their best have gone a long way towards undoing fixed beliefs and practices—and they have a long way yet to go.

Then there are the stories that will have to wait for another telling. For example, the Ganga Fan—the largest sea fan in the world—is an emerging underwater delta built out of the billion metric tonnes of sediment per year that the Ganga and Brahmaputra carry down from the Himalaya. In several hundred million years a new land will exist here. It's possible to go, via trawler, to the Swatch-of-No-Ground, a two-thousand-mile-long canyon in the Bay of Bengal which channels sediment into the Sea Fan. The Swatch is the world's hotspot of cetacean diversity: many species of whales, porpoises, and dolphins—including the occasional river dolphin, which was once common all along the Ganga—congregate here.

I miss not having seen the mahseer—the so-called 'tiger-amongst-fish'. Neither did I encounter the long-nosed gharial, cousin to the crocodile, which emits a mating hiss that can be heard half a mile away on a quiet day. Nor did I follow the river dolphin into a sacred grove like Mandu in Bulandshahr District along the Ganga in U.P., which ecologists consider 'the last refuge' of biodiversity along the Upper Ganga in order to taste the special chiku fruit that grows there (I did, however, touch some mellow, squelchy, soft-shelled Gangetic turtles, which are extinct in the wild, at the shrine of Bayyazid Bostami in Chittagong).

Neither did I share the hopeful tale of how Kolkata discharges all of its sewage—completely untreated—into the East Kolkata Wetlands, which has been recognized as a wetland of international importance by the UN Ramsar Convention. The sewage is channelled into a series of constructed fishponds called bheries, where sunlight, oxygen, and microbial action eventually turn the effluent into fertilizer for the fish to feed on. Almost two-thirds of the fish and vegetables are safely grown in that rich faecal ferment, providing a hopeful model for other megacities around the world, and serving as a positive example of soft infrastructure in the Ganga River basin. Although fishing and farming cooperatives have thrived there despite the best efforts of developers to rezone the land for industrial development, the state environment minister and mayor of Kolkata, Sovan Chatterjee, in recent years, has allegedly encouraged encroachment on this land despite protests by environmentalists, according to a 2017 *Hindustan Times* article. His proposal regarding the construction of a flyover through the wetland was thankfully turned down by the Kolkata High Court in July 2018.

And these are just the tales that I, a lone person of Indian origin with two ears and two eyes and two legs, and the blinkers that come with being diasporic, know of. These stories need to be told, and heard, if we want to change how we address these crises. But even the stories I have shared give rise to more pressing questions: What should be done? What can be done?

The first solution is to amplify what so many are doing: publicize the problems while respecting their complexity but with the belief that humans can solve problems that they have caused. Publicize the mistakes that have been made, and also the successes, in order to lead those in power to confront the present condition of the river as it suggests the river's future.

But what would taking more skilful action with regard to the Ganga really look like? Throughout my travels, I had the opportunity to talk with others about failed leadership. Successful, skilful, inspiring leadership is terribly hard—harder by far than I imagined when I set out on my trek. For me, at least, only the felt reality of being in and around this superhuman river, of meeting those who depend upon it, care for it, exploit it, think they know how to treat it or what to do about it—living daily with its problems and blessings had the power to show me the near impossibility of successful leadership in this regard despite the absolute necessity of it. For the nearly impossible always remains an option for us.

Social conditioning will push back at you when you try to make any change in habits, including the creation of spaces where communities, networks, and organizations feel comfortable shedding patterns that no longer serve. Dialogues across boundaries would allow everyone to have a view of the river that is more whole, but how can this work across differences be enabled in a context as complicated as India? In China, a single state with immense centralized power, the Yangtze River dolphin went extinct—a fact worth mentioning again—after thirty years of debates amongst bureaucrats and conservationists failed to materialize with a plan to save it.

My journey was messy, but it had moments of grace that gave me resilience. Small memories of my travels give me hope in difficult times: the dream of the paradise flycatcher at the foot of the Gangotri glacier and the Himalayan aricha leaf that was given me to chew, curing my altitude sickness; immersing myself in the Ganga at Haridwar, and feeling the water evoke a liveliness of purpose within myself that I hadn't felt in a long time, maybe ever; viewing the total solar eclipse along with thousands of others at Varanasi and learning about the ancient Indian water clock through which time flowed very differently; the unique examples of communal living from the Kumbh Mela near Allahabad and the surprising, if still limited, efficacy of laws to protect public health along the river in Kanpur.

I feel the urgency of learning from these uncomfortable, dangerous places before they disappear, and the discomfort of learning new stories through the body, and letting go of old stories through the body. I remember lifting up my red bucket above my head, about to splash water on my head, longing to utter the words 'Ganga, Ganga', out loud. I remember the exhilaration when I finally dared to do so. I remember how much resistance I had to overcome to ask myself about the Ganga I want to leave for my grandchildren, to ask others about their wildest dreams for the river.

Dr Kazi called for accountability; I suggest that we need re-enchantment with the river in addition to that. I will never forget glimpsing the river dolphin in Bihar. I remember my heart beating like a drum as I considered the existence of the Gangaridae, a tribe whose name could only mean 'Ganga-hearted', or so I believe. I remember tasting delicious river fish in Bangladesh, and meeting the scores of kind, generous people who are living according to a new paradigm, one that still leaves a place in their hearts for the Ganga. The superhuman river has been called down to earth, may have a chance to grow into its new identity as a living human entity. Simultaneously, we humans have become troublingly superhuman with regard to our impact on the earth's living systems. This is an opportunity for a renegotiation of what it means to be human—as individuals, as families, as communities, institutions, and social norms, as mortals who, regardless of religious beliefs, surely wish for toxic infrastructure, inefficiency, inequality, and exploitation to be wiped clean. The first step is to pay attention to how we pay attention to the Ganga.

ACKNOWLEDGEMENTS

In loving memory of: Shudhanshu and Amiya Banerji; Nityanarayan and Narayani Banerjee; Santosh Kumar Mukherjee; Amitava Kumar Banerjee; Chandranath Kumar Mukherjee; Margaret Collins; Dorothy V. Corvino; and Pamela Krasney.

My family in the US: Mahasweta Banerjee; K. K. Collins; George Collins; and Bijoya Banerjee-Collins. This book is theirs as much as mine.

My family in India: Shila Mukherjee, who reinvigorated me with her hospitality, her cooking, and her magic touch many times over the decade it took to complete this book; Samidh Banerjee, who accompanied me to remote parts of Bengal, Bangladesh, and Bihar; Subhra Mukherjee, who supported my unconventional interests; Sarvapriya and Sadapurna Mukherjee, who cheered me on and helped me navigate; Kasturi Banerjee, whose caregiving abilities are surpassed only by her panache; Udayaditya and Parul Banerjee who hosted me in Delhi, took me to NMCG offices, and helped me with legalities; Babu Mama, my great-grandma's sister's son, who helped arrange my visit to Gangotri and Uttarkashi, where I stayed safely and comfortably with his employee's mother-in-law; Pankaj kaka, who accompanied me to Farakka and Murshidabad; Ranjan kaka and Bratati kakima, who validated my interest in the Ganga-hearted people; Rita pishi, who inspired me with her stories about ancient civilizations near and far; Anuradha pishi, Aditi pishi, Bhutin pishi, Babu kaka, Keya kakima, and Kasturi; and Neel and Tai Banerjee, who were supportive and encouraging.

And my mentors: Tom Birt; Mirabai Bush; Cheryl Colopy; Ted Conover; Louise Dunlap; Queen Mutima Rose Imani; Marty Krasney; Amitava Kumar; Perry Lang; Genine Lentine; Bill McKibben; Jeffrey Paine; Esther Perel; Roopal Shah; Chris Shaw; Gus Speth; Fred Strebeigh; Rebecca Solnit; Dev Tayde; Mi'Jan Celie Tho'Biaz; and Marion Weber.

And:

Indicorps crew who teach me how to do Seva: Asha and Rahul Brown; Kohl Gill; Tushar Kansal; Sheel Mohnot; Karthik Raman; Rish and Sima Sanghvi; Tanya Sehgal; Sonal Singhal; and Shaila Parikh.

Forestry Crew who show me how to TGIF: Meredith Cowart; Freddie Ghesquiere; Marion Thorpe; Mira Manickam; Mike Sesko; Justin Freiberg; Seth Zeren; and Melinda Stylos-Alan.

Friends who bail me out: Atreyee Das; Isa Kretschmer; Maceo Montoya and Alejandra Perez; Rebecca Tuhus-Dubrow; Jennifer Russ; Sara Ruiz; Geoffrey Sledge and Michele Tang; James Sumner; and Helen White. Thank you for being at my side for the past 20–35 years.

The Dalai Lama Fellows crew who teach me about courage: Joel Bombarbier; Natalie Conneelly; Bela Shah; Chris Simamora; Mirabai Bush; Marty Krasney; Andy Ng; Steven Chan; Yi Zhang; Dana Pearlman; Greg Hodge; Anamaria Aristizabal; Oscar Medina; Marley Benshalom; Karim-Yassin Gossinger; Rehan Adamjee; Samir Goel; Samir Mohite; Prabhakar Jayaprakash; Cemre Agoaglu; and almost 100 others—you know who you are.

The How We Gather crew who teach me how to gather: Casper ter Kuile; Angie Thurston; and Sue Phelps.

The India Climate Solutions road tour gang: Abisekh Bharadwaj; Caroline Howe; Alexis Ringwald; Deepa Gupta; Kabir Khan; Anna da Costa; Kartikeya Singh; and Alark Saxena.

California friends and inspirations: Tenzin Seldon, Miyuki Baker; Meena Srinivasan; Charles Vogl, Socheata Poev, and Kep Vogl; Molly Roy; Anders Peterson; Melissa Anderson; Joyce Brady; Bhaskar Ghosh and Brinda Natarajan; Gayathri Narayan; Roopa Maurya; Monica Mody; Vijaya Nagarajan; Natasha Singh; Shilpa Jain; Sunita Puri; Nina Rastogi; Tenzin Choedon; Bhuti Sangma; Martha Gramajo; Kevin Shaw, Mia Pixley, and Mikai; Catherine Porter and the American Friends of the Ganges; Jeff Leifer; Evan Steiner; and the Impact Hub Oakland.

Philanthropists: Middlebury Environmental Journalism Fellowship; Esalen Institute; Breadloaf; Yerba Buena Arts Center's Future Soul Think Tank; Yale Tropical Resources Institute; Hedgebrook; Mesa Refuge; and Commonweal.

Coaches: Richard Strozzi-Heckler; Staci Haines; Paola Laird; Michael Kalikow; Nathaniel Shara; and Gabriel Wilson.

Places of awakening: Lake Merritt; Lawrence Yoga Center; The Suigetsukan dojo; Two Rock dojo; Kalighat; Belur Math; and Boulder Aikikai.

Editors: Sam Frank and his staff at Triple Canopy; Simar Puneet, Isha Banerji, and the staff at Aleph Book Company.

Those who offered hospitality during my travels: in Dhaka—Khushi Kabir; Fakrul and Najma Alam; Salma Shafi. In Kolkata—Jhontuda; Shondhadi; Aman-da. In Varanasi—Sankat Mochan Foundation and Vedanidhi Trust.

The names of people I met in my travels and people with whom I had conversations, whose help has been invaluable, appear in the text. But I would like to take this opportunity to thank them as a group.

In addition to my travel and conversations, it is important to note that I have been helped by a number of books. Here are some that deserve special mention. Manik Bandhopadhyay's *Padma Nadir Majhi* (and Gautam Ghosh's excellent film of the same name, available on YouTube); Steven G. Darian's *The Ganges in Myth and History*; Cheryl Colopy's *Dirty, Sacred Rivers: Confronting South Asia's Water Crisis*; Anthony Acciavatti's *Ganges Water Machine: Designing New India's Ancient River*; Georgina Drew's *River Dialogues: Hindu Faith and the Political Ecology of Dams on the Sacred Ganga*; Annu Jalais's *Forest of Tigers: People, Politics and Environment in the Sundarbans*; Ananya Jahanara Kabir's *Partition's Post-Amnesias: 1947, 1971 and Modern South Asia*; the Centre for Science and Environment's *Excreta Matters*; Rahul Mehrotra and Felipe Vera, editors, *Kumbh Mela: Mapping the Ephemeral Megacity*; Kelly Alley's *On the Banks of the Gaṅgā: When Waste water Meets a Sacred River*; Assa Doron, Richard Barz, and Barbara Nelson, editors, *An Anthology of Writings on the Ganga: Goddess and River in History, Culture, and Society*; Amitav Ghosh's *The Hungry Tide*; Richard Eaton's *The Rise of Islam and the Bengal Frontier, 1204–1760*; Iftekhar Iqbal's *The Bengal Delta: Ecology, State and Social Change, 1840–1943*; Madhav Gadgil's *This Fissured Land: An Ecological History of India*; and Willem van Schendel's *The Bengal Borderland: Beyond State and Nation in South Asia*.

Finally, movies like Raj Kapoor's *Ram Teri Ganga Maili,* and Valli Bindana's *Sun Ganges*, and songs like Bhupen Hazarika's 'O Ganga Behti Ho Kyun' were inspiring during the writing of this book.

ENDNOTES

INTRODUCTION

xiii   **indifferent to the 'dirty, sacred river':** I owe this phrase to Cheryl Colopy's terrific book *Dirty Sacred Rivers: Confronting South Asia's Water Crisis*, New York: Oxford University Press, 2012.

xiii   **the 2035 figure was an overstatement:** Damian Carrington, 'IPCC officials admit mistake over melting Himalayan glaciers', *The Guardian*, 20 January 2010.

xiv   **1,109 polluting industries discharge toxic waste:** R. C. Acharya, 'Namami Gange: With 1,109 industries discharging toxic effluents, it is a long way to go', *Financial Express*, 7 March 2019.

xiv   **mercury and pesticides plague the river:** Dipankar Chakraborti et al, 'Groundwater arsenic contamination in the Ganga River basin: a future health danger', *International Journal of Environmental Research and Public Health*, 23 January 2018 <https://www.mdpi.com/1660-4601/15/2/180/pdf> [accessed: 6 May 2019].

xv   **What would the Ganga be like:** The next total solar eclipse (of the kind I had witnessed in July 2009) will occur on 13 June 2132.

xv   **clean-up of the Thames:** Victor Mallett, *River of Life, River of Death: The Ganges and India's Future*, Oxford: Oxford University Press, 2017, p. 233.

xvi   **The Bihari boatman:** I am forced to change his name because, unbelievably, a mafia rules certain stretches of the river.

xvi   **Yangtze River's baiji, which disappeared from this world:** Catherine Brahic, 'Yangtze river dolphin is almost certainly extinct', *New Scientist*, 8 August 2007.

xvii   **Chandrasekhar Kambar's village pond, Mother Ganga:** Chandrasekhar Kambar, 'Our Village Pond Named Mother Ganga'.

xvii   **'living human entity…':** Saptarshi Dutta, '3 years of "Namami Gange": where do we stand?', *Swachh India*, 22 September 2017.

xvii   **Supreme Court suspended the earlier judgment:** A. Vaidyanathan, 'No, Ganga and Yamuna are not living entities, says Supreme Court', *NDTV*, 7 July 2017.

xviii   **more than a billion litres of waste flows into the Ganga:** Radheshyam Jadhav, '1.3 bn litres of waste flows into the Ganga every day', *Times of India*, 20 April 2018.

xviii   **find their way into the Hindu scriptures:** Steven G. Darian, *The Ganges in Myth and History*, New Delhi: Motilal Banarsidass, 2001, p. 49.

xviii   **nomadic Aryans learned how to cultivate rice and barley:** Ibid., p. 57.

xix   **500 million people live in the Gangetic basin:** 'For a living Ganga', World Wide Fund for Nature India (WWF), 2012, accessed via <www.wwfindia.org>.

xix   **fertile goddess who birthed Kartikeya:** Ruth Vanita and Saleem Kidwai (eds.), *Same-Sex Love in India: Readings from Literature and History*, New York: Palgrave, 2001, pp. 78–79.

xix   **we can find a river yielding up gold:** Darian cites the Mahabharata, p. 60; Vana Parvan 86.

xx   **India is the most vulnerable to climate change:** Reuters, 'Why India is most at risk from climate change', 21 March 2018.

xx   **blurred sculptures of gods, rishis, serpent rajas and ranis**: Darian, *The Ganges in Myth* *and History*, p. 19.

xxii **Nitish Kumar, held a conference in 2017 called 'Incessant Ganga':** IANS, 'Bihar CM Nitish Kumar demands national debate on Ganga', *Financial Express*, 25 February 2017. I take the phrase 'more-than-human world', below, from David Abram, *The Spell of the Sensuous: Perception and Language in a More-Than-Human World*, New York: Pantheon, 1996.

xxiv **'the Ganges, the Godavari, any river':** Horace H. Wilson, *Glossary of Judicial and Revenue Terms of British India*, London: W. H. Allen and Co., 1855, p. 165.

xxiv **mode of adjusting an account of borrowed money:** Ibid., p. 165.

xxiv **'Upper castes' regarded this with contempt:** 'Judicial oaths among the Hindus', *Asiatic Journal and Monthly Register for British India and its Dependencies*, Vol. 23, April 1827, pp. 475–78.

xxiv **we'll encounter the Gangaridae:** There's a complicated backstory here. For more, *see* Dineschandra Sircar, *Studies in the Geography of Ancient and Medieval India*, Delhi: Motilal Banarsidass, 1971, p. 171.

xxv **Gangahriday is situated on the banks of the river:** Aniruddha Ghosal, 'Chandraketugarh: the city that never was', *Indian Express*, 19 February 2017.

xxv **The poet Virgil writes about them too:** 'Gangaridae' or 'Gangaridai' as the site was known was called so by Greco-Roman writers, was later indigenized to 'Gangahridaya'. For more *see* Sircar, p. 171.

xxv **Sobhaparvan of the Mahabharata mentions the muslins:** Sircar, p. 139.

xxv **'had an army of 20,000 horse[s], 200,000 infantry…':** 'Did you know why Alexander did not proceed to conquer ancient Bengal?', *Daily Star*, 12 August 2015.

xxv **'beneficent non-habit-forming [drug]':** William Burroughs, *Naked Lunch*, New York: Grove Press, 1991, p. xxxvii.

xxv **represented the edges of the world:** Dante Alighieri, 'Purgatorio Canto II: 1–45 The Angel of God', *Poetry in Translaion*, <https://www.poetryintranslation.com/PITBR/Italian/DantPurg1to7.php#anchor_Toc64099520> [accessed: 9 May 2019].

xxvi **'highly engineered hydrological super-surface':** Anthony Acciavatti, *Ganges Water Machine: Designing New India's Ancient River*, Novato: Oro Editions, 2015, p. 7.

xxvii **'the worst place in the world, [or] close':** Hari Kunzru, 'Drone', *Granta*, No. 130; on the building of large dams, *see* Ramachandra Guha (ed.), *Social Ecology*, Oxford: Oxford University Press, 1994, p. 6.

xxvii **'aviral Ganga, nirmal Ganga':** 'Namami Gange', *Down To Earth*, 4 July 2015.

xxix **similar moral and ethical shifts had helped lead the Chinese civilization:** Adam Hochschild, *Bury the Chains: Prophets and Rebels in the Fight to Free an Empire's Slaves*, Boston: Houghton Mifflin, 2005, pp. 130–33, 221–33; Kwame Anthony Appiah, *The Honor Code: How Moral Revolutions Happen*, New York: W. W. Norton & Company, 2010, pp. 94–100.

xxix **spirituality, science, and the wisdom of our bodies are combined:** M. S. Nawaz, 'IIT professor-turned-seer, on fast for nearly 4 months for clean Ganga, dies', *Times of India*, 11 October 2018.

CHAPTER 1: THE ORIGINS OF TOUCH AND FLOW

3 **'emerges from a spot beyond human reach':** Quoted in Parvathy Suresh, 'The story of the Ganges', *ISSUU*, June 2013.

5 **'So painful indeed is this track…':** James Baillie Fraser, *Journal of a Tour through Part of the Snowy Range of the Himâlâ Mountains, and to the Sources of the Rivers Jumna and Ganges*, London: Rodwell and Martin, 1820, p. 466.

7   **India is almost two degrees warmer:** 'CSE data shows India getting warmer consistently, rapidly', *The Pioneer*, 6 June 2017.

7   **endure an additional two to seven degrees:** 'Stark reality of future global warming', *The Pioneer*, 14 December 2017.

7   **30-kilometre length retreating more than 850 metres since 1975:** 'Retreat of the Gangotri glacier', *NASA Earth Observatory* <https://earthobservatory.nasa.go./images/4594/retreat-of-the-gangotri-glacier> [accessed: 6 December 2019].

7   **retreating in the range of 13 to 33 millimetres per year:** PTI, 'Himalayan glaciers in India are receding at highly alarming rate', *Financial Express*, 2 July 2019.

7   **2.5 per cent of the glacial lakes of the state:** Soma Basu, 'Himalayan states also face risk of glacial lake outburst floods', *Down To Earth*, 17 August 2015.

8   **'the world remains a great enchanted garden':** Max Weber, *The Sociology of Religion*, 1922, Boston: Beacon Press, 1993, p. 270. *See* also Alan Mulhern, *The Sower and the Seed: Reflections on the Development of Consciousness*, London: Karnac Books, 2015, p. 223.

8   **many have sought re-enchantment from wellsprings:** The literature on 'secular magic' (Simon During's term) is large; for a useful survey, *see* Michael Saler, 'Modernity and enchantment: a historiographic review', *The American Historical Review*, Vol. 111, June 2006, pp. 692–716.

10   **'you two make love together':** Vanita and Kidwai, *Same-Sex Love in India*, p. 101.

11   **'Ganga struggled to set herself free…':** 'Bhagiratha: who brought River Ganga to earth' <https://vibhanshu.wordpress.com/2010/03/20/bhagiratha-who-brought-river-ganga-to-earth/> [accessed: 29 April 2019].

11   **Chola bronzes of Shiva Nataraja:** Liesbeth Pankaja Bennink et al, 'Shiva's dance in stone: Ananda Tandava, Bhujangalalita, Bhujangatrasa', *AsianArt*, 29 June 2012.

11   **Jain version of the Sagara story:** Alex McKay (ed.), *Pilgrimage in Tibet*, Surrey: Curzon Press, 1998, p. 151.

11   **Ganga flowed from sage Jahnu's ear:** 'How the Ganga became known as Jahnavi', *Holy Dham* <http://www.holydham.com/how-the-ganga-became-known-as-jahnavi/> [accessed: 29 April 2019].

12   **'looked at the river fearlessly':** The mythological origin-stories are from Robert Goldman (trans.), *Ramayana* of Valmiki and J. A. B. Van Buitenen (trans.), *The Mahabharata*, as excerpted in Assa Doron et al (eds.), *An Anthology of Writings on the Ganga: Goddess and River in History, Culture, and Society*, New Delhi: Oxford University Press, 2013.

14   **the National Council for River Ganga:** 'Cabinet approves the River Ganga (Rejuvenation, Protection and Management) Authorities Order, 2016', *PIB* <http://pib.nic.in/newsite/PrintRelease.aspx?relid=150983> [accessed: 29 April 2019].

14   **'a control commission' should replace the Planning Commission:** 'Planning Commission should be replaced with a new body: Independent Evaluation Office', *Economic Times*, 24 June 2014.

14   **'22 drains that cause 90 per cent of pollution':** 'Cabinet gives Clean Ganga Mission power to fine polluters', *The Hindu*, 22 September 2016.

14   **2013 Interim Report:** 'Ganga River Basin Management Plan-2015', September 2013, <http://cganga.org/wp-content/uploads/sites/3/2017/09/GRBMP-MPD_March_2015.pdf> [accessed: 13 May 2019].

14   **'entire river valley (including the active floodplain)' is 'the river space':** Ibid.

14   **a Tibetan river that merges with the Bhagirathi:** Sathya Narayanan, 'Why is Ganga called Jahnavi?', *Speaking Tree*, 16 February 2016.

15   **'In order to preserve and invigorate the National River Ganga…':** 'Ganga River Basin

Management Plan' p. xix.

15 **'a testimony to our ancient wisdom…':** 'Ganga River Basin Management Plan-2015', January 2015, 'Consortium of 7 "Indian Institutes of Technology"s (IITs)' <https://cganga. org/wp-content/uploads/sites/3/2017/09/GRBMP-MPD_March_2015.pdf> [accessed 20 November 2019].

15 **removal of shanty-town dwellers:** Ibid., p. 57.

15 **open defecation cost India a staggering 5.2 per cent of the nation's GDP:** Sushmita Sengupta, 'Poor sanitation cost India 5.2% of its GDP', *Down To Earth*, 12 September 2016.

18 **second-century BCE Ptolemaic map of Gangahriday:** Ptolemy's map depicting land beyond the Ganges is in public domain, <https://commons.wikimedia.org/wiki/ File:Ptolemy_Asia_detail.jpg> [accessed: 10 May 2019].

CHAPTER 2: 'THE RIVER, VAINLY, IDOLIZED OF YORE' (RISHIKESH AND HARIDWAR)

19 **'What need of expensive sacrifices…':** Padma Purana, 60.39.

20 **word Ganga, often taken to mean 'swift-goer':** Diana L. Eck, *Banaras: City of Light*, New York: Knopf Doubleday Publishing Group, 1999, 2013 (repr), p. 217.

20 **Brahma Kund, one of the most sacred spots in the holy town:** At the beginning of everything, the first salvation story goes, the devas (gods) and the asuras (demons) heard that the nectar of immortality was concealed in the 'Ocean of Milk', the cosmic ocean lying at the foot of Mount Meru, the centre of the universe. Only by cooperating would they be able to find it. So they stuck Mount Meru (the then centre of the universe) into the ocean and wrapped the king of the serpents around it. The devas grabbed the serpent-king's head and the asuras his tail; each side shook its end of the serpent, and together they churned the waves for a thousand years. Finally, they found not just the nectar of immortality but also its obverse—a poison so deadly that it would destroy the world, all the gods included. Since no one knew what to do with it, Shiva consumed it, only to have it lodged in his throat, which turned a blazing blue. So, Shiva must continuously slake that poisonous heat in order to not release it into the world.

20 **'[S]tanding by the Ganges river…':** James Lochtefeld, *God's Gateway: Identity and Meaning in a Hindu Pilgrimage Place*, New York: Oxford University Press, 2010, p. 51.

23 **'superbugs' resistant to most antibiotics:** Z. S. Ahammad, T. R. Sreekrishnan, C. L. Hands, C. W. Knapp, and D. W. Graham, 'Increased waterborne blaNDM-1 resistance gene abundances associated with seasonal human pilgrimages to the upper Ganges River', *Environmental Science and Technology*, Vol. 48, No. 5, 4 March 2014, pp. 3014–20.

23 **a parasitic infection, after swallowing three spoons of river water:** Atul Gawande, *Being Mortal*, New York: Metropolitan Book, 2014, pp. 261–62.

24 **Local water bodies were zealously kept up by community:** Amita Bhaduri, 'The missing water bodies of Western Uttar Pradesh', *India Water Portal*, 1 September 2013.

25 **'a decked boat accommodating two passengers…'** Joyce Brown, 'A memoir of Colonel Sir Proby Cautley, F.R.S, 1802–1871, engineer and palaeontologist', *Notes and Records of the Royal Society of London*, Vol. 34, No. 2, 1980, pp. 185–225.

25 **'the steep slopes that exist…':** Proby T. Cautley, *Report on the Ganges Canal Works: From their Commencement until the opening of the Canal in 1854*, Vol. 1, London: Smith, Elder and Co., 1860, p. 3, quoted by Acciavatti, *Ganges Water Machine*, p. 114.

26 **'almost as large as an elephant…':** Brown, p. 199.

26 **'Every kind of difficulty had to be overcome…':** Georgina Drew, 'Transformation and

resistance on the upper Ganga: the ongoing legacy of British canal irrigation', *South Asia: Journal of South Asian Studies*, Vol. 37, No. 4, 2014, p. 675.

27 'While the Solani River...': Acciavatti, p. 116.

27 'The water bridge is 172 feet wide and 24 feet tall...': Sarah Laskow, '160-year-old Ganges canal super-passages are an engineering marvel', *Atlas Obscura*, 18 January 2016.

27 'The night in which false religion...': Charles Eliot Norton, *The Opening of the Ganges Canal*, Cambridge: Metcalf & Company, 1855, p. 15.

28 'I stood among them...': Henry George Keene, 'The Opening of the Ganges Canal' in 'Young Bengal', *Blackwood's Edinburgh Magazine*, Vol. 75, June 1854, pp. 648–57; quoted in Acciavatti, p. 118.

29 'disproved statements' and 'idle calumny': Proby T. Cautley, *A Disquisition on the Heads of the Ganga and Jumna Canals in Reply to Strictures by Major-General Sir Arthur Cotton*, London: n.p., 1864, p. iv.

29 'imposed infrastructure provided the perfect alibi...': Acciavatti, p. 120; *see* also pp. 215–19 and 235.

30 'there is room for only four persons to pass abreast': Walter Hamilton, *East-India Gazetteer*, Vol. 1, London: W. H. Allen and Co., p. 667.

30 'the British Government expanded the access way...': Kelly D. Alley, *On the Banks of the Gaṅgā: When the Wastewater Meets a Sacred River*, Ann Arbor: University of Michigan Press, 2002, p. 108.

31 there was no water for pilgrims to bathe in: Ibid., p. 109 and 117.

31 decided to dig a new channel that diverted the river: Ibid., p. 109.

31 'Mahamana' by Rabindranath Tagore: Shashi Shekhar, '"Mahamana": A forgotten visionary', *Livemint*, 25 December 2017.

32 no Hindu would place his material prosperity above: quoted in Alley, *On the Banks of the Gaṅgā*, p. 113.

32 '[e]ven if the cost were one lakh or two lakhs...': Ibid.

33 he gave diksha to 'untouchables' by anointing them with Gangajal: Sitaram Chaturvedi, *Madan Mohan Malaviya (Builders of Modern India Series)*, Ministry of Information and Broadcasting, Govt. of India, 1972, p. 52.

33 The Government of India argued that more dams were fine: Nitin Sethi, 'Water resources ministry: No more dams on Ganga in Uttarakhand', *Business Standard*, 28 June 2016. For Acciavatti on tube wells, *see* p. 213.

34 beneath the surface in the region as a 'silent Saraswati': Anthony Acciavatti in Anne Rademacher and K. Sivaramakrishnan (eds.), 'Re-imagining the Indian underground: a biography of the tubewell', *Places of Nature in Ecologies of Urbanism*, Hong Kong: Hong Kong University Press, 2017, pp. 206–38.

34 Indo-Gangetic plains support 900 milion people: Rama Mani, 'Impact of climate change on major river basins in India: The Indo-Gangetic-Plains', *India Water Portal*, 28 August 2009.

CHAPTER 3: THE DEMON OF KANPUR

39 Sitasite-Sarite-Yatra-Sangate/ Tatralupta so Divmutpatanti: A. C. Shukla and Bandana Lal, *Ganga: A Water Marvel*, New Delhi: Ashish Publishing, 1995, p. 32.

40 'The story has not been communicated very well': Interview with Dhruv Kazi, 25, July 2017.

41 Rakeshji and Eco Friends filed a two-paragraph writ petition: 'Court orders', *Eco Friends* <http://www.ecofriends.org/main/courtorders.htm> [accessed: 10 May 2019].

43 It is only because that power must be accessed in radiant place and time: Alley, *On

the *Banks of the Gaṅgā*, p. 220.

43   **to build up assertive public awareness:** In November 1983, the VHP organized its Ekatmata Yatra (All India Harmony Expedition) which originated in different parts of the country and converged at the RSS headquarters in Nagpur; a campaign that utilized, in the words of Christophe Jaffrelot, 'two very tangible symbols: images representing the Ganges and Mother India in the form of divinities', *The Hindu Nationalist Movement and Indian Politics: 1925 to the 1990s*, London: Hurst & Co, 1996, p. 360.

43   **hundreds of tanneries discharge:** Kaveesha Kohli and Neera Majumdar, 'How industrial waste, govt apathy are killing the Ganga in Kanpur', *The Print*, 7 January 2018.

44   **most ETPs are lying unused or are underutilized:** Ibid.

45   **They have no choice but to drink groundwater:** '₹67 crore later', *Down To Earth*, 7 June 2015.

47   **Kashyap alleges that the tanneries paid off this man:** Sunita Narain et al, 'Can we save Ganga?', *Down To Earth*, 17 July 2018.

48   **he calls a 'Mysterious X Factor':** Julian Crandall Hollick, 'Mystery factor gives Ganges a clean reputation', *NPR*, 16 December 2007.

49   **These non-point sources, 5 per cent:** Interview with Rakesh Jaiswal.

49   **the river's ecological flow be increased:** Banjot Kaur, 'Ganga's minimum flow notification too vague to be implemented: Scientists', *Down To Earth*, 17 October 2018.

49   **Ganga really does wash away the sins of humanity:** PTI, 'Floodwater washes away Yamuna's stink, experts say river "healthiest" this year yet', *News18*, 31 July 2018.

50   **the Ganga caught fire and burned for more than thirty hours:** Shareen Joshi, 'Ganga pollution cases: impact on infant mortality', *Ideas for India*, 26 February 2016.

50   **it also banned the dumping of dead bodies:** *M. C. Mehta vs Union of India & Others* Judgment, 12 January 1988, <https://indiankanoon.org/doc/59060/> [accessed: 7 July 2019]; for the subsequent quotation *see* Alley, *On the Banks of the Gaṅgā*, p. 149.

51   **'evidence of a significant drop in both river pollution and health risk':** Joshi, 'Ganga pollution cases'.

51   **infant mortality as a measure of health:** Quay Toan Do, Shareen Joshi, and Samuel Stolpher, 'Environmental policy, river pollution, and infant health: evidence from Mehta vs. Union of India', *International Growth Centre Working Paper*, February 2016.

51   **'The ruling increases the likelihood of the river water…':** Joshi, 'Ganga pollution cases'.

52   **the zero liquid discharge ideal outlined by IIT Kanpur:** Banjot Kaur citing Tare, 'Ganga's minimum flow notification too vague to be implemented: Scientists', *Down To Earth*, 17 October 2018.

52   **CPCB said that tanneries would be held accountable for paying 25 per cent:** 'CPCB gives nod to zero liquid discharge plant at Jajmau', *Times of India*, 2 January 2015; 'Guidelines on Techno-feasability of implementation of Zero Liquid Discharge for Water Polluting Industries' <http://www.indiaenvironmentportal.org.in/files/file/Final-ZLD%20water%20polluting%20industries.pdf> [accessed: 20 August 2019].

52   **state had decided to phase leather industries out of Kanpur and Kannauj:** Nikhil M. Ghanekar, 'I will take care that no dam that hampers Ganga is allowed', *DNA*, 7 May 2017.

53   **transition from a linear to a circular economy:** 'Circular Economy for Sustainable Development in India' <https://www.researchgate.net/publication/312125734_Circular_Economy_for_Sustainable_Development_in_India> [accessed: 20 August 2019].

53   **that the clustering of these tanneries near Kanpur:** Sunita Narain et al, 'Can we save Ganga?'.

53   **And the government has published the names and locations of all these offenders:**

In 2016, a French cartographer and I estimated the latitude and longitude of these industries, and visualized them on a map called 'An atlas of polluters and prayers'. *See* the Guerilla Cartography Collective's *Water: An Atlas* at <www.guerillacartography.org> [accessed: 17 August 2019].

CHAPTER 4: THE CONFLUENCE OF WORLDS (ALLAHABAD)

55 **If like some insubstantial elephant of the sky:** Paraphrased in Steven Darian, 'The Ganges in Indian Art', East and West, Vol. 23, No. 3–4, September–December 1973, p. 312.

55 **'pop-up mega-city':** Tarun Khanna, John Macomber, and Saloni Chaturvedi, *Kumbh Mela: Kumbh Mela: India's Pop-up Mega-city*, Harvard Business School case 214-023, August 2013 (revised January 2019) <https://www.hbs.edu/faculty/Pages/item.aspx?num=45440> [accessed: 3 November 2019].

56 **Dhanvantari, put the nectar in a pot (kumbh):** 'The story of the Kumbh Mela', *Kumbh Mela* <http://www.kumbhmela.com/history-of-the-kumbh-mela/#> [accessed: 20 May 2019].

56 **'In Prayag, Allahabad for modern India, it's the biggest show':** quoted in Kama Maclean, *Pilgrimage and Power: The Kumbh Mela in Allahabad, 1765-1954*, New York: Oxford University Press, 2008, p. 34.

56 **'I have had an attachment for the Ganga and Yamuna':** Ibid., p. 84.

57 **'By this simple process, the Hindu thinks…':** Ibid., p. 89.

58 **the body count was supposedly 18,000—in 1760:** Kama MacLean, 'Making the Colonial State Work for You: The Modern Beginnings of the Ancient Kumbh Mela in Allahabad', *The Journal of Asian Studies*, Vol. 62, No. 3, August 2003, pp. 873–905.

58 **'[squeeze] those who come for salvation':** Arvind Krishna Mehrotra (ed.), Last Bungalow: Writings on Allahabad, New Delhi: Penguin Books, 2006.

58 **'a nest of pryagwalas [*sic*] has been very troublesome…':** James Clement Moffat, *The Story of a Dedicated Life*, Princeton: Princeton Press, 1887, p. 115.

59 **The spot opposite the confluence is covered with rude flagstaves:** Ibid., p. 95.

60 **The 1993 short story 'Pul Mela' by Vikram Seth:** Vikram Seth, 'Pul Mela', *New Yorker*, 22 February 1993.

60 **a stampede started by an elephant killed up to 800 people:** Maseeh Rehman, 'Holy man's gift blamed for 39 dead in stampede', *The Guardian*, 28 August 2003.

60 **100 million pilgrims attended the Kumbh Mela:** 'Over 100 million gather for Kumbh Mela, world's largest religious event', NDTV, 15 January 2019.

60 **'all the Hindu Gods [are] congregated in the landscape and river setting':** Diana Eck and Kalpesh Bhatt, 'Understanding the Kumbh Mela', in Rahul Mehrotra and Felipe Vera (eds.), *Kumbh Mela: Mapping the Ephemeral Megacity*, Ostfildern: Hatje Cantz; Cambridge: Harvard University, South Asia Institute, 2015, pp. 32, 39, 50, 54; Mehrotra and Vera, 'The Ephemeral Megacity', Ibid., pp. 70, 74; Tarun Khanna and John Macomber, 'Government and the Minimalist Platform: Business at the Kumbh Mela', ibid., pp. 336, 349; Benjamin Scheerbarth, Alykhan Mohamed, and Vineet Diwadkar, 'Governance and Organizational Structures', ibid., p. 373.

62 **stampede at the Allahabad railway station that left thirty-six people dead:** Sharat Pradhan, 'Allahabad stampede kills 36 Kumbh Mela pilgrims', *Reuters*, 11 February 2013.

63 **The current budget is almost 4,200 crore rupees:** Aman Sharma, 'Kumbh 2019 budget estimate: over ₹4,200 crore', *Economic Times*, 26 July 2018.

63 **Infrastructure included building 45,000 toilets, and 9,000 sweepers:** 'Relationship between Kumbh Mela, urban infrastructure and economic development of Allahabad'

<http://shodhganga.inflibnet.ac.in/bitstream/10603/186329/5/chapter-5.pdf> [accessed: 20 May 2019].

63   **the illiterate pilgrims were blamed by the government:** Kama MacLean, *Speaking to Subalterns/Subalterns Speaking: Pilgrims, Governments and the durghatna at the 1954 Kumbh Mela* <https://web.archive.org/web/20070607031911/http://www.sasnet.lu.se/panelabstracts/22.html> [accessed: 9 September 2019].

64   **Tata Group of Companies added to this resource:** Annu Baranwal et al, 'Managing the earth's biggest mass gathering event and WASH conditions: Maha Kumbh Mela (India)', *PLoS Currents*, 2015.

66   **'…we made small investments in cleaning up the river…':** Recent developments support Kazi's point. For example, the National Green Tribunal finds Allahabad may be on the verge of an epidemic, and the news came out that the Baswar plant—the only solid waste treatment facility in Allahabad—'has been practically closed since September 2018, which is why the garbage is lying untreated…and the plant is overflowing with filth'. The report also stated that 'The plant has five machines installed for processing waste, all of which are currently closed… 60,000 metric tonnes (mt) of solid waste had been collected at the Baswar solid waste treatment plant. Of this, 18,000 mt was generated during the Kumbh'. *See* Dheeraj Mishra, 'Why NGT thinks Allahabad is on the verge of an epidemic after the Kumbh Mela', *The Wire*, 21 May 2019.

CHAPTER 5: MODEL BEHAVIOUR IN THE AGE OF DISSOLUTION (VARANASI)

71   **all non-polar glaciers might disappear by *2350*:** Kotlyakov, 'V.M. variations of snow and ice in the past and at present on a global and regional scale' (published in 1996 but apparently written in 1991) <https://unesdoc.unesco.org/ark:/48223/pf0000106523> [accessed: 20 May 2019]. *See* also Bidisha Banerjee and George Collins, 'Anatomy of IPCC's mistake on Himalayan glaciers and year 2035: undoing 'the curse' of a chain of errors', *Yale Climate Connections*, 4 February 2010 <https://www.yaleclimateconnections.org/2010/02/anatomy-of-ipccs-himalayan-glacier-year-2035-mess/> [accessed: 20 May 2019].

73   **At dawn on the ghats of Ganga as pilgrims dip:** John McKim Malville and Rana P. B. Singh, 'Time and the Ganga River at Asi Ghat, Banaras: pilgrimage and ritual landscape', Envis Centre on Eco-Tourism, 2012, p. 2.

73   **five sacred pilgrimage routes in Varanasi:** Rana P. B. Singh and Pravin S. Rana, 'Kashi and cosmos: spatial manifestation and the five pilgrimage journeys of Banaras', *International Journal of Religious Tourism and Pilgrimage*, Vol. 4, No. 6, 2016, p. 3 <https://arrow.dit.ie/cgi/viewcontent.cgi?article=1153&context=ijrtp> [accessed: 20 May 2019].

73   **'A total of 108 sacred sites and shrines are found…':** Ibid., p. 67.

74   **'receive the highest religious merit…':** Ibid., p. 11.

74   **'a vital part of the energy vortex behind all life':** Singh is quoting Harland Margold, *The Alchemist's Almanach*, Santa Fe, New Mexico: Bear & Co, 1991, p. 47.

74   **located between the Vishwanath Temple and the Gyanvapi Mosque:** Piyush Srivastava, 'Gyanvapi mosque wall concern', *The Telegraph*, Online Edition, 27 October 2018.

75   **capitalism idealizes cleanliness and orderliness:** Assa Doron, 'The cultural politics of shit: gender and public space in India', *Postcolonial Studies*, Vol. 19, No. 2, 2015, pp. 189–207. Doron is quoting historian Dipesh Chakrabarty.

75   **eco-san (ecological and sanitary) toilet:** Colopy, *Dirty, Sacred Rivers*, p. 37.

75   **an 80,000-square-foot physical scale model of the Ganga:** Binay Singh, '29-year-old Ganga lab suffers negligence of authority', *Times of India*, 12 September 2014.

76 'state of the art scientific and technical knowledge' accommodating 'traditional and local knowledge': Binay Singh, '29-yr-old Ganga lab suffers negligence of authority', *Times of India*, 19 September 2014.

77 'The twenty-five-year-old centre is without funds.': 'Ganga Lab issues: BHU prof seeks Prez's intervention', *Times of India*, 19 January 2011.

79 This number has since risen to ₹7,000 crores: PTI, '₹7,000 cr spent on Ganga in 2 yrs without improvement: NGT', *Economic Times*, 14 July 2017.

80 80 per cent of the Ganga's waters: 'Assessment of water quality and sediment to understand the special properties of river ganga', pp. 1–9 <https://nmcg.nic.in/writereaddata/fileupload/NMCGNEERI%20Ganga%20Report.pdf> [accessed: 20 May 2019].

80 most of the river's water is removed by the Narora Barrage: 'Narora Barrage, fish ladder, Ganga and memories', *South Asia Network on Dams, Rivers and People* <https://sandrp.in/2016/11/24/narora-barrage-fish-ladder-ganga-and-memories/> [accessed: 20 May 2019]. Some studies demonstrate that the barrages have changed the shape of the river; for example, *see* Prachi Singh et al, 'Assessment of recent changes in planform of river Ganga from Mirapur Khadar to Narora barrage', *Sustainable Water Resources Management*, first published February 2018, June 2019, Vol. 5, No. 2, pp. 575–86.

80 antiquated 1916 agreement reached by Malaviya with the British government: Nitin Sethi, 'NDA revives a 1916 pact for dams on the Ganga', *Business Standard*, 21 January 2016 which argues, 'The lives of millions in the Uttarakhand hills and the Gangetic plains are dependent on an ambiguous reading of the agreement.'

83 NGRBA with the PM as the chairman and Tripathi as an expert adviser: PTI, 'Existence of Ganga in danger, says environment scientist Prof B D Tripathi', *Indian Express*, 8 June 2014.

84 'it deems necessary for abatement of pollution: 'Function and power of NGRBA', *NMCG* <https://nmcg.nic.in/ngrbaread.aspx> [accessed: 20 May 2019]; for more, *see* 'The Gazette of India' <https://nmcg.nic.in/pdf/2493.pdf> [accessed: 20 May 2019].

84 'the amount of dissolved oxygen…': 'Biochemical Oxygen Demand – BOD', *YSI* <https://www.ysi.com/parameters/biochemical-oxygen-demand-bod> [accessed: 20 May 2019].

84 BOD rose to 7.4 mg per litre on 14 January: Ram Dutt Tiwari, 'India Kumbh Mela dip "raised Ganges river pollution"', *India Today*, 24 January 2013.

84 recorded the river at its lowest in five years: Harveer Dabbas, 'Ganga water level lowest in 5 yrs in Bijnor', *Times of India*, 12 April 2016.

84 'There are 300 million litres of sewage per day…': Moushumi Basu, 'Clean Ganga Plan to see the light of day?', *The Pioneer*, 5 June 2014; Amita Bhaduri, 'Ganga clean up: It's all talk and no action', *India Water Portal*, 19 September 2018.

85 lives of approximately 500 million people will be threatened: Shyam Krishnakumar, 'Could making the Ganges a "person" save India's holiest river?', *BBC News*, 5 April 2017.

88 'a nearly 280-ft straight rigid boundary channel': Binay Singh, '29-year-old Ganga lab suffers negligence of authority', *Times of India*, 12 September 2014.

94 Jhatkaa, which had launched only six months prior: *Jhatkaa.org* <https://jhatkaa.org/about-us/> [accessed: 6 August 2019].

94 Sankat Mochan Foundation, which Veer Bhadra Mishra…had founded: *Sankat Mochan Foundation*, <http://sankatmochanfoundationonline.org/>.

94 'Let's use this spotlight on Varanasi…': Rajesh Ahuja and Moushumi Das Gupta, 'Ganga water cleaner than it was in 1986?', *Hindustan Times*, 4 February 2018.

94   his son, Bedu, has taken over the Foundation: Omar Rashid, 'Warrior for a river', *Hindustan Times*, 16 March 2013.

96   'whoever does not see another as different...': Agni Purana, 165: 10–12.

CHAPTER 6: THE SOUND OF RESILIENCE: VIKRAMSHILA GANGETIC DOLPHIN SANCTUARY (BIHAR)

97   **'Some observers are not optimistic...':**.Colopy, *Dirty, Sacred Rivers*, p. 303. The geological age of the Himalayas is controversial. Recent estimates suggest that the mountain range may be up to 50 million years old, far older than the 33 million year estimate that was common earlier.

97   **Its clicks are inaudible to human ears:** Kazuhiro Mizue, Masaharu Nishiwaki, and Akira Takemura, 'The underwater sound of Ganges river dolphins (Platanista Gangetica)', *The Scientific Reports of the Whales Research Institute*, Vol. 23, 1971, pp. 123–28.

98   **a pioneer in researching the Ganga River dolphin:** Niramala Ganapathy, 'India conducts first official survey of Ganges dolphins', *The Guardian*, 28 July 2015.

98   **In 1998, he found some Indus River dolphins:** G. T. Braulik et al, 'One species or two? Vicariance, lineage divergence and low mtDNA diversity in geographically isolated populations of South Asian River Dolphin', *Journal of Mammalian Evolution*, Vol. 22, No. 1, March 2015, pp. 111–20. Both the Ganges River dolphin (*Platanista gangetica gangetica*) and the Indus River dolphin (*Platanista Minor*) are subspecies of the South Asian River dolphin (*Platanista gangetica*).

98   **document outlines best practices for river dolphin conservation:** R. K. Sinha, S. Behera, and B. C. Chaudhary, 'The Conservation Action Plan for the Gangetic dolphin 2010–2020', Ministry of Environment and Forests Government of India, 2010.

99   **less than 2,000 alive:** 'Ganges River dolphin', *WWF*.

99   **declared it an endangered species:** Sinha, Behera, and Chaudhary, 'The Conservation Action Plan for the Gangetic dolphin 2010–2020', p. 8.

99   **multi-million-year-old history of the Ganga River dolphin:** Braulik et al, 'One species or two?'. According to Healy Hamilton et al, 'Evolution of River Dolphins', [Royal Society] *Proceedings. Biological Sciences*, Vol. 268, December 2001, pp. 549–56, the Ganga river dolphin's ancestor evolved in the Middle Miocene.

99   **'There was no straight-line march of terrestrial mammals...':** Riley Black, 'How Did Whales Evolve?', *Smithsonian Magazine*, 1 December 2010 <https://www.smithsonianmag.com/science-nature/how-did-whales-evolve-73276956/> [accessed 7 December 2019; adapted from Brian Switek (now Riley Black), *Written in Stone: Evolution, the Fossil Record, and Our Place in Nature*, New York: Bellevue Literary Press, 2010, pp. 155–73.

99   **reconstructed forty-eight-million-year-old fossil:** J. G. M. Thewissen et al, 'Whales originated from aquatic artiodactyls in the Eocene epoch of India', *Nature*, Vol. 450, December 2007, pp. 1190–5; *see* also Ian Sample, 'From Bambi to Moby-Dick: How a small deer evolved into the whale', *The Guardian*, 20 December 2007.

100 **'shallow' and 'acoustically-cluttered':** F. H. Jensen et al, 'Clicking in shallow rivers: short-range echolocation of Irrawaddy and Ganges River dolphins in a shallow, acoustically complex habitat', *PLOS*, April 2013.

100 **gangapuputaka:** Bhavani Prakash, 'King Ashoka and Gangetic Dolphin protection', *Gangetic Dolphin Protection Group* <https://gangeticdolphin.wordpress.com/tag/emperor-ashoka/> [accessed: 20 May 2019].

100 **the shushuk is known as the 'water-hog':** Som Prakash Verma, *The Illustrated Baburnama*, New Delhi: Routledge India, 2016, p. 327.

100 **Ganga's mythological mount, the Makara:** Janaki Lenin, 'My husband and other animals—the beast within', *The Hindu*, 14 January 2011.

101 **gracing the lintels of Hindu and Buddhist temples:** 'Makara (Hindu mythology)', *Academic Dictionaries and Encyclopedias* <http://www.enacademic.com/> [accessed: 3 November 2019].

101 **flourishing up and down the length of the Ganga:** S. Jones, 'The present status of the Gangetic susu', *Platanista gangetic* (Roxburgh), with comments on the Indus susu, Platanista minor Owen', FAO Advisory Committee on Marine Resources Research Working Party on Marine Mammals. FAO Fish. Ser. (5), Vol. 4, 1982, pp. 97–115.

101 **that was more than fifty dams ago:** *See* also <http://india-wris.nrsc.gov.in/wrpinfo/index.php?title=Dams_in_Ganga_Basin> [accessed: 26 June 2019].

101 *Platanista*'s **upper limit is the Bijnor barrage:** Harveer Dabbas, 'Dolphin census begins in 400km stretch of Ganga from Bijnor', *Times of India*, 15 October 2016.

101 **the 1,800 remaining members of the species:** 'WWF-India applauds the declaration of the Gangetic River Dolphin as India's National Aquatic Animal', *WWF*, 6 October 2009.

102 **many Tantric texts were taught there** Pranava K. Chaudhary, 'ASI to develop ancient site of Vikramshila Mahavihara', *Times of India*, 10 October 2009.

102 **Shambhu Lal:** Name changed to protect identities.

102 **Bhuvan:** Name changed to protect identities.

102 **Dolphin Mitra programme:** Sinha, Behera, and Chaudhary, 'The Conservation Action Plan for the Ganges River dolphin 2010–2020', p. 25. For the relationship between fishermen and dolphins, *see* Nachiket Kelkar et al, 'Coexistence of fisheries with River dolphin conservation', *Conservation Biology*, Vol. 24, No. 4, August 2010, pp. 1130–40.

109 **re-birthed the Ganga from his ear or his thigh:** 'How the Ganga became known as Jahnavi'

111 **feudal water-lords, known as panidars:** 'Unshackling the Ganga', *Down To Earth*, 7 June 2015.

111 **The Ganga Mukti Andolan started in 1982:** Ibid.

114 **to protect a nearby lake that serves as an important sanctuary:** 'Nests of rare storks discovered in Bihar', *Wildlife Trust of India*; *see* also Avijit Biswas, 'Foreign tourists visit greater adjutants breeding site in Bihar, spark new interest', *Hindustan Times*, 7 February 2017.

115 **the river can run up to 33 metres deep:** There are now plans to build a new bridge parallel to the Vikramshila Bridge; *see* Piyush Tripathi, 'Centre paves way for bridge parallel to Vikramshila Setu', *Times of India*, 7 September 2018.

116 **more than 200 bird species come to this stretch of the river:** Gautam Sarkar, 'Deluge shadow on sanctuary of Gangetic dolphins', *The Telegraph*, 4 September 2016.

116 **they are called chakwa, chakwi, or 'Laal Surkhab':** *Indian Bird Names*, p. 90, Accessed from Internet Archives.

117 **their status is of 'least concern':** 'Ruddy Shelduck', *IUCN Red List* <https://www.iucnredlist.org/species/22680003/86011049> [accessed: 20 May 2019].

117 **Yangtze River dolphin in China:** Simon Turvey, *Witness to an Extinction: How we Failed to Save the Yangtze River Dolphin*, New York: Oxford University Press, 2009.

118 **tourists pay top dollar to see a single river dolphin:** 'River dolphins under threat in Nepal', *WWF*.

118 **transport coal along 'National Waterway 1':** 'Shipping minister launched inland waterways projects at Kolkata' <http://pib.nic.in/newsite/PrintRelease.aspx?relid=100825> [accessed: 20 May 2019].

118 **'...impacted the number of dolphins':** Mohd Imran Khan, 'Dolphin population declines

in India's only dolphin sanctuary', *Down To Earth*, 19 July 2018.

120 **dire consequences of the National Waterways Act:** 'The National Waterways Act, 2016', *The Gazette of India*, New Delhi, 26 March 2016.

120 **World Bank has pledged $375 million:** 'World Bank approves $375 million to help India Develop its first modern waterway', *The World Bank*, 12 April 2017.

120 **'envisions the centralized, unitary control...':** Nachiket Kelkar, 'Digging our rivers' graves?', *SANDRP*, Vol. 14, No. 1–2, 19 February 2016.

122 **discourages dredging and sand-mining:** 'Ganga River Basin Management Plan – 2015', GRBMP – January 2015: Main Plan Document.

122 **'Despite the diverse geographies...':** Kelkar, 'Save the Ganga, sully the Ganga', *Indian Express*, 23 April 2017.

122 **'river dredging is rampant...':** Ibid.

122 **'we have to do more than clean a part of it...':** Ibid.

124 **dolphins only give birth once every two to three years:** 'Ganges River dolphin', *WWF*.

126 **Three Gorges Dam was built in 2006:** Michael Bristow, 'China acknowledges Three Gorges dam "problems"', *BBC News*, 19 May 2011.

126 **Chinese alligator became 'critically endangered':** *IUCN Red List*.

126 **led to the baiji's demise in 2006:** Stefan Lovgren, 'China's rare river dolphin now extinct, experts announce', *National Geographic News*, 14 December 2006.

126 **increased dolphin mortality in Vikramshila:** Arati Kumar-Rao, 'Blind dolphins in Ganga waterway', *The Third Pole*, 25 August 2016.

127 **The act plans to scale this up to 21.89 MT by 2021:** PTI, 'Cargo traffic on Ganga waterway may rise to 21.89 MT by 2021: Nitin Gadkari', *Economic Times*, 2 October 2018.

127 **'...the transport cost through waterway...':** Shripad Dharmadhikary and Jinda Sandbhor, 'National Inland Waterways in India: A Strategic Status Report', Manthan Adhyayan Kendra and SRUTI, 20 March 2017, p. 25.

129 **'ways to create obstacles in India's energy plans':** 'From Greenpeace to Ford Foundation: Modi govt's controversial crackdown on NGOs', *Firstpost*, 2 June 2016.

129 **'In four years, Modi govt released only one-third of pledged amount...':** Anand Patel, 'In 4 years, Modi govt released only one-third of pledged amount for cleaning up Ganga: RTI disclosure.' *India Today*, 13 October 2018.

CHAPTER 7: TRIANGULATING THE BENGAL DELTA: FALLING OFF THE MAP (BANGLADESH)

135 **multi-decade gap in cross-border train service:** Aniek Paul, 'Cross-border ride: Maitree Express', *Livemint*, 17 April 2008.

138 **on the arsenic contamination in the water:** Jessica Dittmar et al, 'Arsenic in soil and irrigation water affects arsenic uptake by rice: complementary insights from field and pot studies. environmental science & technology', *Environ. Sci. Technol.*, 2010.

138 **77 million people were at risk of arsenic poisoning:** Andrew Buncombe, 'How the West poisoned Bangladesh', *The Independent*, 21 March 2010.

138 **15 billion metric tonnes of sediment flowing downstream:** Dipankar Chakraborti et al, 'Groundwater arsenic contamination in the Ganga River Basin: a future health danger', *International Journal of Environmental Research and Public Health*, January 2018 <https://www.mdpi.com/1660-4601/15/2/180/pdf> [accessed: 23 May 2019].

138 **groundwater overuse increased, so did arsenic poisoning:** Ibid., p. 3.

138 **one in five deaths in affected areas:** Maria Argos et al, 'Arsenic exposure from drinking

water, and all-cause and chronic-disease mortalities in Bangladesh (HEALS): a prospective cohort study', *The Lancet*, Vol. 376, 24 July 2010, pp. 252–58.

138 **the worst case of mass poisoning in history:** Buncombe, 'How the West poisoned Bangladesh'. For the mapping of Bangladesh aquifers, *see* Abhijit Mukherjee (ed.), *Groundwater of South Asia*, Singapore: Springer, 2018, p. 209.

139 **Indian plate slammed into the Eurasian plate:** 'Continental/Continental: The Himalayas', *The Geological Society*.

140 **SONO filter had a much shorter lifespan under actual conditions:** 'Arsenic primer: guidance on the investigation & mitigation of arsenic contamination', 2018, p. 50; *see* also pp. 23, 23–29, 52 and 65 <https://www.unicef.org/wash/files/UNICEF_WHO_Arsenic_Primer.pdf> [accessed: 20 May 2019].

142 **Dombipada belonged to the Sahajiya sect of Buddhism:** Darian, *The Ganges in Myth and History*, p. 146.

143 **Man is as deep as the Ganges?:** Ibid., p. 147.

143 *Men and Rivers*: Humayun Kabir, *Men and Rivers*, Bombay: Hind Kitab, 1945. The quotation in the next paragraph by Manik Bandhopadhyay is from *Padma River Boatman*, St Lucia: University of Queensland Press, 1973, p. 98, 2nd edition, New Delhi: National Book Trust, 1977. *See* also Ananya Kabir, *Partition's Post-Amnesias: 1947, 1971 and Modern South Asia*, New Delhi: Women Unlimited, 2013.

147 **'When a caged bird wants to be free…':** Quoted in Donna Pankhurst, *Gendered Peace: Women's Struggles for Post-War Justice and Reconciliation*, Geneva: Routledge, 2008, p. 198.

CHAPTER 8: GRAVES OF THE GANGA (GAUR, FARAKKA, AND SAGAR ISLAND)

150 **'It is a land of dead and decaying rivers':** Riaz Uddin and Naz Hasan Huda, 'Arsenic poisoning in Bangladesh', *Oman Medical Journal*, Vol. 26, No. 3, May 2011, p. 207.

151 **eight out of fifteen rivers are dead:** Kalyan Rudra, *Rivers of the Ganga-Brahmaputra-Meghna Delta: A Fluvial Account of Bengal*, Cham, Switzerland: Springer, 2018, p. 23. *See* also <http://en.banglapedia.org/ index.php?title=Bengal_Delta>, which features a clearly marked map of the different stages.

151 **Austroasiatic language called Munda:** Paul Sidwell, 'Austroasiatic Studies: State of the art in 2018', Presentation at the Graduate Institute of Linguistics, Taiwan: National Tsing Hua University, 22 May 2018.

152 **intelligible to the Maoris and the Polynesians:** C. F. Voegelin and F. M. Voegelin, 'Languages of the World: Indo-Pacific Fascicle One', *Anthropological Linguistics*, Vol. 6, No. 4, April 1964, pp. 1–106.

152 **successful human strategies to influence the superhuman world:** For more context, especially involving transformations of Buddhist practices and varieties of human/superhuman cosmologies during this time, *see* Richard M. Eaton, *The Rise of Islam and the Bengal Frontier, 1204–1760*, Berkeley: University of California Press, 1993, pp. 13–14, 69–70, 303.

152 **Ganga left behind its western and southern channels:** Ibid., p. 307. To qualify my dates for the first British census: 'The first 1871–72 census was the first attempt at a complete enumeration of British India. However, not all provinces were included, and local censuses made between 1868 and 1875 supplement that census. The 1881 census, 'the first synchronous enumeration' of British India, contains report on the census of British India taken on 17 February 1881 (India, Census of India 1871–72) <http://

id.lib.harvard.edu/alma/990058098920203941/cataloge> [accessed: 3 November 2019].

153 **area was mostly populated at that time by tribes:** Kingshuk Nag, 'How did Bengalis become Muslims?', *Times of India*, 8 August 2012.

153 **integrated into Indian Sufism:** Eaton, *The Rise of Islam*, p. 78.

153 **who were worshipped by Nath yogis:** Carl W. Ernst, 'Being careful with the goddess: Yoginis in Persian and Arabic texts', *Performing Ecstasy: The Poetics and Politics of Religion in India*, Pallabi Chakrovorty and Scott Kugle (eds.), Delhi: Manohar, 2009, pp. 189–203.

153 **'I found the king and minister in myself.':** Eaton, p. 80.

153 **'yoga and Sufi ideas resisted true fusion':** Ibid., p. 81.

154 **Lord Curzon annulled the first partition in 1911:** Joya Chatterji, *The Spoils of Partition: Bengal and India, 1947–1967*, New York: Cambridge University Press, 2007, p. 9.

154 **'imbues other particles with mass':** Kelly Dickerson, 'Stephen Hawking says "God Particle" could wipe out the universe', *Live Science*, 8 September 2014.

155 **'needed to keep the universe on the brink of instability':** Ibid.

155 **gave the green light to Cotton's proposal:** Kumar-Rao, 'The nowhere people', *Peepli. org* <http://peepli.org/stories/the-nowhere-people/> [accessed: 26 May 2019].

155 **Cambridge historian Joya Chatterji:** Joya Chatterji, *Bengal Divided: Hindu Communalism and Partition, 1932–1947*, Cambridge: Cambridge University Press, 1994; *The Spoils of Partition: Bengal and India, 1947–1967*, p. 267.

155 **to ensure the navigability of the Port of Kolkata:** 'About us', *Farakka Barrage Project* <http://fbp.gov.in/> [accessed: 26 May 2019].

155 **had started constructing the Farakka Barrage in 1961:** A barrage is a dam whose purpose is to divert water or increase the depth of a river by barring the free flow of water

156 **Farakka caused damages of up to 3 billion USD for Bangladesh:** M. A. Kawser and M. A. Samad, 'Political history of Farakka Barrage and its effects on environment in Bangladesh', *Bandung: Journal of the Global South*, 2016.

156 **the dry season had considerably decreased:** Ishtiaq Hossain, 'Bangladesh-India relations: The Ganges Water-sharing Treaty and beyond', *Asian Affairs: An American Review*, Vol. 25, 1998, p. 142.

156 **20 million Bangladeshi environmental refugees:** Colopy, *Dirty, Sacred Rivers*, p. 315.

156 **'The river may have been shifting and silting up…':** Ibid., p. 316 and 312.

157 **'the tendency to replay the scene of the Farakka loss…':** Ibid., pp. 316–17.

157 **stronger reason to increase their allyship:** Ibid., p. 321.

157 **'The lack of small meanders…':** E. Addink and M. G. Kleinhans, 'Recognizing meanders to reconstruct river dynamics of the Ganges', *GEOBIA*, ISPRS, Session 3, Calgary, Canada, 2008, p. 2.

157 **I witnessed how fisheries have been devastated up-river:** M. Sinha, M. K. Mukhopadhyay, P. M. Mitra, M. M. Bagchi and H. C. Karamkar, 'Impact of Farakka Barrage on the Hydrology and Fishery of Hooghly Estuary', *Estuaries*, Vol. 19, No. 3, September 1996, pp. 710–22.

158 **cautions against using the term 'interlinking':** Cheryl Colopy, personal communication, 14 February 2019.

158 **stays in the system and then blows up again:** Colopy, *Dirty, Sacred Rivers*, p. 271.

158 **highlights experts who propose alternatives to interlinking proposals:** Colopy, personal communication, 14 February 2019. See also *Dirty, Sacred Rivers*, p. 317.

159 **whose ports have long since 'dried up':** Swati Chattopadhyay, 'Cities and peripheries', *Historical Research*, Vol. 83, No. 222, November 2010, p. 654.

159 **'I have seen whole villages thus deserted…':** R. H. Phillimore, *Historical Records of*

the Survey of India, Vol. 1, Dehradun: Surveyor General of India, 1945, p. 64.

159 'became obsessed with documenting these changes...': Chattopadhyay, 'Cities and peripheries', p. 659.

159 'Having surveyed this part of the Ganga in 1797...': Phillimore, *Historical Records of the Survey of India*, p. 388.

160 'On Recent Changes in the Delta of the Ganga': James Fergussen, 'On recent changes in the delta of the Ganga', *Quarterly Journal of the Geological Society*, Vol. 19, 1 February 1863, pp. 321–54.

160 'geological history was a hovering presence in his surveys': Chattopadhyay, 'Cities and peripheries', p. 663.

160 meanders which are clearly visible to the eye: Addink and Kleinhans, 'Recognizing meanders to reconstruct river dynamics of the Ganga'.

160 '[V]isual comparison of the channel map...': Ibid., p. 6.

161 its documented history begins around 1198 CE: Rabiul Hasan and Andrew Eagle, 'History beyond reach', *Daily Star*, 4 October 2017.

161 'The market is everywhere and everything...': Richard M. Eaton, *The Rise of Islam*, pp. 98–99.

162 Gaur became a dead city: W. W. Hunter, *The Annals of Rural Bengal*, New York: Leopoldt and Holt, 1868, p. 39.

166 'Abyssinian Interlude': Prabhash K. Dutta, 'Africans in India: Forgotten history of slaves, soldiers and rulers', *India Today*, 30 March 2017; S. N. Das (ed.), *The Bengalis: The People, their History and Culture*, New Delhi: Cosmo Publications, 2002.

168 'Then I saw/ In the midst of the charnel ground...': Thanissaro Bhikkhu (trans.), *Kisagotami Theri*, 2006 <https://www.accesstoinsight.org/tipitaka/kn/thig/thig.10.01.than.html> [accessed: 26 May 2019].

169 heads 1,200 miles back upstream: 'Farakka barrage construction dries up hilsa, jumbo prawns supply in state', *Times of India*, 10 August 2016.

169 a fraction of the hilsa to swim upstream: Kaushik Das Gupta, 'Why new plan to "unlock" Farakka for hilsa recalls old debate on fish passes', *Indian Express*, 21 February 2019.

169 the proposed algal wastewater ponds in Varanasi: Binay Singh, 'Jai Ganga Maiyya...', *Times of India*, 26 May 2009.

171 A smothered scream, a ripple upon the water: Darian, *The Ganges in Myth and History*, p. 155.

171 signs of human habitation: Patrick Olivelle, *Between the Empires: Society in India 300 BCE to 400 CE*, Oxford: Oxford University Press, 2006, p. 9.

172 PUPA (Paribesh Unnayan Parishad): 'Organisation's profile', *Paribesh Unnayan Parishad* <http://pupaamargram.org/> [accessed: 3 November 2019].

CHAPTER 9: THE WILD WOMAN'S GANGA (THE SUNDARBANS)

179 River connects the village to the rivers Raymangal, Durgaduani, Bidya, and Matla: Annu Jalais, *Forest of Tigers: People, Politics, and Environment in the Sundarbans*, New Delhi: Routledge India, 2010, pp. 40–43, 73, and 178. For the Sundarbans' diversity of species, *see* Asish Ghosh, *Natural Resource and Conservation and Environmental Management*, New Delhi: APH, 2003, p. 55.

181 deadly mask approach to man-tiger confrontation: Caroline Alexander, 'Tigerland: a journey through the mangrove forest of Bengal', *New Yorker*, 14 April 2008.

190 there operates an entire economy: Abhijit Mitra, 'Shrimp seed collection in Indian Sundarban estuaries: a threat to overall estuarine ecosystem services', *Journal of Environmental*

and *Social Sciences*, 2017 <https://www.researchgate.net/publication/316790049_Shrimp_Seed_Collection_in_Indian_Sundarban_Estuaries_A_Threat_to_Overall_Estuarine_Ecosystem_Services> [accessed: 27 May 2019].

191 **prawn-seed collecting becomes more common:** Annu Jalais, 'Braving crocodiles with Kali: being a prawn-seed collector and a modern woman in the 21st century Sundarbans', *Socio-Legal Review*, Vol. 9, 2010, pp. 1–23.

192 **committed to protecting the Bengal tiger:** Rajat Ghai, 'Sundarbans' "swamp tigers" could be gone in 50 years, warns study', *Down To Earth*, 13 January 2019.

192 **oil spills may severely diminish the number of tigers:** 'Sundarbans National Park', UNESCO <https://whc.unesco.org/en/list/452> [accessed: 26 June 2019].

192 **Mission report called for tightening regulations:** Alexander, 'After oil spill, unique mangrove forest faces more threats', *National Geographic*, 7 May 2015.

CONCLUSION

195 **'Ganga bathed to wash away the sins…':** Darian citing the *Archaelogical Survey of India* in *The Ganges in Myth and History*, p. 62.

195 **imagines a disembodied India of the future:** Kunzru's 'Drone', cited in the next paragraph, appeared first in *Granta*, No. 130.

198 **'Behaviour changes, changes of cognition…':** Leon Festinger, *A Theory of Cognitive Dissonance*, Stanford: Stanford University Press, 1957, p. 31.

198 **out of 261 projects, only 76 had been completed:** Shreya Jai, 'Namami Gange moves slow: of ₹2,300 cr allotted, only ₹700 cr used', *Business Standard*, 3 February 2019.

199 **'make everyone responsible for his or her own shit':** Colopy, pp. 36 and 43; for quotation from Shetty, *see* pp. 36–37.

201 **affecting 88.23 lakh people in 31 out of 38 districts:** P. N. Rai, 'Innovative measures taken to reduce the impact of Flood', Disaster Management Department, Government of Bihar, 2016 <https://ndma.gov.in/images/ppt12formationday/Bihar.pdf> [accessed: 27 May 2019].

201 **'innovations' failed to address the systemic challenges:** Sanjiv J. Phansalkar et al, 'Development profile in flood prone areas', *Studies in Development Processes*, No. 1, 14 May 2016 <http://www.vikasanvesh.in/wp-content/uploads/2018/07/Download-full-report-2.pdf> [accessed: 27 May 2019].

201 **Ganga's fate as a sewage canal was sealed by 1960:** Laskow, '160-year-old Ganges canal super-passages are an engineering marvel'. *See* also *Science,* NS Vol. 188, 9 May 1975, pp. 611–16.

202 **'All of the seemingly disparate…':** Acciavatti, *Ganges Water Machine*, p. 8.

203 **'the last refuge' of biodiversity along the Upper Ganga:** Vineet Singh, 'Mandu sacred grove in Upper Ganga Ramsar site, Uttar Pradesh', *Current Science*, Vol. 104, No. 4, February 2013, pp. 409–10.

204 **allegedly encouraged encroachment on this land:** Snigdhendu Bhattacharya, 'West Bengal may lift building limits in fragile wetlands', *Hindustan Times*, 13 December 2017.

204 **construction of a flyover through the wetland was thankfully turned down:** 'Wetlands flyover: Centre nod not enough, HC to take call', *Times of India*, 7 July 2018.